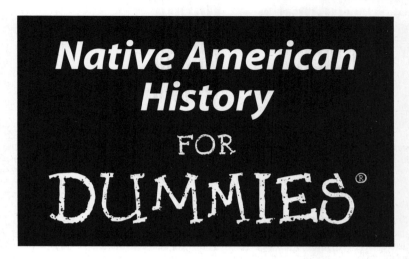

Native American History FOR DUMMIES®

by Dorothy Lippert, PhD and Stephen J. Spignesi

BICENTENNIAL
1807
WILEY
2007
BICENTENNIAL

Wiley Publishing, Inc.

Native American History For Dummies®

Published by
Wiley Publishing, Inc.
111 River St.
Hoboken, NJ 07030-5774
www.wiley.com

WILEY

About the Authors

Dorothy Lippert, PhD: Dorothy is Choctaw and an archaeologist. She received her BA from Rice University and her MA and PhD from the University of Texas at Austin. She works in the Repatriation Office of the National Museum of Natural History. Dorothy serves on the Executive of the World Archaeological Congress and on the Board of Directors for the Society for American Archaeology. Her research interests include the development of Indigenous archaeology, repatriation, ethics, and the archaeology and bioarchaeology of the Southeastern United States.

Stephen J. Spignesi: Stephen Spignesi is a best-selling author of more than 40 books, including his highly-acclaimed debut novel, *DIALOGUES* (Bantam). His latest book is *George Washington's Leadership Lessons* (Wiley) written with James Rees, the Executive Director of George Washington's Mount Vernon. He is also the co-author of *Second Homes for Dummies* (Wiley). His book, *JFK Jr.* (Citadel), was a New York Times best-seller.

Dedication

Stephen J. Spignesi: For Adrienne, who was with me in spirit all the way through this, and who never failed to say the exact right thing at the exact right moment.

Authors' Acknowledgments

Dorothy Lippert: I was privileged to work with Stephen Spignesi in the production of this book. His energy and hard work were what made the book what it is. I would also like to thank Phil Konstantin whose research and writing were such an invaluable part of the process.

Stephen J. Spignesi: Five people deserve all the thanks in the world for their help, support, and above all, friendship:

Dorothy Lippert, PhD, the co-author of this book, has my gratitude for her insights, patience, and for teaching me about not only her tribe, the Choctaws, but also about all of Native American history and culture. Thanks, Dorothy, for taking me on a classic journey of discovery and enlightenment. It was an honor to work with you.

Jennifer Connolly, our Project Editor, for her smarts, wit, grace, sense of humor, forbearance, and charm, and for her good nature when providing the answers we needed — even when the questions were staggeringly convoluted and had "from left field" written all over them! Thanks, Jenn.

Mike Lewis, our Acquisitions Editor, for putting everything together, overseeing it all, and maintaining a placid and controlled manner that was always encouraging, even when I knew circumstances warranted anything but unruffled calm! Thanks, Mike.

Phil Konstantin, a Cherokee who is also a real paesan. Phil, your help was of enormous value and immeasurable excellence, and your performance made the dictionary makers rewrite the definition of prompt! Thanks, Phil.

John White, my literary agent, a man of integrity and great moral strength who has been an inspiration and role model for me for over two decades now. Thanks, John.

Publisher's Acknowledgments

We're proud of this book; please send us your comments through our Dummies online registration form located at www.dummies.com/register/.

Some of the people who helped bring this book to market include the following:

Acquisitions, Editorial, and Media Development

Project Editor: Jennifer Connolly

Acquisitions Editor: Mike Lewis

Copy Editor: Jennifer Connolly

Technical Editor: Phil Konstantin

Editorial Managers: Jennifer Ehrlich, Michelle Hacker

Editorial Supervisor: Carmen Krikorian

Editorial Assistants: Erin Calligan Mooney, Joe Niesen, Leeann Harney, David Lutton

Cover Photos: © Swift/Vanuga Images/Corbis

Interior Photos: © Florida Center for Instructional Technology

Cartoons: Rich Tennant (www.the5thwave.com)

Composition Services

Project Coordinator: Erin Smith

Layout and Graphics: Carl Byers, Melissa K. Jester, Laura Pence, Christine Williams

Proofreaders: Laura Albert, Glenn McMullen

Indexer: Glassman Indexing Services

Publishing and Editorial for Consumer Dummies

Diane Graves Steele, Vice President and Publisher, Consumer Dummies

Joyce Pepple, Acquisitions Director, Consumer Dummies

Kristin A. Cocks, Product Development Director, Consumer Dummies

Michael Spring, Vice President and Publisher, Travel

Kelly Regan, Editorial Director, Travel

Publishing for Technology Dummies

Andy Cummings, Vice President and Publisher, Dummies Technology/General User

Composition Services

Gerry Fahey, Vice President of Production Services

Debbie Stailey, Director of Composition Services

Contents at a Glance

Table of Contents

Introduction

*T*he history of Native Americans is, ultimately, the history of America. They were, after all, here first, right?

And we cannot truly know who we are today without looking back at the first occupants of this land and understanding how their presence, cultures, and beliefs influenced and shaped everything that was to follow.

The indigenous people who were here hundreds of years before Columbus arrived are now known by several terms, including the most common:

- ✔ Native American
- ✔ American Indian
- ✔ Indigenous peoples
- ✔ First Nations (in Canada)

In this book, we basically use them all, mainly selecting which identifying term to use based on clarity and historical accuracy. For example, we often use "indigenous people" when referring to a time hundreds of years before European contact. Why? Because there was no "America" at the time and referring to the native peoples of that period as "Native *Americans*" or "*American* Indians" is just plain silly.

"Indian" is the legal term for all tribal people in the U.S., including Alaska, so even though it's a misnomer (this ain't India, folks), the term has become part of American law, and so we use it freely.

"Native American" is the more popular term these days, but even that one has its opponents. Why? Because it's technically inaccurate. Anyone born in America is native to America. Thus, your second-generation Italian-American next-door neighbor can logically (albeit ludicrously) refer to himself as a Native American. But we use it anyway, because it's part of the American lexicon.

About This Book

Native American History For Dummies is a general interest reference work that presents much of what you might want to know about Indians in America, from the earliest migration theories, to the newest techniques for identifying remains for repatriation.

Plus, the organization of this and every other *For Dummies* book makes it perfect for either reading straight through, selective browsing, or the reading of individual, self-contained chapters. Each chapter is like a mini-book unto itself. And within each chapter, the content is organized by headings for ease of reading and for continuity. Unto itself.

You can even skip material in each chapter — specifically, the sidebars — and still absorb the info of the chapter with no problem.

Conventions Used in This Book

When this book was printed, some Web addresses may have needed to break across two lines of text. If that happened, rest assured that we haven't put in any extra characters (such as hyphens) to indicate the break. So, when using one of these Web addresses, just type in exactly what you see in this book, pretending as though the line break doesn't exist.

Also, because this book is about Native American history, you will find some rather challenging proper names and tribal names. In every case we've gone with the most traditional and accepted spelling, but have omitted pronunciation guides, mainly because on a page with several names and tribes mentioned, we'd be devoting an awful lot of page space to parenthetical pronunciation information. It's not necessary, since we assume you're not going to be reading this aloud and so you can scan over the names and still understand the material.

What You're Not to Read

Like we said, you don't have to read the sidebars if you don't want to or don't have the time. They're second-tier material but, in all honesty, you'll really enjoy them if you read them anyway! (Prejudiced much?)

What we mean is that sidebars are often used for ancillary material that, while it isn't critical to know, can certainly be fun to know! And what's wrong with that, right?

Foolish Assumptions

What we assume about you, oh dear *For Dummies* reader, is that, for one thing, you know how to read. (Sorry. Little joke.)

Seriously, though, this *For Dummies* book assumes that you have a basic foundation in simple American History: "In 1492, Columbus sailed the ocean blue . . ." and so forth and so on.

We also assume that if you bought this book, you are more than a little interested in the history of pre-Columbian peoples on the North American continent. And that you are open to having stereotypes exploded, myths debunked, and sacred assumptions de-sacredized. (De-sacredized is probably not a word, but we think you know what we mean.)

How This Book Is Organized

This book is structured into parts, chapters, and headings:

- ✔ Parts are all-encompassing, single-theme, topic-based collections of chapters grouped together.
- ✔ Chapters zoom in on specific topics and look at these topics in detail.
- ✔ Headings and subheadings are how chapters are organized and they zoom in on the material even closer.

Let's put it this way: imagine you're the Hubbell telescope. (C'mon, just play along, okay?) As you read through the book and move from part, to chapter, to heading, it's sort of like you're turning the thing that makes the Hubbell zoom in on a planet, a star, a UFO, or the guy in the apartment building across the street playing the oboe in his underwear.

Here's a look at the individual parts of the book and what they cover.

Part 1: America Before It Was "America"

These chapters look at how the people who were here before October 12 became Columbus Day got here, the different cultures and peoples, where they settled, what America looked like thousands of years ago, and how the tribes formed and where they migrated.

Part II: Interacting with Others

These chapters talk about what happened after the first Indian said, "Honey, we've got company!" Plus, they look at great leaders and warriors, how the Spanish and French explorers often made a mess of things, the fighting that went on and still goes on, and how Indians have interacted with the U.S. from the nation's earliest days up through today.

Part III: Working for a Living

Food, shelter, clothes, and travel. These chapters look at these basic needs of all Indians and how they provided them.

Part IV: All in the (Native American) Family

Tribal structures, families, how languages developed, and how signs and pictures served as communication tools. Also, this part looks at the religious beliefs and creation myths of tribes and talks about how artifacts like peyote and totem poles are used in ritual and worship.

Part V: In a Modern World Not of Their Making

This part looks at the often grim picture of Native American life today. But it also points out how things are getting better and highlights Indian endeavors like gaming, offshore mineral rights, forestry, coal mining, and individually owned businesses.

Part VI: The Part of Tens

This fun section looks at Native American museums and cultural centers, movies and documentaries, and great books about Native American history.

Icons Used in This Book

An icon is a visual symbol that tells you you're about to learn something cool.

This one is commonly a piece of advice about Indian culture or protocol, or a tip on how to make use of Native American resources to continue your learning and study.

This is information you should try to remember, if possible. The fact that we're saying "remember" (this) should be a tip-off that it's valuable and worth learning.

Remember *Lost in Space*? "Danger, Will Robinson!" No, this icon doesn't really warn you against dangerous stuff. It's more like "watch what you say" or "don't do this" type info.

This is ignorable info, mainly because it's usually highly specialized technical information that we felt obligated to include (to show off for our mothers, mostly) but which most of you probably won't be too concerned about knowing.

Where to Go from Here

You can read this book anyway you want to. Start anywhere and go anywhere.

Part III, "Working For a Living" is probably a good place to start, since it's a "daily life" kind of chapter and will immediately acclimate you to the whole Native American mojo, to boldly mix cultural references.

Remember, *For Dummies* books are meant to be fun to read and to make finding out more about a topic easy. The entire series is a unique blend of both discovery and entertainment.

So go explore. And be entertained while so doing, okay?

Part I
America Before It Was "America"

The 5th Wave — By Rich Tennant

In this part . . .

The United States is just over two hundred years old, yet the land the country occupies has been here for millions of years, and there have been people living here for tens of thousands of years.

The debate as to how the Native peoples arrived here is ongoing, and include both overland and "by water" theories. The point is, the North American landmass has a lengthy history, and in this part we will look at what the land was like eons ago, how the first people arrived here, how tribes developed cultures, and where they all settled.

Chapter 1

The Rich, Troubled Past of the American Indian

All Americans need to know the undeniably wonderful, oftentimes troublesome, commonly awe-inspiring, sometimes regrettable history of our country. Economic miracle and global influence? Great. Slavery and the near-extinction of the Native American peoples? Not so great.

The "American identity" is multifaceted and has been forged in a cauldron of countless influences, one of the most important being the fact that the Indians were here first. Why is that important? For the same reason that many states have passed resolutions apologizing for slavery. The Indians were here when European explorers arrived and claimed the land as their own, using authority they believed was given to them by God himself.

That's pretty powerful validation, when you think about it, and it helps explain how European settlers had zero qualms about taking what they wanted and eliminating Native peoples at will. They were doing God's work.

The Price of Greatness

Knowing and understanding the genesis of what many believe is the greatest country in the history of civilization is important because it puts this achievement known as the United States in perspective. It illustrates that greatness often comes with a price, and that price is commonly the exploitation or elimination of others.

But don't get me wrong: This is not a diatribe against the great American success story. It is simply a reminder that one of the signs of a truly evolved society is its willingness to admit the travails of its past, which America consistently does with dignity and grace.

The history of the American Indian is the story of ancient civilizations, ancient cultures, glorious rites and rituals, and evolved societies that were fully developed and functional when they first met the European explorers and settlers.

In *Native American History For Dummies*, you look at who Indians were, what happened to them, and who they are now. You can find out more about:

- ✔ Their homes
- ✔ Their hunting, trapping, fishing, and other survival practices
- ✔ Their rites of passage
- ✔ Their battles, both with Anglos and each other
- ✔ Their creation myths
- ✔ Their cultural practices

You will hear from great warriors and leaders, and hopefully gain that aforementioned perspective on how the creation of America impacted an entire race of people.

In the Beginning . . .

The first part of this book discusses the many theories put forth to explain how the Native peoples who were here when the first Europeans arrived got here.

Some say by land, some say by sea, but the bottom line and the undeniable historical and scientific fact is that there were certainly hundreds of thousands, and more likely millions of indigenous people already inhabiting the North American landmass when it was "discovered."

The theories

A few theories as to how this huge population came into being in North America are looked at, including:

- ✔ The migration across the Bering Sea theory via the Beringia land bridge
- ✔ The arrival along the western coast by boat

> ✔ The theory that the Chinese may have been here first
>
> ✔ A similar theory that the Celts may have stopped by earlier

Why should you care about how the people we now know as Indians, Inuits, and Aleuts got here in the first place? Why is this important?

Because their history is *your* history, and it is critically important that science pinpoints the genetic ancestry of as many of the earth's populations as possible. Such information has consistently been used to pinpoint important genetic and medical facts that have been used in the battle against disease and ethnic-specific medical problems.

Plus, it can't be denied that even though Santayana's reminder about those who don't know their history are bound to repeat it is now something of a cliché, there is a huge amount of truth in it, and the reason history is studied is to not make the same mistakes over and over and over again.

The stages and waves

While studying Native American history, it is also of value to identify and discuss the different stages of cultural development and the geographical migration waves of Indian tribes and ethnic groups.

You will look at:

> ✔ Clovis and Folsom cultures
>
> ✔ Na-Dene culture
>
> ✔ The Inuits and the Aleuts

You also journey through the development stages that have come to be known as:

> ✔ Archaic
>
> ✔ Plano
>
> ✔ Pueblo

And don't forget the K-Man

The discovery of the Kennewick Man was a huge step forward in . . . well, in making scientists and tribal peoples even more confused about the Paleoindian Period and who lived where, and when.

The K-Man was not supposed to be where they found him. Or it could actually be the other way around: The K-Man was not who scientists expected to find where they found him.

Controversy has raged ever since the remains of the indigenous male known as Kennewick Man was discovered in 1996. As many as five tribes initially claimed ownership of the remains of someone they believed was their ancestor, and it took a court ruling rejecting their claims for kinship to get them to drop their suits.

So who owns the Ancient One?

Right now, we do. Yeah, that's right. I'm talking to you. The American people own the remains of Kennewick Man. Well, more accurately, the U.S. Army Corps of Engineers, a federal agency, owns the remains because they were found on land controlled by the Corps. (See Chapter 2 for more on Kennewick Man.)

The Tribes of Then and Now

The tribal migration patterns resulted in Indian settlements all across North America, from the northwest forests and western shores, to the plains, the southeast and southwest, and the northern woodlands.

Some tribes were enormous; many were very small. An overwhelming number of tribes are now extinct.

The Five Civilized Tribes were the tribes that had the largest populations, inhabited the most land, and had the most influence, both among other tribes and with the white man. The Five Civilized Tribes are the tribes the Anglos negotiated with, and did business with.

They consisted of:

- ✔ The Cherokee
- ✔ The Choctaw
- ✔ The Seminole
- ✔ The Chickasaw
- ✔ The Creek

Other important tribes included the Navajo, the Lakotas, Nakotas, and Santee, the Chippewa, the Pueblo, the Apache, the Iroquois, and the Arctic tribes.

Native American History For Dummies provides concise "biographies" of these varied tribes, with emphasis on how and where they lived, what they were known for, and what their status is today.

Unexpected Visitors

Once the Europeans arrived, the Indian tribes had to deal with them.

Whether they liked it or not. Whether they wanted to or not.

Columbus was first to come in contact with tribal peoples, specifically the Arawaks on the Bahamas, and later Haiti, and that intercourse didn't go all that well for the Natives. Columbus put them to work as slaves, sent many back to Spain as slaves, and, as the historical record unequivocally shows, treated them . . . well, let's just say it was as though the Golden Rule didn't exist for the Italian explorer and his men.

Spanish and French explorers soon followed Columbus. After all, the so-called "New World" was like a bottomless treasure chest of natural resources, fur-bearing wildlife, game, fish, and other riches that were absolutely irresistible to Europeans.

Soon to follow were such explorers as:

- John Cabot
- Amerigo Vespucci
- Ponce de Leon
- Hernando Cortez
- Jacques Cartier
- Hernando De Soto
- Francisco Vasquez de Coronado
- Marquette and Jolliet
- La Salle

A Plethora of Persistent Personalities

Tribes always were, and still are, the foundation and cornerstone of Native American life and culture. (See Chapter 17 for more on the familial and organizational structures of American Indian societies.)

Indians identify themselves by their tribe. "I'm Choctaw. I'm Navajo. I'm Cree." Tribal identity is as important to American Indians as national ethnicity is to European-descended people of America: "I'm Italian American. "I'm African American. I'm Polish American."

Yet it is commonly the fascinating *people* of the tribes, specific tribes' memorable individuals, that are spoken of most often these days. Native American leaders and warriors have permeated white culture. Their names have truly become household names:

- ✔ Geronimo
- ✔ Cochise
- ✔ Sitting Bull
- ✔ Crazy Horse
- ✔ Pocahontas
- ✔ Tecumseh
- ✔ Chief Seattle
- ✔ Sacagawea

From the 16th century through today, Indian tribes have produced great leaders who have often been visionaries working diligently to maintain the aforementioned tribal identity and not allow their pasts to fade away into the annals of time.

Their aspirations have not always been fulfilled, and many iconic American Indian leaders have watched sadly as their tribes were dispersed, or their land was taken, or their past was forgotten.

Things are somewhat better these days.

Native American culture is thriving and many tribes have Web sites and historical foundations and museums working to educate people — both tribal and Anglo — about Indian history and the roles tribes have played before, during, and currently in the history of America.

The U.S. government, through the Bureau of Indian Affairs, strives to support Native American community efforts, and laws have been passed to protect rights that have been commonly trampled on in the past.

The Smithsonian Institute's Museum of the American Indian also works diligently to chronicle Indian history and culture.

War Stories

The history of Indians in America has been violent.

But not always.

Treaties were signed and peace did exist for great lengths of time between tribes and the white, as well as between rival tribes.

But warfare was one of the main causes for the devastating population losses tribes suffered through in the 16th through 19th centuries. Interestingly, both the whites and the Indians had advantages and disadvantages. Whites had superior firepower, but Indians were incredibly skilled at surreptitious movement and attacking from concealment.

Some of the more important battles — meaning influential and impacting both the Indians and the Europeans (see Chapter 11 for more on our violent past) — in chronological order, covered in this volume include:

- ✔ King Philip's War
- ✔ The French and Indian Wars
- ✔ Pontiac's Rebellion

Also, Indians fought — on both sides — in the major wars as well:

- ✔ The American Revolution
- ✔ The War of 1812
- ✔ The Civil War

Many battles with Indians have now become an iconic part of our history and their names have morphed into having more meaning than simply identifying where the conflict took place.

Movies are made, books are written, and even people who have limited knowledge of history have heard of "Little Big Horn" and "Wounded Knee."

Dysfunction Junction

Relations between the United States government and American Indians have been troubled from the start. That's an undeniable historical fact. This reality resonates throughout the Native American community today, and permeates the Indian culture and zeitgeist.

The U.S. was formed at the expense of the indigenous peoples, yet great effort has been consistently made to remedy the wrongs and repair the damage.

Treaties were broken; tribes were "relocated"; children were taken from their parents and placed in government schools. Reservations were offered as a trade-off for land grabs, yet they were often inferior in all ways.

Sovereignty works

There's still a lot of catching up to do, but Indian self-determination is, as Harvard professor Joseph P. Kalt, author of a 2005 Harvard American Indian Project survey, says, "the best policy in 100 or 200 years for solid progress in taking the tribes out of poverty."

"'Self-rule,' Kalt wrote, "brings decision making home, and local decision makers are held more accountable to local needs, conditions and cultures than outsiders."

The seven ways

Over the centuries of U.S.-Indian relations, the United States has implemented seven specific approaches to "dealing with" the Indians.

They were/are:

- ✔ Treaties (1608–1830)
- ✔ Removal (1830–1850)
- ✔ Reservations (1850–1871)
- ✔ Assimilation (1871–1928)
- ✔ Reorganization (1928–1942)
- ✔ Termination (1943–1968)
- ✔ Self-determination (1968–present)

Currently, self-determination is the official policy of the United States government. Indian tribal nations are sovereign entities, and the U.S. deals with them like individual countries. They make their own laws, impose and collect their own taxes, and yet are still an important part of America.

Stepping up

The U.S. has not shirked from remedying wrong. In the last 35 or so years, many acts, bills, and programs have been passed and launched to benefit the Native American community, including:

- ✔ The Indian Self Determination and Education Assistance Act (1975)
- ✔ The Indian Health Care Improvement Act (1978)
- ✔ The American Indian Religious Freedom Act (1978)

✔ The Indian Child Welfare Act (1978)

✔ The Native American Graves and Repatriation Act (1990)

Daily Life

The history of any ethnic group is also told by how it lived and continues to live on a day-to-day basis.

A group's living arrangements, its eating habits, the clothes it wears, the games its children play, its religious beliefs, its parenting practices, its art and music . . . all these elements combine to paint a rich and textured portrait of a people.

Regarding sustenance, Native Americans relied for food on

✔ Hunting

✔ Trapping

✔ Fishing

✔ Crops

Trading also played a huge role in the daily lives of many Indian tribes. The Indian's talent for trapping and skinning fur-bearing animals created an economic dynamo to satisfy the European demand for North American animal furs.

Natives also made their own clothing from deer and buffalo hides, which included footwear in the form of boots, moccasins, and snowshoes.

All parts of the animals were used, plus Indians made use of the other bounties of the natural world including:

✔ Shells

✔ Stones

✔ Bark

✔ Feathers

Home Is Where the Hearth Is

Native American tribes were markedly different in how and where they lived. It often comes as a surprise to people that Indians employed many more types of homes and domiciles than just the tipi.

Some of these included

- ✔ Plankhouses
- ✔ Longhouses
- ✔ Hogans
- ✔ Chickees
- ✔ Tipis
- ✔ Wigwams
- ✔ Lean-tos
- ✔ Igloos
- ✔ Earth homes

Prey tell

The white man introduced the Indian to the rifle and that enormously changed the way Native peoples hunted.

Prior to the use of firearms, Indians used bows and arrows for distance hunting, knives for close-up killing, and traps for prey that they couldn't spend time stalking. They would set the traps and return days later, usually to find an animal snared.

All aboard

Traveling on foot was de rigueur for tribal peoples, although they were also very adept at figuring out labor- and time-saving other ways of traveling. Waterways were especially useful for covering long distances in a short period of time, and some of the vehicles they used included:

- ✔ Dugout and bark canoes — water
- ✔ Kayaks and umiaks — water
- ✔ Balsa boats — water
- ✔ Bull boats — water
- ✔ Snowshoes — snow
- ✔ Plank boats — water
- ✔ Travois — land
- ✔ Sleds and toboggans — snow

Family First

An important facet of Native American societies is the family, which forms the core unit of the tribe. In Chapter 17 the family structure of American Indians is discussed, including the difference between patriarchal and matriarchal family types.

A woman's work

The role of women in Native American culture was an enormous surprise to the Europeans, who were quite literally shocked at the authority women wielded in both the family and the tribe.

Tribal women in the 16th through 19th centuries were enormously important in terms of tribal solidarity and the continuing maintenance of a sense of community, and their duties included:

- Keeping the household supplied with whatever it needed
- Constructing the home
- Cooking for the family
- Monitoring and restocking the water supplies
- Having almost total responsibility for and oversight of the family's children
- Maintaining the vegetable garden
- Tanning the hides, if the tribe was in the fur business

The kids are alright

In the pre-reservations era for Native Americans, children were somewhat indulged, yet also expected to contribute to the welfare of the tribe, and achieve certain ritualistic milestones in order to officially move into adulthood.

Puberty and first menses were epic transitions into adulthood for tribal children, and for males this commonly required some type of fasting, isolation, or physical endurance tests (or all of the above) for "graduation" into the world of tribal adults.

Language Lab

There were almost as many Native American languages as there were tribes prior to contact with the Europeans explorers and settlers.

There was very little written down, and tribes both communicated and passed down tribal traditions and legends through the use of sign language, the spoken word, and pictographic symbols.

Language groups

The Native American language families included these groups:

- Algic (Algonquin)
- Iroquoian
- Muskogean
- Siouan
- Athabaskan
- Uto-Aztecan
- Salishan

Today, there are approximately 175 Native American languages, yet a staggering 90 percent of them are what is known as "moribund." This means they are not being used enough, or passed down enough to younger generations, to survive much longer.

More than words . . .

Indians did, in fact, use smoke signals to communicate among tribes.

They also used pictures when communications needed to be recorded on paper or bark. The Native American pictographic symbols and drawings illustrate the validity of the old adage about a picture being worth a thousand words. A simple line drawing could easily recount a history, give instructions, chronicle the change of a season, and provide at a glance detailed information that would take lots of words (even if, perhaps, not a thousand), to write or speak.

Words as weapons

Language is a tool that can be used to educate, communicate, and do damage.

The historical record is awash with racist essays and diatribes against Native Americans by white writers, and today there exists Indian literature that not only counters such stereotypical hogwash, but paints a rich and multifaceted portrait of Indians.

If you want to know what real Indians are like, then it is critical that you read literature by real Indians, like:

- Louise Erdrich
- Leanne Howe
- Susan Power
- Wendy Roses

Pray Tell

Native American spirituality is a topic that can, and has, filled many, many books.

And as with Indian languages, there are almost as many tribal belief systems and creation myths as there are/were tribes.

Although it has become something of a cliché to describe Native American religious beliefs as "nature based," it is true that the natural world informed and validated tribal beliefs in a nature spirit (commonly called Wakan Tanka) that was, in one sense, the manifestation of God and the spirit of life in the world.

Animal spirits

Animals play a large role in Indian spirituality and have their own spirits as well as having participated in the creation of the universe.

Animals and birds that appear in Indian creation myths include

- Beavers
- Buzzards
- Coyotes
- Crows
- Deer
- Dogs
- Ducks
- Eagles
- Foxes
- Geese
- Hummingbirds
- Mountain lions

- Parrots
- Serpents
- Tarantulas

- Turtles
- Water beetles
- Wolves

Water

Many Indians believe that all life comes from the water. Many creation myths are very specific: Before there was *anything*, there was water. Some creation myths state that all of reality was beneath the water at the beginning of time. This sacred belief has been validated by science, which uncovered the secrets of how life sprang from the sea and moved onto dry land.

Indians also have creation myths revolving around:

- A first man and a first woman
- The wind
- The underworld

See Chapter 19 for details on these and other tribal deities.

Rituals

Native American spirituality commonly employs rites, ceremonies, and rituals to focus the percipient's spirit and enhance the experience.

These include

- Chanting
- Dancing
- Meditation
- Prayer
- Singing

A church where drugs are legal?

The Native American Church is the only religious establishment in the United States in which members that can legally use the drug peyote in their religious ceremonies.

> ✔ Sweat lodges
>
> ✔ Vision quests

Some of the "tools" used for these rituals include

> ✔ Drums
>
> ✔ Foods
>
> ✔ Musical instruments, especially flutes
>
> ✔ Peyote
>
> ✔ Prayer beads
>
> ✔ Rattles
>
> ✔ Sacred garments
>
> ✔ Stone and wood fetishes

Christian Indians

Many Native Americans today are practicing Christians who strive to incorporate traditional Indian beliefs and practices into Christian dogma and rituals.

Some crossover practices include

> ✔ Using "holy water" and crosses in ceremonies
>
> ✔ Saying Christian prayers during tribal ceremonies, like sweats
>
> ✔ Calling peyote a "sacrament," a common Christian term
>
> ✔ Incorporating sacred Indian pipes into Masses and other Christian ceremonies
>
> ✔ Christian ministers and Catholic priests participating in sacred Sun Dances

The Indian Population Decline . . . and Hope for the Future

It is estimated that nine out of ten Native Americans died in the period between initial European contact and the end of the 19th century.

The causes for this enormous number of deaths were

- ✔ Exposure to diseases for which they did not have immunity
- ✔ Violent conflict with Anglos
- ✔ Violent internecine conflicts among tribes
- ✔ Starvation and death from illness from forced relocation

See Chapter 20 for details on the staggering population loss experienced by Indians in North America during the period of European exploration and settlement.

Native American Identity Today

Today, tribes must be federally identified as an official tribal nation in order to avail members of government programs, as well as establish and implement sovereignty regarding laws and official policies.

Not every tribe that requests federal recognition gets it.

And not every person who wishes to claim membership in a particular tribal nation is granted "citizenship." There are "blood quantum" requirements that effectively determine whether or not someone is officially Cree, or Cherokee, or Navajo, and so forth.

Don't all tribes own casinos?

There is a pervasive misconception in America today that all tribes own casinos and all tribes are getting rich from owning casinos. Would that this were true, eh?

The truth is somewhat different.

Of the over 560 federally recognized tribal nations, only around 200 or so own and operate casinos. There are currently around 360 Indian casinos in the United States, and the overwhelming majority of them are nowhere near as successful as the ones we read about in the papers all the time, like the Mashantucket Pequot and Foxwoods casinos in northeastern Connecticut.

It's been estimated that of the 360 casinos, around 10 percent of them — maybe 30, 35 establishments — generate three-quarters of all the tribal casino revenue in the country. Obviously this means that the 90 percent of the remaining casinos share a very small piece of the gaming pie.

Problems and solutions

The American Indian in today's U.S. has problems, although the progress being made in education, income, health, life expectancy, and entrepreneurship is encouraging and ongoing.

Education

Educational levels are improving steadily. In 2000, almost 71 percent of all Native Americans had earned a high school degree.

This was around 15 points below the national U.S. average, but this was a marked improvement over this same statistic in 1990.

Alcoholism

The trend in Native American communities is toward reversing the devastation alcoholism has wreaked upon their people. Alcohol abuse is a huge problem among American Indians, yet as they say, knowing you have a problem is the first step toward correcting it.

And today, there are programs and a new attitude about alcohol that bodes well for the future and for Native American children who currently abuse alcohol at ten times the average national rate among other children.

Offshore banking

Some Indians are in the international banking business these days and they're making serious money at it, too.

The Blackfeet Tribe of Montana, for example, led the way in 1999 with the formation of their groundbreaking endeavor, the Glacier International Depository.

Mineral rights

Many tribal nations now look to the mineral rights on the lands they own as a source of income to the tune of $245 million in the U.S. in the year 2000.

What minerals are Indians selling for profit? Here's a breakdown:

- **Gas**: 45 percent
- **Coal**: 27 percent
- **Oil**: 22 percent
- **Other**: 6 percent

Tribes are also into wind farms, biodiesel, hydroelectric plants, and biomass (logging and mill residue).

A Bright Future

Native Americans have suffered in the past, and it has taken decades to begin the process of turning around the headlong rush into poverty, lack of education, and dependence on the government.

Today, a new generation of Native Americans are PhDs, doctors, lawyers, accountants, computer designers, and every other profession in America. College is now considered very important for young Indians (although for many, it is still an unattainable dream) and the number of Native American self-owned businesses climbs annually.

In *Native American History For Dummies,* you'll find out about not only the rich and troubled past of the American Indian, but also about the opportunities and achievements taking place today, and the ones that will assuredly take place in the future.

Chapter 2

The Great Migrations

In This Chapter

▶ Exploring how American Indians arrived in the Americas

▶ Checking out the three waves of immigration

▶ Uncovering early periods of development

The following key questions regarding the origin of the Indian population of the North American continent have still *not* been answered with absolute certainty:

✔ Who was here?

✔ How'd they get here?

✔ How many people were there?

Although valiant efforts have been made to accurately account for the creation of the Indian population of North America, no theories to date have answered everyone's questions with certainty, nor can scientists, historians, and Native Americans agree to the validity of one theory over another.

In this chapter, you get a glimpse at some of the wide-ranging and varying theories as to how the people now who are now known as American Indians, Native Americans, Alaska Natives, and First Nations in Canada got here in the first place. You can also discover details on their culture, tools, and how their way of life evolved during the early periods of their civilization on the American continents.

How'd Everyone Get Here Anyway?

The most commonly accepted scientific theory on how American Indians came to be in the Americas is that they came from Asia. Sure, this is now being challenged (like, on a daily basis) but many historians and scholars still consider the "from Asia" theory the most likely explanation.

How they got here exactly, is subject to some debate. In fact, some people believe they came by another route, or even originated here. Some of the artifacts found in North America contradict different theories. The following sections explore these theories and the evidence to support them.

Crossing a bridge to somewhere: Beringia

The standard scientific theory on how North America was populated is that groups from Asia migrated into Alaska (sometimes referred to as the overland migration theory). The waters in the Bering Strait are relatively shallow. During some of the occasional ice ages, sea levels dropped as much as 200 feet around the world. This lowering of the level of the ocean exposed this section of land between the Chukchi Sea and the Bering Sea of the north Pacific.

This land bridge is often called Beringia. It stretched from the eastern point of modern-day Siberia to western Alaska. Experts believe this area could have covered as much as 1,000 miles from north to south.

When did Beringia appear and when did people start moving across it from Asia? That answer is up for debate. This is just one of the many controversies surrounding the origins of the Native people of the Americas. Many experts agree that during several of the short ice ages during the last 100,000 years, land was exposed in Beringia.

Does DNA divulge any details?

Research in mitochondrial DNA has suggested that people were in North America at least 25,000 years ago. This research is based on DNA mutations found in people of American Indian ancestry. The current theory is that mutations occur in DNA at a fairly regular interval. By looking at the differences between two different groups, you can tell when they split off from each other. The 25,000-year figure is derived by comparing certain American Indian groups and other groups that remained in Asia.

The general consensus is that the major exodus along this route took place between 10,000 and 20,000 years ago. There is evidence to show there were several waves of migration into North America.

Even CSI would be stumped

Why is there such a discrepancy in the dates of the migration? Very few ancient artifacts made by humans have been found in this area. The constant advance and retreat of the glaciers of the polar ice cap have scraped much of the land clean. Many of these areas are still under ice or sedimentation. Without artifacts that can be dated, it is difficult for scientists to accurately determine when people first appeared here.

Another commonly accepted part of the land bridge theory is that during the ice ages northern Alaska and Canada were covered by glaciers that were many hundreds of feet thick. This was also believed to be the case along the coastal areas or the northeastern Pacific. However, there was a wide central area that might have been clear of ice. This area ran along the eastern edge of the Rocky Mountains into the Great Plains. Soil core samples of some sections of this part of North America have shown there were areas that were free of ice during these short ice ages. This would have left a wide path open for migrating groups to follow in a general southeasterly direction.

Why'd they come?

Why would people leave Asia and travel through unknown areas into North America?

The most commonly held belief is that these people were nomadic in nature. They would often follow the large herds of migrating animals. These animals were their main source of food. Humans often made their clothing, shelter, and the simple tools they had from these animals. With fresh pastures opening up because of the creation of the land bridge, some herds migrated to the east. As the herds moved east, the human nomads followed them.

It is also possible that some animals that originated in North American might have moved west into Asia. Some groups might have moved east to find their source. Some anthropologists think part of the reason for the migration might have also been due to conflicts with other groups in Asia. Some tribes might have traveled east to look for lands of their own, or were pushed that way by more powerful groups.

Some scientists debate whether the Dyuktai Culture of Siberia and/or the Ainu people of Japan were some of the earliest explorers into North America by way of Beringia.

The first noted documentation of the Beringia theory of the peopling of North America was by José de Acosta. De Acosta was a Jesuit who lived from 1540 to 1600. He wrote a great deal about the agriculture, culture, and geography of the Americas.

Arriving by water

Another theory regarding the arrival of people in North America from Asia is that they took a water route. These explorations are thought to have taken place between 15,000 and 10,500 years ago. There is evidence that many of the people who lived along the northwestern shores of the Pacific during this time period had boats. Some scientists believe these groups could have followed the shoreline across the northern Pacific until they found areas that were not covered in ice.

This theory is not as widely held as the overland migration theory. Many scientists feel that too much of the Alaska and British Columbia coastline was completely covered by glaciers. Any groups traveling along this route would not have been able to find any anchorages. There would have been no place to go ashore in order to repair boats or get needed supplies. With much of the coastal shelf now under the ocean, it has been hard for researchers to find artifacts to support this theory.

Other theories

That people traveled along the Bering landmass is not the only theory on how people first came to North America. In the following sections, you can check out the other possibilities that have been suggested.

Many scientists have found reasons to believe that people from Africa, Asia, and Europe settled in North America. Many of these theories propose that the peoples of the Americas all found their origins in other continents.

The Chinese

Some scientists have suggested that Chinese sailors might have helped to first populate the coastal areas of North America. Chinese junks were able to endure long ocean voyages. Whether their eastward travels were intentional, or as the result of encountering storms at sea, it is not beyond the realm of possibility for Chinese to land in North America and thrive. Some scholars have made the same proposal for Japanese sailors as well.

This bulleted list shows you some of the reasons supporting the possibility of Chinese visits to the Americas:

- ✔ A few researchers have found many artistic similarities between the ancient Chinese and cultures in Central America.
- ✔ There have long been stories told of a Chinese treasure fleet that might have visited Mexico in the 1420s.
- ✔ To some researchers, some ancient Olmec graphics appear to be similar to ancient Chinese texts.
- ✔ Fifth-century Chinese explorer Hui-Shen described his travels to the land of Fu-Sang. One of the plants there is very much like the corn — maize — that only grows in Central America. Was Fu-Sang Central America?

The Solutreans

There is another theory about Europeans traveling to North America that has been gaining some supporters of late. This involves people whose archaeological culture has been called Solutrean. Solutrean people had established themselves in areas of Spain and France. They had some distinctive methods of fashioning arrowheads and lance points.

And here's the interesting part: Points that look similar can be found in *eastern parts of the United States*. The time range on these discoveries is about 16,000 years ago. The scientists who put forward this theory have also discovered some genetic similarities between certain American Indian groups and those of certain modern-day Europeans. These similarities are not found among Asian groups. Like most of the other theories, this one is not yet widely accepted. Scientists are continuing to search for evidence to bolster this idea.

The Africans

Norwegian explorer Thor Heyerdahl mounted several expeditions to show that the Americas could have easily been reached by seafaring groups from Africa. Heyerdahl sailed from Morocco to North America. Heyerdahl never seriously suggested North America was populated by Africans, but he did show that people might have been capable of going between the two continents. To date, no substantial evidence has been located to back up the idea of African colonists.

And we can't forget Atlantis

There are also the old theories of explorations of the world by ancient mariners such as the Phoenicians. These theories can also be found in "new age" stories that ancient explorers were people from Atlantis. While scholars acknowledge the possibility of Phoenicians reaching North America, Atlantis remains the substance of myth in academic circles.

Indigenous theory

Finally, there is the indigenous theory of the origins of the people of North America. Some American Indian groups do have oral histories of there being very long travels before they finally came to the lands they occupied at the time of the onset of the organized European explorations of the 15th and 16th centuries.

However, many more indigenous groups have creation stories that say they originated in North America. Many tribal traditionalists say they were created here, and they stayed here. The Nez Perce tribe point to the "Heart Of The Monster" in Kamiah, Idaho, as their place of origin. Similar stories are told by many other tribes.

According to a 1995 United States Census Bureau survey, 49 percent of indigenous people preferred being called *American Indian,* 37 percent preferred *Native American,* 3.6 percent preferred "some other term," and 5 percent had no preference. The common phrase used in Canada is First Nations or First People.

The Three Immigration Waves

Most scientists believe there were several waves of immigrants moving into North America over the Bering Land Bridge.

One theory says there were three major waves of immigrants into North America. These different migrations can easily be divided into three groups:

- Clovis, Folsom, and Plano
- Na-Dene
- Inuit and Aleut

The two significant differences between these groups are the dates when they first moved into North America and their basic language.

The dates associated with each of these groups vary considerably from scholar to scholar.

Clovis, Folsom, and Plano

According to the most widely held theory, the first significant group to migrate into North America crossed Beringia sometime around 15,000 to 20,000 years ago.

As they traveled along the ice-free corridor east of the Rocky Mountains, they eventually spread across the Great Plains. Most of these groups moved to areas south of modern-day Canada. Continuing cold weather made these areas too harsh to merit long-term habitation. Many scientists believe these original groups are the basis for most tribal groups south of Canada.

By the end of the last ice age, around 12,000 years ago, they came into the eastern parts of North America. At the same time, they traveled south through Central America into South America.

Cultural linguists believe that most of the languages of North and South America, south of Alaska and Canada, developed from this initial group of immigrants.

Clovis

Around 11,000 years ago, these groups began to share some common characteristics. They tended to be nomadic hunters. Preferring larger animals, they developed specialized hunting techniques and tools. One of their most distinctive inventions was the spear head they devised. It was usually made from flint, and had a long narrow point. One of the first of these points was discovered in the 1930s in Clovis, New Mexico. This group would be named for this town: the Clovis Culture.

Around 10,000 years ago, the largest land animals of North America became extinct. This would include such animals as:

- ✔ Mammoths
- ✔ Mastodons
- ✔ Saber-toothed cats

Many scientists speculate that the Clovis groups were the reason for the depopulation of these North America animals. As these larger animals disappeared, cultures and methods began to change.

However, recent studies by scientists Donald Grayson and David Meltzer suggest that Clovis people did not instigate the extinction of approximately 35 major groups of mammals. Their theory is that Clovis people just happened to live at the same time as a natural extinction occurred.

Folsom

To deal with these changes, new techniques and methods led to the development of a new cultural group. This newest group was called the Folsom Culture. They were at their peak from about 10,500 to 8,500 years ago.

They added some refinements to the original Clovis point. The Folsom culture developed the atlatl. This stick would be used to help them throw their spears faster and farther. (See Chapter 11 for more on the atlatl.) They also became adept at herding animals into marshes or cul-de-sacs.

One of their more common hunting techniques was the animal jump. Some of the hunters would drive a herd of large animals toward a cliff. Other hunters would wait at the bottom of the cliff to butcher the animals after they jumped to their deaths.

The word *atlatl* comes from the Aztec language of Nahuatl. It can be translated as spear thrower or hand thrower. Atlatls were used by many ancient cultures throughout the world.

The Folsom people are best known for their hunting of a now-extinct form of American bison called the *Bison antiquus*. Whether the Folsom people hunted the *Bison antiquus* into extinction is a matter of debate among scientists. The Folsom people flourished until around 8,000 years ago.

The *Bison antiquus* (ancient bison) was often as tall as 6 feet at the shoulders. They could easily weigh as much as 2,000 pounds.

Plano

After the Folsom culture came the Plano Culture.

The Plano people were a further development of the Folsom people. Their period of existence is usually estimated to be from 6,000 to 8,000 years ago. With the eventual extinction of the *Bison antiquus*, the Plano people turned their attention to the smaller modern American bison (commonly called the American Buffalo) and other small game.

Some of their ancient sites showed dwellings that were circular in shape. This has led some scientists to believe they employed skins over poles for shelters. The Plano people also refined the spear points that had been used by the Clovis and Folsom people.

Collectively, the Clovis, Folsom, and Plano people are often called Paleoindians.

Na-Dene

As with most of the early history of North America, exact dates are hard to come by.

The second major migration into North America can be estimated to have happened around 9,000 to 10,000 years ago. This group, on whole, has remained in Alaska and Canada. They are distinguished by their common language base: Na-Dene.

The major language groups are composed of:

- Athabaskan
- Haida
- Tlingit

One theory says the Na-Dene were stranded in Beringia for some time by encroaching glaciers. When the ice finally retreated, the Na-Dene groups moved out of Beringia into Canada and parts of Alaska. The Navajos (or Diné, as they call themselves) and the Apache, of the southwestern United States, are also part of this group.

The Inuits and Aleuts

The third migration into North America included the Inuits and the Aleuts.

This immigration is believed to have occurred about 4,000 to 6,000 years ago. Most of this group has remained in Alaska, northern Canada, and Greenland.

This migration is also called the Eskimo-Aleut migration. No other major migrations have taken place since this last group crossed from Asia into North America.

Some scientists believe the Na-Dene may have immigrated out of Beringia after the Inuits. As with all of these theories, precise dates are hard to establish.

Even older ancient sites have been discovered in the Americas. If the estimated dates of these sites have been accurately determined, they could have people in the Americas at least 1,000 years earlier than previously thought.

Dating ancient sites is a very tricky business. Scientists often disagree about the exact dates. Some of these possibly older sites are

- Meadowcroft Rockshelter in Pennsylvania
- Monte Verde in Chile

The Stages of the Earliest Americans

Archaeologists and anthropologists have divided the development of the original inhabitants of North America into several different stages.

While there are generalized time frames involved in these different periods, some things happened in different times in different areas. Different climates and terrains lead to different lifestyles. An area thick with trees would allow for wooden shelters. Deserts or plains would require another type of shelter design.

The major developmental periods and areas of the earliest Americans are

- Paleoindian
- Archaic
- Post-archaic
- Woodlands
- Pueblo

We discuss these developmental periods in more detail in the sections that follow.

The Paleoindian period

The Paleoindian period generally covers the time period of 6,000 to 15,000 years ago. This period includes the spread of humans across the Americas. The people are represented by the Clovis, Folsom, and Plano groups already discussed.

If the Paleoindians had their own theme song, it would be Dion's "The Wanderer." (Because, y'know, they wandered around like the guy in the song. Wasn't that obvious?) Seriously, though, the Paleoindians were nomadic and moved according to the migration patterns of the mammoth and buffalo.

They were hunters, mainly, but also gathered what edible vegetation they could find. During the Paleoindian period, they essentially spread out southward and eastward from what is now Alaska into the North American continent and down into what is now South America.

They used atlatls and spears to bring down their prey, and the dominant characteristic of the people of this period was constant movement. (See Chapter 11 for more on the weapons of choice of Native peoples.)

The Archaic period

The Archaic period is usually dated from about 3,000 to 10,000 years ago, depending on the area. One of the distinctions of the Archaic period is a change in the climate of North America. As the ice age came to an end, temperatures began to rise. This led to the creation of some the desert areas of North America. Glaciers began to retreat, ocean levels began to rise, and the depressions of the Great Lakes began to fill.

The inhabitants of North America were also starting to change their ways of life. The types of animals they hunted began to expand. As more of the larger animals were killed off, the people of this period began to make use of smaller and smaller animals, and more plants. Some groups changed from hunters to foragers.

Finding the Ancient One

In 1996 a skull and some 300 other bones and bone fragments were discovered in the shallow waters of the Columbia River, near Kennewick, Washington. Radiocarbon dating of the remains revealed that the bones were over 9,000 years old.

Scientists who examined the remains found that this person's cranial shape did not match that of local groups. Instead of being short from front to back and round, the cranium was long and narrow. The person likely looked a lot like the other early people from the Americas, but if he has to be placed into a modern population, his cranium looks most like the Ainu of Japan.

Because these remains had been found on lands that were traditionally part of the territory of Indian tribes, several groups asked to have him returned for reburial. Scientists objected and in good old-fashioned American tradition, the case went to court. In the end, the remains were not deemed to be "Native American" under the Native American Graves Protection and Repatriation Act.

A wider variety of tools were being developed. Grinding rocks in order to form tools was used in addition to the older method of chipping off pieces.

Previously, tools were most often made from flint or obsidian. These stones could easily be chipped to the desired shape. During the Archaic period, stone points decreased in size and changed in shape. By the end of the Archaic, people had developed arrowpoints. Other tools, such as nets, were also developed and refined.

The Post-Archaic period

The Post-Archaic period ranges from present day to 3,000 years ago, depending on the location. There were considerable differences in the types of development between those areas that were the East Coast, the Great Plains, the deserts, and the west coastal regions. The distinctive changes of this period were

- ✔ Invention of pottery
- ✔ Increasing use of agriculture
- ✔ Development of textiles and leather goods
- ✔ Tools made from bone
- ✔ Improvements of stone tools
- ✔ Improvements in the construction of shelter
- ✔ Invention of the bow and arrow

The Woodlands

In what would become the United States, several cultural groups developed. Having significant amounts of wooded areas, groups were able to utilize trees for a variety of purposes.

East Coast Areas

The Hopewell and Adena cultures left a significant number of artifacts. Both groups were noted for their construction of mounds. Copper began to be used for tools and jewelry.

Great Plains

Village life would become the central focus of much of the Great Plains along many of the year-round rivers. While some groups would still be nomadic hunter-gatherers, many others would settle down. Hunting would remain a major activity for Great Plains groups.

West Coast Areas

The west coast offered a variety of climates and habitats. Some groups developed significant fishing operations. The Pacific Northwest had a significant population. The desert areas of California and the Great Basin saw smaller population levels.

The main form of agriculture of this period was the cultivation of corn, beans, and squash. These agricultural products are often called the "three sisters."

The Pueblos

The Pueblo peoples of the American Southwest had their own unique development. According to their own histories (similar to the Hopi and Zuni), they are the descendants of the *ancient ones*.

The "ancient ones" were formerly referred to as Anasazi, but are now known as Ancestral Puebloan.

The earliest groups lived in caves or simple mud-and-pole structures. They harvested wild grasses and eventually cultivated corn, beans, and squashes. They also domesticated the turkey. As they matured, these cultures developed pottery. Weaving was also a significant part of their culture.

Around 750 B.C. they began building aboveground adobe structures for living quarters. They also maintained underground structures called *kivas,* which were often used for religious or ceremonial purposes. Their initial settlements appeared around 2,000 years ago in the northern part of the American Southwest. As the climate changed, they tended to move toward the south.

The following sections discuss each of the Pueblo periods in more detail, showing you how their way of life changed as the years passed.

Pueblo III

The Pueblo III period dates from approximately 1050 to 1300 B.C. This period is also known as the "Classic Pueblo" period.

There appear to have been fewer outlying villages during this period, as much of the population moved into the larger communities. It is during this time that many of the large, multi-storied villages were built. These could be free-standing structures, or structures built into hollow areas in cliffs. The largest structures had hundreds of rooms. Some of the more well-known structures of this period are

✔ Mesa Verde in Colorado

✔ Chaco Canyon in New Mexico

- ✔ Aztec Ruins in New Mexico
- ✔ Casa Grande in Arizona
- ✔ Canyon de Chelly in Arizona

This era saw most of the communities located in southern parts of modern-day Colorado and Utah and the northern sections of Arizona and New Mexico. The end of this chronological period is dated to the abandonment of these large communities.

A drought covering over 20 years struck the American southwest in 1276, and many scientists believe this was one of the major reasons why most of the major structures were abandoned by the end of this period. Some scientists have suggested that the appearance in the area of more aggressive groups, such as the Navajo and Apache tribes, also led to the exodus of the ancient Pueblo people.

The two oldest continuously inhabited settlements in the United States are in this area. Oraibi, on the Hopi Reservation in Arizona, and Acoma (Sky City) in New Mexico, date back to around 1150. San Augustine, Florida, is the oldest European-founded continuously inhabited city in the United States.

Pueblo IV

The Pueblo IV period dates from approximately 1300 to 1700 C.E. This period is also known as the "Regressive Pueblo " period. With the abandonment of the large communities of the Classic era, the population moved to the east and to the south. While there were some large communities, the architecture was not as refined as that of the Classic era.

Cotton was used for textiles, and corn continued to be a major source of food. Pottery tended to have bolder designs during this era.

In 1598, Spanish conquistador Juan de Oñate Salazar began a major expedition into the lands north of the Rio Grande. Oñate claimed most of New Mexico for Spain. He then established a capital city in Santa Fe.

The first Spanish expedition into Pueblo areas was that of Francisco Vasquez de Coronado in 1540. When he did not find the fabled "Seven Cities of Gold," he left the area.

Spanish efforts to dominate the daily life of the Pueblos, including religious conversions, led to considerable resistance by the Pueblos. In 1680, a Tewa Pueblo Indian named Popé led a revolution against the Spanish. Starting in the Taos pueblo, the revolt was successful. The Pueblos managed to rid much of New Mexico of Spanish forces. The end of the Regressive Pueblo era is marked by the return of significant Spanish forces into the area around 1694.

Pueblo V

The Pueblo V period dates from approximately 1700 to the present. This period is also known as the "Modern Pueblo" period. This period is marked by continuing control of the territory by Spanish, Mexican, and American authorities. During this time, the number of thriving Pueblo communities was significantly reduced.

Many of the domesticated animals (cattle, goats, horses, and sheep) introduced by the Spanish were adopted by the Pueblos early in this period. While cotton was still used for textiles, wool from their sheep and goats soon became the predominant fiber.

The Pueblos have been relatively successful in establishing sovereignty over their local governments.

Chapter 3

The Development of the Ancient Cultures

*N*ative American history is an epic story spanning centuries. More importantly than its chronological duration, though, are the many types of cultures that evolved on their own based on geography and resources, and then either died off or assimilated as migration patterns changed, or contact was made with other tribes.

This chapter looks at the ancestral cultures of the Indian past whose spear points, and drinking vessels, and, yes bones are telling their story to us today as we dig deeper, both literally and figuratively, into the lost ages of this land's first inhabitants.

Clovis, Folsom, and Plano (11,500 B.C.)

After arriving on the North American continent, the first explorers spread across the land not covered by ice.

As it was then, and as it has always been for humans, they had two main concerns, sustenance and protection from the elements. Food and shelter.

People learned to adapt to the environment and to exploit the flora and fauna of the continent. As people traveled throughout the land, they analyzed the available resources and developed technology to best utilize them. The first inhabitants invented specialized stone tools to hunt the animals they discovered.

Two of the most well-known tool types were named after the places that archaeologists first identified these artifacts. Clovis and Folsom points are among the most highly recognized types of artifacts that are found in the Americas. When they are found, they provide evidence that humans were present at that location many thousands of years ago.

Clovis

The Clovis culture has long been believed to be one of the oldest types of people in North America. Many scientists believe they were the first group who successfully spread across the continent. This theory is called *Clovis First.*

The Clovis people are identified archaeologically by a distinctive type of spear point. The spear point is characterized by a groove down the middle. This made it much easier to attach to a wooden shaft. The edges of the stone were also chipped down to an almost razor edge. The stones are usually 4 to 6 inches long, and up to 2 inches across. The points narrowed to a point at the very end. They were mostly flat on the top and bottom.

These points were made skillfully using percussion, or hammering blows and pressure flaking with bone and antler tools.

The first of these spear points was located near the town of Clovis, New Mexico, in 1936. It was near the fossils of an extinct American mammoth. Organic material around the stone suggested it was from about 11,500 years ago.

These kinds of spear points were especially good for hunting the very large animals which populated North America at the time. The American mammoth was a perfect example of one of these large beasts. In essence, the people who used Clovis points were big-game hunters.

Clovis points have been found over much of North America, and the exact dates of the Clovis period are under debate by archaeologists. Scientists generally agree that these points date to the period of time in which megafauna were present in the Americas. The length of time during which these points were used is still being evaluated.

The "Clovis First" theory has changed significantly in the last few decades. The following list discusses some of those changes:

✔ Scientists Michael R. Waters and Thomas W. Stafford have suggested that the discovery of isolated sites in North and South America seem to pre-date Clovis times by as much as several thousands of years.

✔ Another theory relating to the Clovis people is that they might have hunted the largest land animals to death.

✔ A similar layer of soil has been discovered at many of the archaeological sites where Clovis points have been found. According to a new theory, this is evidence of something affecting both the weather and the living beings on this continent.

Folsom

The first points of the type that were later named Folsom were discovered by an African-American cowboy named George McJunkin. McJunkin, a former slave, was interested in the bones of extinct animals he saw while working on a ranch near Folsom, New Mexico. While examining the bones, he also noticed some interesting spear points mixed in with the animals. While the points interested McJunkin, it took longer for professional archaeologists to take notice.

The Folsom culture follows the Clovis culture. Folsom points are similar to Clovis points in that they are manufactured with a shallow groove in the middle of the point. Unlike Clovis points, the grooves are wider and run the length of the Folsom point. This may represent a change in hunting practices.

As with the Clovis era, the exact dates of the Folsom period are debatable. Generally, they range from about 10,000 to 10,900 years ago. Some scientists place these dates as much as a thousand years sooner and later.

More knives were being produced at this time. These knives were often much thinner than the knives made by the Clovis period and are believed to be related to the need to quickly and efficiently process meat and hides of bison. Folsom craftspeople also made hide scrapers. One of the other tools they are believed to have produced was the atlatl. This was a notched stick which could be used to throw a spear faster and farther. (See Chapter 11 for more on the atlatl.)

The following list gives you an idea of what these tools were like:

✔ **Spear points:** The spear points became more fluted and were thinner. These points often had notches cut in the side, so they could be attached more easily to wooden staffs with sinews.

✔ **Knives:** More knives were being produced. These knives were often much thinner than the knives made by the Clovis period.

✔ **Hide scrapers:** Folsom craftspeople also made hide scrapers.

✔ **Atlatl:** One of the other tools they are believed to have produced was the atlatl. This was a notched stick which could be used to throw a spear faster and farther. (See Chapter 11 for more on the atlatl.)

Plano

The Plano people were a further development of the Folsom people. Their period of existence is usually estimated to be from 6,000 to 8,000 years ago. Some of their ancient sites showed dwellings that were circular in shape. This has led some scientists to believe they employed skins over poles for shelters. The Plano people also refined the spear points that had been used by the Clovis and Folsom people.

The Folsom people are best known for their hunting of a now-extinct form of American bison called the *Bison antiquus*. Whether the Folsom people hunted the *Bison antiquus* into extinction is a matter of debate among scientists. With the eventual extinction of the *Bison antiquus*, the Plano people turned their attention to the smaller modern American bison (commonly called the American Buffalo) and other small game.

The *Bison antiquus* (ancient bison) was often as tall as 6 feet at the shoulders. They could easily weigh as much as 2,000 pounds.

Adena and Hopewell (1000 B.C.– A.D. 1000)

Another significant period of time in the development of the people of North America occurred as the weather started to stabilize into conditions which are similar to what we experience today. In the Southeast, the Woodland period covers sites that were occupied between the Archaic period and the Mississippian period.

The Woodland period people were the first to create and use pottery, and the earliest type came from the coast and was tempered with fiber. Woodland groups deliberately cultivated plants such as sunflowers, instead of simply gathering plants.

Some Woodland groups built large earthen mounds that were elaborately designed in the shapes of animals and birds. The size of the mounds indicates that there was some form of organized political control over the communities. A typical settlement would range from three or four dozen in the winter to as many as 100 people during the summer.

Woodland groups developed new tools, and it was during this period that the bow and arrow was first utilized. In addition to hunting, Woodland period people fished using nets and traps. In the Late Woodland period, reliance on plants increased and corn, beans, and squash were all grown.

Adena

The Adena culture belongs to the Early Woodland period, and may date to as early as 500 B.C. You may have noticed that archaeologists like to name cultures after places near which they were first uncovered, and — surprise — this culture was first identified during excavations at a plantation named Adena.

Adena sites are centered in the Ohio River Valley. Other sites in the eastern U.S. have some similarities, but these may not actually belong to the same culture.

Adena people lived in circular houses, but may also have moved seasonally to take advantage of resources. Like other Woodland-period people, they utilized pottery and created mounds. Circular earthworks were sometimes built near the mound sites.

The burials of important Adena people were incredibly elaborate, and could result in the creation of a mound that eventually reached 60 feet in height! It's unclear whether this was the original intent of the burial practice, because the mounds usually began as smaller affairs that grew with each event associated with them.

Hopewell

The change from the Adena era to the Hopewell era seems to have occurred gradually, and one of the most distinct changes was in their pottery.

While the Adena culture did have pottery, it was very basic in shape and design. Hopewell pottery became very ornate and detailed. Their mounds and earthworks also grew in size and complexity. The Hopewell Culture also covered more territory.

Generally, the Hopewell Culture is dated from around 100 B.C.–A.D. 400 or A.D. 500. They had a much more developed agriculture than did the Adena. They expanded the number of foods they raised. However, they were one of the few early American Indian societies not to have a significant use of corn.

They also made refinements to the tools that they used. Hopewell craftwork made sizable improvements. Their jewelry was very detailed and was constructed out of many different types of material. Copper, mica, and ceramics were all used. Their pottery took on some very intricate designs and patterns.

Hopewell trade networks covered considerable territory. Excavations at ancient Hopewell settlements have discovered shells from the Gulf of Mexico, the

Great Lakes, and the Atlantic. Minerals from as far as Lake Superior and northern Georgia have been found.

Hopewell earthworks and mounds were significantly larger and more elaborate than the Adena. One earthwork surrounded over 100 acres. They used geometric shapes such as circles, octagons, and squares. Many of the earthworks were designed to be outlines of animals such as birds and bears. Such large structures hinted at a much more complex society and political organization.

The name Hopewell comes from the name of the owner (Mordecai Cloud Hopewell) of a farm where one of these mounds was first excavated in the late 1890s.

Hohokom and Mogollon (A.D. 200–1450)

A different type of development took place in other parts of North America. The desert southwest saw several different societies grow and prosper for a time.

The eruption of Sunset Crater in 1064 distributed a layer of ash over much of this area, and people were soon drawn to the much-improved growing conditions.

The three main groups in this area were the Hohokam, Mogollon, and the Ancestral Puebloans.

Hohokam

Hohokam is generally thought to be a Pima (Akimel O'odham) word for "those who have gone" or "all used up."

The Hohokam were a group of people who lived in the central and southern part of Arizona from before 200 B.C. until around 1450 of the common era. They may have originated in Mexico or they may be the descendants of local hunter-gatherers. While they have a couple of distinct characteristics, they are perhaps best known for their irrigation systems.

Water, water everywhere

The Hohokam canals are an amazing accomplishment considering that all the builders had to build the canals with were stone hand tools. Over the course of history, the Hohokam built well over 500 miles of canals. Some canals were narrow, short, and shallow. Canals were up to 15 miles long, 60 feet wide, and over 10 feet deep. Many of these canals still exist, including in modern Phoenix.

With the availability of water from the Gila and Salt rivers, the Hohokam were able to produce crops year-round. They raised beans, corn, cotton, and a variety of squashes. With a good food supply, they often had surpluses. This helped them to develop a thriving amount of trade with neighboring groups.

Their pottery was very distinctive. It was often based on the colors of red and tan. A unique part of their design was the use of distilled plant juices to etch their pottery. They were also skilled artisans, specializing in working with shells from the Gulf of California.

Their ceremonial dress had a certain central Mexico flair because of their use of feathers. While they also had ball courts like the central Mexicans, Hohokam courts were often oval, rather than rectangular like the Mexicans. Many of their towns had raised central platforms.

Historians have divided the experiences of the Hohokam into several time periods. They are

- The Pioneer Period

- The Colonial Period

- The Sedentary Period

- The Classic Period

The Pioneer Period

As is often the case with the chronology of Native American history, the starting date for the Pioneer Period varies depending on which historian you ask. Genesis dates range from around A.D. 1–A.D. 300. The year A.D. 775 is the commonly accepted ending date for this period.

During this time, the Hohokam were farmers situated around the Gila River in Arizona and the southwestern United States. They lived in simply constructed homes made from a framework of woven small branches that would often be covered with mud. This design is usually called wattle and daub.

They also had pit houses. (See Chapter 15 for more on the types of homes American Indians lived in.)

A village often had a central plaza. A village was often built on the design of a large ranch. Fields were located around a central housing complex. The Hohokam had begun to make simple jewelry from shells and locally produced turquoise. Their pottery during this time was for basic purposes and was simple in design. As more time passed, the designs became more colorful and intricate. They also designed simple pots which they often used to bury the remains of the dead.

Starting with corn and beans, as the years passed, they acquired a wider variety of crops. Living in river valleys, they could irrigate their crops with shallow wells. Toward the end of this period, the villages increased in size, and the irrigation canals began to appear. Notably, the villages of Pueblo Grande and Snaketown developed.

The Colonial Period

The standard time for the Colonial Period is from A.D. 750–A.D.775 to A.D. 950–A.D. 975.

The most significant development of this period is the growth of the population. Villages and houses increased in size and spread out over a larger region. Groups of houses will often circle a courtyard. Raised central mounds in the plaza will increase in size. These seem to be built atop trash heaps and may have served as dance grounds. Some towns may now have as many as 1,000 residents.

Ball courts were built in some of the larger towns. Irrigation canals continue to grow. They now have over 20,000 acres in crops. They continue to harvest a very wide variety of naturally occurring plants. Local animals are also a source of food.

The color and design of the pottery is further developed. More red is used. Minerals are added to give the pots a two-tone color. Funeral pots also become much more elaborate.

Based on excavations of some of the ruins, it appears that classes had started to develop among the population. Some areas had larger homes, bigger trash pits, and more elaborate funeral materials.

Trade with Mexico and their surrounding neighbors continued to increase.

The Sedentary Period

The Sedentary Period ranges from around A.D. 950–A.D. 1150. As the population continued to grow, so did the towns, the canals, and the complexity of society. Pit houses were being reinforced by posts. More house clusters were being built around central courtyards. Larger ovens are constructed. Society developed determinedly, and the Hohokam built more, traded more, and employed what could justifiably be called mass-production practices.

Artisans continue to develop new designs, materials, and crafts. Feathers from birds, a wide variety of minerals, especially copper, shells and jewels are now either being discovered, or reaching the Hohokam through trade. Macaw feathers and mosaic pyrite mirrors were among the items that were traded from MesoAmerica. Using distilled plant juices, pottery and jewelry are now being made using a technique called "acid etching." The Hohokam may be one of the first cultures in the world to utilize this method.

The Hohokam were now trading extensively throughout Mexico and their surrounding area, including California. Definite social classes were present by this time. The social structure essentially had three levels — here they are in descending order:

- ✔ The cultural elites
- ✔ The artisans
- ✔ The common laborers

Business was good. Even pottery and shell work were now being manufactured in bulk for sale.

Larger towns were developing, more urban areas developed with a raised platform in the central plaza, and ball courts were appearing all over the region. Toward the end of this period, Snaketown was abandoned. It was later excavated in 1934, which provided an enormous wealth of information about the Hohokams during this period.

The Soho Phase

The Soho Phase is the first part of the Classic Period. It lasts from around A.D. 1150–A.D. 1300.

What is acid etching?

The Hohokam achieved designs and patterns on shells and pottery using a technique called acid etching.

The Hohokam discovered that fermenting cactus juice resulted in a highly acid liquid that they could use to burn away unprotected areas of their pottery and decorative shells.

They got so good at it, that today we credit them with "perfecting" the skill.

During this period, the indigenous population slowly started to decline. Fewer new villages were being built; some old ones were abandoned. The larger towns started to build walls around their perimeters. Multi-storied buildings (in the classic Pueblo style) started to expand. Pit house construction seemed to end. Fewer canals were built, and the main canals were strengthened and deepened.

Based on architecture alone, the Hohokam seem to have developed a siege mentality. Casa Grande, Mesa Grande, and Pueblo Grande were the largest towns. The Hokokom had reached their peak.

Contacts with the distant world seemed to be fewer, as trade with nearby neighbors increased. Polychrome (three or more colors) pottery was developed and no new ball courts were being built.

The Civano Phase

The Civano Phase is the second half of the Classic Period. It runs from around A.D. 1300–A.D. 1450. Many settlements were abandoned. The population dropped considerably. No major construction projects took place, but facilities were seldom maintained. Agriculture ranged between extremes, and river levels were well above normal for several years, and then well under normal levels for several years. For all practical purposes, the society collapsed.

So, what happened to the Hohokam?

That is a question which experts can only guess at, and, as you would certainly expect, there are several theories, including:

- **Drought:** There was a significant drought in the late 1200s. Then there was extensive flooding after that. A large population cannot long survive without a reliable source of food.

- **Devastating raids:** Another theory says that raiders entered the area and plundered mercilessly. In a region that was relatively peaceful for a long time, this would have been a major jolt to the society.

- **Corrupt leaders:** Another theory is that the leaders of the culture demanded too much of the population, while they took too much of the spoils of society. A story among the Pima (Akimel O'odham) says that the population revolted against corrupt leaders. Without leaders, the society broke up.

So where are the Hohokam today? Are they still around, or did they die out? This is still a matter of debate among historians and anthropologists. The Pima (Akimel O'odham) and Tohono O'odam (Papago) may be the descendants of the Hohokam. If that is true, then the Hohokam are still alive in the same relative area. There are also stories among the Hopi and Zuni which suggest some of the Hohokam drifted into their areas and merged with the Ancestral Puebloans and the Mogollon.

The Mogollon

The Mogollon people's name comes from where they lived, the Mogollon Mountains, which were named after Spanish official Juan Ignacio Flores Mogollón.

The Mogollon lived in parts of Arizona, New Mexico, Texas, Sonora, and Chihuahua. Their "turf" ranged from the Little Colorado River in the north, to the Pecos River in the east, to Verde River in the west, and central Chihuahua in the south. This area includes mountains, valleys, high deserts, canyons, and forests.

Common bonds

The Mogollon were really a group of different people who had certain things in common. They are separated into certain branches, which were usually based in a certain geographic area. Two of the better known Mogollon groups were the Mimbres (southwest New Mexico) and the Jornada Mogollon (southeast Mexico and Texas).

Dates are a bit hazy, but the Mogollons existed from around 150 B.C. to the 1500s. Initially, they lived in narrow mountain valleys or mesa tops. There was little fertile ground, so they were primarily hunter-gatherers. They lived off of nuts, grasses, and small game. Their earliest homes were often pit houses. They eventually developed aboveground houses in the traditional pueblo style.

Stargazers?

There is some evidence that the Mogollons made astronomical observations. Certain images on pottery, pictographs, and petroglyphs appear to be of star patterns or astronomical events. An "astronomy circle" has been discovered in the Casa Malpais ruins near Springerville, Arizona. Measuring about 80 feet across, certain notches or openings appear to match up with astronomical events such as solstices. While this is still being researched, it is not the only such site among the Mogollon.

Their pottery

The Mogollon are known in large part by their pottery. Their pottery started out in the color of the clay they used. Eventually, it evolved into a very distinctive black-on-white color scheme. They buried their dead, often in or accompanied by pottery or special earthenware.

By around the period A.D. 600–A.D. 700, the Mogollon had been able to develop significant crops of corn, beans, and squash. By this time, they had often found more fertile areas in which to live.

Early on, their homes were pit houses. These would consist of a circular or rectangular hole about 3 feet deep. Poles were set up around the perimeter. Thin poles or branches were placed across the top. Sometimes, mud was applied to the roof. These types of homes were well insulated and could handle extreme cold and heat fairly well. Villages started out with just a few families, and slowly grew over the centuries. These were most common until around the year 1000.

Hot and cold

After 1000, the Mogollon began living in the typical aboveground style of adobe pueblo. These would have somewhat thick walls and roofs to help keep out the heat and cold of their environment. Desert temperatures are often over 100 degrees Fahrenheit during the day. Winter temperatures could get under zero degrees.

In the northern part of their territory, there are many similarities with Ancestral Puebloan cliff dwellings during this time. Gila Cliffs is an example of this. In the south, they appear to have been influenced by Mexican styles. In both cases, these structures could have over 100 rooms. Casa Grande (Paquimé) in Chihuahua is a good example of this.

Many of these villages had underground ceremonial pits called *kivas*. Similar to the other groups of the region, these were believed to be used for religious and civic purposes. The Mogollon were believed to have shamans and very developed religious and burial ceremonies.

Mimbres, Grasshopper, and Jornada cultures

Also after A.D. 1000, the Mimbres branch of the Mogollon were reaching their peak. They lived in southwestern New Mexico and are especially known for their very artistic pottery. They had a variety of designs that included wildlife and intense mystical and abstract designs. Kokopelli, a humpbacked flute player, was a very common character on their pottery. It is from these pots that many archaeologists believe they have learned a lot about Mimbres culture. As with the Hohokam, they also had detailed pots used for burials.

Starting around A.D. 1200, the culture slowly began to decline, moving slowly from the north to the south. However, Casa Grandes in Chihuahua, Mexico, continued to thrive during this time. Casa Grandes (or Paquimé, as it is more commonly known now) was a very large village. It had a central plaza and large buildings. It seemed to be a trading center between Mexico and the northern regions.

One of the other communities which did see some population increase during this time was called Grasshopper. It was in central Arizona situated on what is called the Mogollon rim. It is speculated that Ancestral Puebloans moving away from their drought-stricken areas may have moved into this area.

The Mogollon Rim is a very long escarpment that often abruptly rises several thousand feet from the lands below. It is considered the southern part of the Colorado Plateau. It runs from central Arizona, north of Phoenix, to almost the New Mexico border.

The Jornada Mogollon were centered in western Texas, west of the Pecos River. They were one of the last of the Mogollon people. There are some ruins (Firecracker) which appear to have still been occupied in the 1400s.

So, what happened to the Mogollon people?

This is the difficult question asked regarding the fate of all of the ancient southwestern cultures. All of the reasons listed in the earlier section "So, what happened to the Hohokam?" can be applied to the Mogollon. They may have died off, drifted away, or evolved into what would become the Pueblos.

The Ancestral Puebloans: The people formerly known as Anasazi

The Ancestral Puebloans are perhaps the best known of all the ancient people of North America, but many people know them by their former name: Anasazi.

The ruins of their villages can be found all over the "four corners" area of the United States. Their old name, Anasazi, comes from a Navajo word meaning "ancient enemies." (See Chapter 2 for more info on the Ancestral Puebloan.)

Other names for this group of people are

- ✔ Ancient Ones
- ✔ Ancient Pueblos

- ✔ Basketmakers
- ✔ Hisatsinom (Hopi for "ancient people" or "those who came before")
- ✔ Se'da (Tewa for "ancient ones")

Archaeologists have established several timelines for the Ancestral Puebloans. It is difficult to be precise on the boundaries between periods. Many of the different timelines overlap, as well.

Here is a combination of some of the many Ancestral Puebloans timelines:

- ✔ 6500–1200 B.C. Archaic
- ✔ 1200 B.C.–A.D. 50 Basketmaker II (Early)
- ✔ A.D. 50–A.D. 500 Basketmaker II (Late)
- ✔ A.D. 500–A.D. 750 Basketmaker III
- ✔ A.D. 750–A.D. 900 Pueblo I
- ✔ A.D. 900–A.D. 1150 Pueblo II
- ✔ A.D. 1150–A.D. 1350 Pueblo III

People have been living in the southern part of the Colorado Plateau for many thousands of years. The Archaic people were hunter-gatherers. The start of culture is often picked as the time when these people started developing agriculture. This happened around 2,000 years ago. These ancient crops were centered around corn and squash.

Unlike the Hohokam and the Mogollon, in the early days the Ancestral Puebloans did not produce many pots. They were known for their basket-making skills. This is why they are often called Basketmakers. Their lived in pit houses, or structures made from logs sealed with mud.

They were able to make fabrics from the fiber of naturally growing plants. These were used for mats, bags, blankets, and to cover the dead for burial. The Ancestral Puebloans also seem to have domesticated dogs. They used spears and small arrows or darts to hunt the small game of the area. Rabbits were important for food and fur.

Ch, ch, ch, changes . . .

Starting around A.D. 450–A.D. 500 (Basketmaker II period), changes became apparent in Ancient Puebloan culture.

More pit houses were being built closer together. These dwellings began to be developed in large caves or under overhanging rock walls. This would be the classic look of Ancient Puebloan structures. Toward the end of this period, kivas began to be built. These ceremonial structures were often found in the front sections of a village. Some jewelry was being made with local materials and stones (turquoise). Also during this time beans were first seen as one of their crops.

In the Pueblo I period, starting around A.D. 700–A.D. 750, the Ancient Puebloan began building mud and adobe brick homes. Slowly, these developed into multi-storied buildings. It is right around the transition into this time period that bows and arrows were developed. Spears would ultimately be discarded.

They also started making pottery and growing cotton during this time. This led to an increase in craftwork and clothing. Some birds, such as turkeys, became domesticated. The feathers would be used for many purposes.

Chaco

The Pueblo II period, starting around A.D. 950, saw the development of what would be called the Chaco Phenomenon. Centered around Chaco Canyon in northwestern New Mexico, this became a widespread series of villages. Trade was highly developed throughout the area, with their neighbors and into Mexico.

The Chaco area seemed to develop a highly structured society. There are thousands of small structures and nine major building complexes in the valley. One of them, Pueblo Bonito, was five stories tall, and had over 600 rooms and dozens of kivas. They built roads which went on for over 100 miles. They had many irrigation ditches. Stairways were carved into the cliff faces. There are several examples of structures and drawings that showed their interest in astronomy.

Chaco Canyon is the home of some interesting carvings (petroglyphs) called the Sun Dagger. First discovered in 1977, located behind three large slabs near the top of a butte in Chaco Canyon are two spirals carved in the rock. Light shining between the two large rocks forms a narrow strip of light which is similar in shape to a dagger. As the sun moves through the sky, the light moves across the wall. On the summer solstice, the dagger went directly through the middle of the larger spiral. On the day of the winter solstice, two sun daggers perfectly bracket the larger spiral. The sun dagger goes through the middle of both spirals during both equinoxes. Unfortunately, damage caused by bad weather has caused the large rocks to shift. The sun dagger now only lives on in photos and movies.

This period is marked by the largest expansion of then Ancestral Puebloan culture. More multi-tiered structures are being built in cliff alcoves, mesa tops, and cliff bases. Trade expands and brings lots of goods into Ancestral Puebloan areas.

The Pueblo III Period is marked by the relatively quick abandonment of the major towns. Between 1277 and 1300, a 20-year drought developed and was centered in the area of the San Juan River basin. It is during this time that populations declined and people started migrating to the south and east. Many archaeologists now believe the Ancestral Puebloans moved toward the Rio Grande River valley.

Chapter 4

Hardly a Vast Wasteland: America before 1492

*T*here must have been a lot of European jaws dropping when explorers from Spain, England, and other countries first laid their eyes on the natural wonders that abounded in the New World.

Sure, many European countries were (and still are) similarly resplendent with verdant veldts, winsome waters, tall trees, and mountainous mountains, but remember, these guys had been on boats for a long time. And back in those days, ocean travel was, shall we say, less than luxurious. (Does the word "scurvy" ring a bell?) So when they set foot on this sea-to-shining sea land of ours, they were almost certainly stunned by the magnificence laid out before them: endless stretches of virgin forest, enormous bright green and yellow fields, stately snow-capped mountains, their sides carpeted with trees, thundering herds of bison, plus rivers and lakes that probably reminded them of the ocean they crossed to get here.

This chapter takes you on a journey through pre-Columbian North America, showing you the developments and cultural advances Indians made to the land. Also, we debunk several of the myths and stereotypes of pre-Columbian peoples.

Taking Advantage of Vast Resources

The word "pristine" has often been used to describe the pre-Columbian state of the North American landmass. But "pristine" means "not yet altered by human encroachment," and ongoing research is utterly refuting the notion that Indians "trod lightly" on the Earth and did not do anything to alter their environment. The following sections describe just how pre-Columbian North America was changed through Indian development.

Altering the lay of the land

Across the Americas, many different tribal groups found ways to alter their environment to benefit themselves. These changes included everything from pyramids to burial mounds to paved roadways to enormous mounds designed to look like animals.

A variety of different tribes built structures that altered the landscape, including the:

- Olmecs
- Toltecs
- Maya
- Aztecs

The Indigenous people were known for their temples and giant sculptures. Between them, they built many thousands of buildings and pyramids. The pyramid at Cholula, Mexico, is larger by volume than any of the pyramids in Egypt.

The Maya built paved, elevated roads (called sacbes), which traveled through the countryside from one community to another. Yes, pre-Columbian America had paved roads. Today, many ancient sacbes have been incorporated into modern highways and railway lines.

But it wasn't just the people of Central America and Mexico who built large buildings.

The Ancestral Puebloans (Anasazi) of the American southwest built structures which were up to five stories high and had hundreds of rooms. These communities also had roads that were wide and ran up to 100 miles long. (See Chapter 3 for more about the Hohokam.)

Outside of St. Louis, Missouri, are the Cahokia Mounds. The largest one of the 100-plus mounds here is over 100 feet tall and covers over 14 acres. The area also had a stockade which was over 2 miles long. All of this was built by hand.

Other mound sites in the Southeast covered acres and were created in the shapes of animals or in abstract designs.

The Aztec completely modified their surroundings to point of even creating land. Being one of the last tribes to arrive in the valley of Mexico, the Aztec could only find a place to live on an island no one wanted in the middle of a large, shallow lake. Needing more land, they would anchor floating woven mats to the lake bottom with poles. They would then scrape up the lake bed and pile it up on the mats. After stacking up enough mud, rocks, and gravel, the pile would be above water. Eventually, it would dry enough to stand on. Over many years, they built a city called Tenochtitlan in this manner.

The Maya also practiced this kind of land building in their swampy areas. They would also find a low-lying area and dig a ditch around it. This would allow the water inside the area to drain off into the ditch. They would throw the soil from the ditch into the middle, thus creating more land. These elevated growing platforms can be found all over the Maya lowlands.

Changing course — the river's course

Many different cultures modified the flow of rivers to provide them with drinking water, as irrigation for their crops, or to help them catch fish:

- The Hohokam of the American southwest built hundreds of irrigation canals and dams. Some of their canals were over ten feet deep and stretched for miles. (See Chapter 3 for more about the Hohokam.)

- In the northeastern United States, several tribes built V-shaped rock dams across their rivers. An opening at the tip of the V would canal the fish into a narrow area where they could easily be caught in nets. This was also practiced by tribes in southern California.

- The Aztec city of Tenochtitlan was on a lake that covered 3,000 square miles. To get to their city, they built a series of causeways from the shoreline to their city. The water in the lake was not good to drink. So, they built two aqueducts to bring them water from the nearby mountain springs and streams. They had two aqueducts so one could be working in case the other needed to be worked on. Their engineering was so good that they had public and private fountains that flowed with good water.

Going after game

Across North America, there were many different ways that the American Indians modified and used their environment in order to hunt game or keep domesticated animals. Stockades would often be used to keep smaller domesticated animals from getting away. Some of these stockades in the Mississippi River valley and around the Great Lakes could be quite large.

The Alaska Natives would often wait in mountain passes for the annual migration of the elk, which were also called *wapitit*. These tremendous herds were much easier to hunt in these circumstances.

In the Great Plains, tribes would use several different methods to capture some of the animals who traveled in herds. The following list discusses one of the simplest methods and one of the most effective methods:

✔ **Herding the herds:** The simplest method would be to try to stampede a herd in the direction of some waiting hunters. Without something to contain the animals to a small area, this method was not very effective. Prairie grasses could be set on fire in order to direct the herd toward an area where the hunters waited. This was most often used for smaller game.

✔ **Using the buffalo jump:** One of the most effective methods used hundreds of years ago was called the *buffalo jump*. This involved quite a bit of preparation. The most important part of this operation was a cliff near lands where the buffalo roamed (to describe it in a particularly familiar way). The cliff did not have to be too high. At the bottom of the cliff, a corral was built. The hunters would stampede the herd off the cliff. Sometimes, a V-shaped wall of rocks, brush, or people would be set up near the cliff in order to direct the herd into a small area. If any of the bison survived after falling off the cliff, the corral would keep them from escaping. The bison were hard to kill using weapons, so this method was very efficient.

In the past, some Alaska Natives would often wait in mountain passes for the annual migration of the elk. These tremendous herds were much easier to hunt in these circumstances.

Valuing vegetation

Almost all of the tribes all over North America practiced farming to some extent or another. In some of the larger towns, many tens of thousands of acres of crops were grown.

Some studies say that over half of all the foods being eaten in the modern world had their origins in the Americas. These foods were domesticated here and then exported to the rest of the world. Everything from potatoes to tomatoes, and beef jerky to chewing gum originated here. After all, it was a search for things to spice up the food that brought most of the explorers here in the first place.

Many different methods were used to aid in plant growth:

- ✔ **Slash and burn:** Many tribes used the slash-and-burn method for farming. Each year they would cut down the remnants of the previous crops and burn them. The ashes would help to return some vital nutrients to the soil. However, this was not a very good long-term method. So, every few years, or so, a field would have to be abandoned to help it revive itself.

  In some area, tribes would cut down large areas of trees. They would chop the trees into small pieces and spread them across the area. These would then be burned. This was similar to slash and burn. It also created new fields for future use.

- ✔ **Crop management:** In many parts of the Americas, crop rotation was practiced in one form or another. Sometimes it was from necessity because a certain crop could no longer grow in the nutrients that were left in the soil. In other cases, it was a planned activity. Tribes as diverse as the Hidatsa, Hurons, Mohawks, and the Timacua did this in one way or another.

- ✔ **Controlled burn:** A common method of crop management was the controlled burn. For example, in California, many tribes lived off of acorns. They noticed that lightning strikes would often start major fires. If there was significant underbrush, these fires would destroy the trees which produced the nuts they needed to live.

  By trial and error (an early, yet accurate application of the scientific method, in a way), they discovered that setting a fire when there was only a small amount of underbrush would burn off the forest floor without burning down the big trees. This also opened up the ground for new growth. With new growth come tender new plants. These are very appealing to animals like deer. So, a controlled burn could help the acorn harvest and deer hunting as well. This was practiced in many different parts of the continent.

Cultural Diversity That Was Hardly Primitive

When the Spanish first arrived in the Aztec capital (which is now Mexico City), they were in awe. The Indigenous cultures were quite highly advanced. The city was bigger and more lavish than any city in Europe. The Maya also had a significant written language. The sections that follow discuss some of their cultural advances in more detail.

Native medical wonders

Along with the food value of crops (see the section "Valuing vegetation," earlier in this chapter), organic material found other sophisticated uses in North America. Many tribes discovered that certain natural substances could be used for medical purposes, including:

- Foods
- Herbs
- Barks
- Roots
- Other plant parts

Heart problems in the northeastern part of the continent were treated by using part of the foxglove plant. The active ingredient (digitalis) is still used today. In fact, many of the early Spanish colonists commonly preferred going to an Indian herbalist than to their own doctor. Even the king of Spain sent doctors to the New World to learn medical practices.

Watching the skies

Many North American cultures were very advanced in astronomical observations:

- **Calendars:** The Maya had a very sophisticated calendar that was based on observations of the sun, moon, the planets, and stars. The Maya were particularly interested in Venus. They could predict its movements across the sky with amazing accuracy. They could also predict solar and lunar eclipses.
- **The number zero:** The Maya are only one of three civilizations in the world to have invented the concept of the number zero (Babylon and the Hindus did, too).
- **Observatories:** Many tribes established observatories or *star wheels*, which could be used to predict when the equinoxes and solstices would happen. (See Chapter 3 for more about the Anasazi.)

We, the people . . .

The Iroquois Confederacy is often thought of as the model for the government of the United States. Their form of government had separation of powers and democratic principles. The American Constitution is very similar to the laws of the Iroquois.

Debunking Pre-Columbian Stereotypes

There are many stereotypes related to the Indigenous people of North America at the time of Columbus's visit. Many of these stereotypes are contradictory. Here are just a few:

- ✔ The continent was mostly a pristine area populated by just a few Natives.
- ✔ The Natives were very primitive in their cultural and technological development.
- ✔ The Natives were peaceful, eco-friendly, mystical people.
- ✔ The Natives were ignorant, savage heathens.
- ✔ The Natives came across a land bridge from Siberia around 13,000 to 15,000 years ago.
- ✔ The Natives all had red skin.
- ✔ The Natives all lived in tipis and worked animal skins.
- ✔ The Natives had very few tools and no metal.
- ✔ The Natives gained everything by being "civilized" and gave little back.
- ✔ The continent was populated by one large homogeneous group of people.
- ✔ The Europeans brought culture and religious enlightenment.
- ✔ The Europeans brought, disease, oppression, bigotry, and intolerance.

The sections that follow bring out the truth about the Indigenous people of North America.

Playing with numbers

The population of North America in 1492 has been debated almost ever since then.

The numbers range from 500,000 to over 100,000,000. Each side accuses the other of under or overestimating their numbers. Most "experts" tend to believe the population was somewhere between 1,000,000 and 15,000,000.

In any case, what happened to all of them? Most experts believe that a very large number percentage of the ancestors of the population in 1492 would eventually die from diseases brought by the Europeans. The percentage is often estimated to be around 85 to 95 percent.

Some experts are of the opinion that by the 1600s and 1700s, much of the North American continent was free of its earlier population. Without the American Indians to continue their stewardship of the land, it reverted to a more "pristine" environment, closer to like it was before the Indigenous peoples used the land for their communities. The large tribes de Soto saw in the 1500s were dramatically removed by the time La Salle came through 100 years later.

Dumpster diving for truth

The Native people of this continent often made significant changes to their environment (you can find out more about this in the section, "Taking Advantage of Vast Resources," earlier in this chapter). In many cases, they changed the environment so much that they had to move on to better lands quite often, or their civilizations collapsed. Much of the knowledge gained about certain tribes has been learned by going through their very ample trash heaps. These answers refute several stereotypes.

The early Indigenous people created tools that were found only here. They also independently developed tools that are found around the world. Some of them worked with metal, too, such as gold in Central and South America, silver in South America, and copper throughout the Southeast.

Many groups have extremely complex societies with extensive knowledge and even written texts. They had detailed religious beliefs and even democratic institutions. And yet, others were very autocratic or run by the religious elites. Some tribes seldom fought wars; others were seldom ever at peace.

With the significant variations in recent archaeological discoveries, the time period of the population of North America seems to be getting further in the past. While it was once almost universally held belief that the original Americas came here by way of a land bridge from Siberia, there are now many theories which have them coming by boat and land across the Pacific and the Atlantic.

Culture clash

There was a vast exchange of goods and ideas between the Old World and the new. While the New World was often not in control of the exchange, they did profit from some new technologies. The Old World reaped a bounty of valuable goods, foods, and culture.

There are vast differences between the many different tribes of North America. The Maya are different from the Tlingit, which are different from the Hopi, who are different from the Abenaki. They speak different languages, have different beliefs, and different life styles.

The cultural exchange between Old and New Worlds was based on a power system which was hard for the New World to overcome. According to some anthropologists, the radical change of the culture of the North American peoples due to their massive population loss made it very hard for them to resist the invading European cultures. Had not so many of the Native people died from their exposure to diseases, for which they had no immunity, they might have fared better.

Chapter 5

Settling Down: Tribal Settlements after the Great Migrations

In This Chapter

▶ Understanding what culture areas are about

▶ Discovering details about tribal settlements

▶ Looking at life in culture areas

*T*he identification and study of Indian culture areas provides us with an interesting look at how societies and civilizations evolve. Each specific culture area can be viewed as a microcosm of larger, more expansive societal constructs such as towns and cities — yet with an important difference: The Indians had no technology to utilize to compensate for nature's shortages or complications.

The different culture areas developed based on the natural resources of the area in which the tribes found themselves, or to which they migrated. It's reasonable to say that the indigenous cultural evolutionary model consisted of *environment equaled adaptation*, or at the very least *directed* said adaptation.

While there are many similarities among the various tribes of North America, there are also many differences. Hundreds of different languages are spoken; rules of kinship and religious practices vary. It is a common misunderstanding to assume there is only one "American Indian" way to do something.

The Major Culture Areas

As the earliest groups of American Indians spread across the North American continent they encountered many different kinds of geography. Each area had its own unique combination of land, weather, native plants, and animals. Eventually, these groups began to settle. When they lived off the land, they had to adapt to that land. After spending a long enough period of time in one area, these ways of life became societies. Scientists, anthropologists, historians, and people with OCD always like to put things in categories. And these societies were no exception!

One of the ways which the early inhabitants of North America were categorized by anthropologists and historians was by *culture areas*. While different tribal groups had different ways of life, they often shared certain activities with other tribes living in similar areas. For example, the shelters required for a normally hot climate would share similar features, such as ventilation, sun reflection, lightweight portability, and so forth — even if the shelters were different in structure and appearance. Anthropologists and sociologists noted many of the common lifestyles among tribes that lived in certain regions. This led them to try to group together those tribes who shared the same basic environments. These areas became known as culture areas.

While the numbers vary a bit, there are eight major culture areas in North America:

- ✔ Arctic and the Subarctic
- ✔ Eastern Woodlands
- ✔ Southeast
- ✔ Plains
- ✔ Southwest
- ✔ Plateau and Great Basin
- ✔ Pacific Northwest
- ✔ California

As is commonly the case when experts start coming up with "definitions," opinions varied. Many scientists established different boundaries for each culture area. Some culture areas were bounded by major obstacles to travel such as mountain ranges, lakes, or deserts. Other culture areas were set up to match similar weather patterns or similar languages. Initially, the number of major culture areas ranged from as few as 5 to as many as 20. Cultural scientists seem to have settled on from 5 to 9 major areas. Similar geographical regions have become the major deciding factor for setting up the boundaries of these areas.

The Arctic and the Subarctic

The Arctic and Subarctic culture areas are usually grouped together. While there are some differences between them, they are more similar than most of the other areas. The sections that follow discuss these culture areas, their similarities, and differences in detail.

Location, location, location

On a map, the Arctic culture area covers the western coast of Alaska, across the Arctic Ocean, including the Yukon, the Northwest Territories, and Nunavut to the northeastern part of Labrador in Canada. Included in this area are the Arctic islands of Canada and the northern half of Hudson's Bay.

The Subarctic culture area included the inland part of eastern Alaska and most of southern half of Canada. The Subarctic was the area where trees were able grow year-round. There was more abundant plant and animal life, too. Like the Arctic culture area, this area is extremely cold for much of the year.

Braving the brrrrr!

Among the common factors of tribes living in the Arctic culture area is their adaptation to year-round cold weather. The northern *tundra* (a cold, treeless, rolling plain with a short growing season where often the earth just a few feet under the surface remains frozen year-round) has a very short growing season for the limited number of plants that grow there. There are almost no trees here. So, many of the houses were made from skins, sod, stone, or snow (igloo). Today, people may still use traditional houses at hunting or fishing camps, but most live in regular houses made of brick or wood.

The communities in Alaska have been identified politically as Alaska Native villages. It may be confusing to think of each village as a separate tribe, but this is the easiest way to compare communities to those in the lower 48 states. Villages that are quite close to each other may contain members of the same cultural group, but as a political entity, each has its own tribal or village council.

An igloo is a structure built from blocks of snow. The walls are usually built in a circular fashion. Each new layer of blocks is of a smaller diameter. This eventually forms a domed roof. Later, a door is cut into the wall. (See Chapter 15 for more on the various types of domiciles of the American Indians.)

Catching up on their culture

Socially, in the Arctic the nuclear family was quite common. Family relationships were important in this region as people needed to depend on each other for social and economic support. Thus, extended families were usually in contact with each other. In the eastern Subarctic, families were *patrilineal* (centered on the father and his family). In the western Subarctic, the Athabascan groups were often *matrilineal* (a family which is based around the mother and her family).

In the Arctic, traditional religion was oriented around myths, spirits, and the practice of shaman. Most groups believed that both humans and animals had souls. Many Subarctic groups believed in witchcraft.

The inhabitants of the Arctic culture area are not normally called American Indians, while this is usually the case with people living in the Subarctic Culture areas and farther south. Historical events have meant that tribal people situated in mainland Alaska are referred to as Native Alaskan and tribes on the Aleutian peninsula are known as Aleut or Unangan. Tribes, such as the Tlingit, Haida, and Tsimshian that are located along the Alaska panhandle are referred to as American Indian.

Eskimo was the word previously used to describe all of the peoples of the Arctic and Subarctic, but using one term for all these different groups is misleading. It's kind of like saying "Anglo" when you're talking about all the people in New York City. Today, there are very strong distinctions between communities in the Arctic and Subarctic. *Inuit* is the word that can be used for people in the north, *Yup'ik* for people in the middle, *Athabaskan* for other groups in the middle, and *Aleut* for people on the chain of islands.

The most common language family in the western part of the Subarctic culture area is Athabascan. Algonquian is the basis for most of the groups in the east. Native Alaskan languages can be divided into Inuit, Yup'ik, or Aleut.

Hunting wildlife

Wildlife in Arctic culture areas was and is somewhat limited. As you can imagine, this limits the ways a person could live. Many of the early settlers lived by fishing and hunting the few animals that grazed here in the summer months. The Unangan, or people of the Aleutian Islands, are believed by anthropologists to have been the most recent Native settlers of North America.

Parts of the Subarctic culture area are the summer home of large herds of migrating animals. Elk (wapiti) and caribou herds could travel through the area in the thousands. Fur from large game is used for clothing and shelter. The early settlers in the area would occasionally cleverly build low stone walls in valleys along the migration routes. These walls would help to "funnel" the caribou into a smaller area where they could be more easily hunted.

Some Arctic and Subarctic tribes

The Arctic Tribes are so-called because, duh, their areas of inhabitation are in the Arctic! Interestingly, the term "Arctic tribe" is also used to describe tribes in northern Europe, especially in the Scandinavian countries. This is a list of the most well-known Arctic tribes:

- Aleut
- Inuit (Eskimo)
- Yupik

The Subarctic culture area is huge and spans most of the northern half of the North American continent, and extends into Canada. These peoples lived with long, hard winters and were skilled trappers. These are the Subarctic tribes:

- Bear Lake
- Beaver
- Carrier
- Chipewyan
- Cree
- Dogrib
- Han
- Hare
- Kaska
- Koyukon
- Kutchin

- Malecite
- Micmac
- Montagnais
- Naskapi
- Ojibwa
- Sekani
- Slave
- Tanaina
- Tanana
- Tutchone
- Yellowknife

The Eastern Woodlands

The Eastern Woodlands culture area essentially consisted of the entire western half of the United States. There are many different types of trees in this area. Lakes and rivers were abundant. Rain was frequent enough for a wide variety of vegetation to prosper.

Getting the lay of the land

The Eastern Woodlands culture area includes the following areas in the United States:

- Along the southern part of the Great Lakes
- The Mississippi and Ohio River valleys
- The lands along the eastern Atlantic from Virginia to southern Labrador

The area had a moderate climate with cold winters and warm summers. There were large forests covering much of the region.

Housing was often a series of poles covered by bark shelving. These types of housing were often seen as *wigwams* (a round, domed structure). It usually has wooden pole supports and bark or plank walls and roofing. It is similar to the wickiups and long houses. *Long houses* were long (go figure), rectangular, usually narrow structures with poles for support and a curved or peaked roof. The siding and roof covering was often from bark. Wigwams and long houses were used as long-term housing as they could not easily be moved. They were fairly durable and stable. (See Chapter 15 for more on the various types of domiciles of the American Indians.)

Understanding what life was like

The early settlers were hunter-gatherers. Some of the earliest cultural groups defined by archaeologists are the people belonging to the Adena and Hopewell cultures. These people were the earliest agriculturalists and developed basketry and distinct pottery styles. Hunting and fishing were also important means of subsistence.

Later Woodland peoples were among the first to encounter permanent settlers in the Northeast and were among the first to face dissolution as a cultural group.

The density of the population in the Eastern Woodland area means that communities exercised careful control over their territory. Disputes could arise over the use of hunting grounds, and these were sometimes settled through outright war. Societies within the tribes developed to structure this type of behavior, and distinct rules could be applied to fighting.

Housing styles varied throughout the region and through history. For early Algonquian groups, housing was often a series of poles covered by bark shelving. These were described by Europeans as wigwams and long houses.

Many of these societies were communal in nature. The goods of the tribe were shared by the members of the tribe. Families around the Great Lakes were often patrilineal. Mom was often the clan boss in groups in the northeast.

Traditional religions of the Eastern Woodlands employed the use of music and masks to connect with the sacred world. In addition, religious societies organized people's relationship to the spirit world.

Many tribes had a specific leader. Tribal groups in these areas often had conflicts with their neighbors over hunting grounds. Warrior societies developed with many groups. Bows, arrows, and clubs were common fighting and hunting tools. Some disputes could often be solved without killings, but many areas appeared to be in a state of constant conflict. *Counting coup* (a way to prove a person's bravery) was an occasional practice.

Tag, you're hit!

Counting coup was a way to prove a person's bravery. An individual would find a way to approach an enemy warrior. He would touch the enemy with his hand or a stick, and then run away. You could call it an adult version of tag, but the other person might strike you back, and it could have deadly consequences. (See Chapter 11 for more on counting coup.)

Religious practices could include:

- ✔ Shaman
- ✔ Spirits
- ✔ Medicine societies

There are four major language groups in this culture area:

- ✔ Macro-Algonquian
- ✔ Algonquian
- ✔ Iroquoian
- ✔ Macro-Siouan

Some Eastern Woodlands tribes

The names of the Eastern Woodlands tribes are some of the most remembered names in Native American history: Algonquin, Iroquois, and Mohican. Many tribes are still extant and some, like the Pequot and Mohegans, have become extraordinarily successful in gaming. Here's a list of some Eastern Woodlands tribes:

- ✔ Abenaki
- ✔ Algonquin
- ✔ Cayuga
- ✔ Chickahominy
- ✔ Chippewa (Ojibwa)
- ✔ Conestoga
- ✔ Delaware (Lenni Lenape)
- ✔ Erie
- ✔ Fox
- ✔ Huron (Wyandot)
- ✔ Illinois
- ✔ Iroquois
- ✔ Kickapoo
- ✔ Mahican
- ✔ Massachusetts
- ✔ Menominee
- ✔ Miami

- Micmac
- Mohawk
- Mohegan
- Mohican
- Montauk
- Nanticoke
- Narragansett
- Neutral
- Niantic
- Oneida
- Onondaga
- Ottawa
- Passamaquoddy
- Pennacook
- Penobscot

- Penacola
- Pequot
- Podunk
- Potawatomi
- Sauk
- Schaghticoke
- Seneca
- Shawnee
- Susquehanna
- Tuscarora
- Wampanoag
- Wappinger
- Wea
- Winnebago (Ho-Chunk)

The Southeast

The Southeastern tribes' lifestyles and culture were impacted by the warmer climate and their coastline locations. Here you get a glimpse of their styles of homes, how they led and fed themselves, and how they communicated.

The area

The Southeastern culture area includes the United States south and east of the Mississippi and Ohio River valleys to the Atlantic south of Virginia to the Gulf of Mexico. Many scientists often place Florida in its own culture area.

The area had a moderate climate with cool winters and hot summers. Forests covered much of the area. Pine was the most common type of tree. There were numerous freshwater lakes and rivers. A very wide variety of vegetation was able to be grown due to the temperate climate and the abundant rainfall. There were also coastal lowlands and extensive marshes.

Housing varied somewhat depending on how far south you were. The more northerly areas often had a large community hall. Individual houses were often round using a wattle-and-daub construction (a durable construction made by loosely weaving a frame made from sticks and/or reeds, which is then covered with a combination of clay, mud, and sand). In the marshy coastal areas and in Florida, many of the houses were on raised platforms. In the warmer area, the houses would have a roof but no walls. This would allow for better ventilation and cooler temperatures during the very hot summer months.

Farming, fishing, and hunting

Many of the groups in the Southeast came to rely mainly on agriculture, but also exploited the rich food resources of the river valleys. Some groups developed a very complex social and religious structure that in some places involved the construction of elaborate settlements. Mound groups were built under the authority of a central leadership. These sites are quite impressive and some, such as Cahokia, rivaled later European settlements in size and grandeur.

Many of the tribes in the Southeast relied on a main leader and had developed complex class systems. Relationships among groups were structured as well, and it was not uncommon for tribes to fight with each other. Some tribes divided themselves up into clans based on belonging to a red or white town, meaning that they were devoted to war or to peace. Artifacts recovered from some of these sites show elaborate warrior outfits.

Today, the Southeastern tribes still fight with each other, but it's more likely to be over who has the best museum or the newest healthcare facility!

Corn, beans, and squash were common crops. The climate in Florida was temperate enough that crops could be grown much of the year. Many of these groups had highly developed agriculture with a wide variety of plants being harvested for food, construction, and handicrafts.

There was a fair amount of small game, especially deer and turkeys. Hunters would often cover large areas in order to find enough game. Fishing was very common along the coastal areas.

Life, leaders, and language

The early settlers were hunter-gatherers, but they switched quickly to stationary farming. Some of the early settlers were mound builders. These societies seemed to be highly class conscious. A royal or priestly caste was found in such ancient groups as the Natchez. Many of the villages were situated along the river valleys. See Figure 5-1 for an idea of what a typical Indian village looked like.

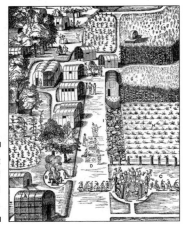

Figure 5-1:
A typical
Indian
village.

Many tribes had a king-like leader. In some groups there was a leader for peace and another one for war. Warrior societies developed within many of these groups, too. Bows, arrows, and clubs were common fighting and hunting tools.

Many of the North American early societies divided responsibilities along gender lines and were communal in nature — goods were shared by the entire tribe. Men were responsible for the hunting, women for planting. Some of these societies, such as the Cherokee, were matriarchal. The home and the children belonged to the women. Clan societies were also quite common in many of these tribes, a characteristic which continues to this day. A man would become part of his wife's family. Often, a male child was mentored by his mother's brother, rather than by his father. Basket and pottery making was often done by the women and children.

The languages of the culture area are based on these language groups:

- Algonquian
- Iroquoian
- Muskogean
- Siouan

Some Southeast tribes

If you wanted to sum up the Southeastern tribes in three words (y'know, if the opportunity ever arises when someone says to you, "Hey, could you sum up the Southeastern tribes in three words"?), those three words would be corn, cotton, and mounds. Here are some of the more prevalent Southeastern tribes.

- Alabama
- Atakapa
- Biloxi
- Catawba
- Cherokee
- Chickasaw
- Chitimacha
- Choctaw
- Creek
- Koasati
- Hitchiti
- Houma
- Meherrin
- Mikasuki
- Natchez
- Nottaway
- Ofo
- Pascagoula
- Powhatan
- Saponi
- Seminole
- Timucua
- Tunica
- Tutelo
- Yuchi

The Plains

If there were ever a more dead-on accurate word to describe a geographical location than "plain" to describe the Plains, we don't know what it is.

The Plains have few wooded areas and extend for light-years in all directions. Survival wasn't easy and most Plains tribes hunted rather than grew crops, since buffalo were plentiful.

Taking a peek at the Plains

The Plains culture area includes much of the United States between the Mississippi River and the Rocky Mountains and areas from southern Canada to the Mexico border.

The area had a variety of climate areas ranging from very cold winters to hot summers. It is covered by a variety of grasses. The few wooded areas are along the river valleys. Rainfall is light to moderate. The elevation ranges from about 300 feet to 5,500 feet. There are three major river systems: Arkansas, Missouri and Red Rivers.

Traditional housing came in two basic types. It was often a series of long thin poles covered by animal skins. This tipi (teepee) allowed for quick setup and removal. They were well ventilated. They were only partially effective against hard rain or very cold temperatures. Some of the non-horse tribes of this area had sod houses. These types of building were used as long-term housing as they could not easily be moved. They were fairly durable and stable.

The religious beliefs of the Plains tribes are among the most exploited by non-Native people. Practices such as vision quests and sweat lodge ceremonies have been appropriated and used improperly by outsiders. For members of these tribes, these are not activities to be trifled with! (See Chapter 15 for more on the various types of domiciles of the American Indians.)

Living life in the Plains

There were few early settlers in this area. Most of the population that traveled through here was hunter-gatherers. Some farming took place along the river valleys, with corn, beans, and squash being the natural choice. Baskets and pottery were produced by most groups.

The great herds of American Bison (buffalo) allowed for adequate hunting to take place. When the domesticated horse arrived on the Plains in the late 1600s, a few more tribes moved into the area. In fact, this is the rare culture area where the population actually was *greater* after the initial contact with Europeans. From around 1650 to 1880, the Plains horse culture led to the spread of several American Indian tribes. It is these tribes which are most known to the general public. Through books, films, and television, the exploits of such tribes as the Cheyenne, Comanche, and the Sioux entered the American consciousness.

Many tribes had a group of leaders, rather than a single "boss." Tribal groups in these areas often had conflicts with their neighbors over hunting grounds. Warrior societies were highly organized within many groups. Bows, arrows, lances, and clubs were common fighting and hunting tools. Some disputes were resolved through prolonged negotiation, but fighting was also common. "Counting coup" was an honorable activity during war.

There are three major language groups in this culture area:

- ✔ Algonquian
- ✔ Siouan
- ✔ Uto-Aztecan

Some Plains tribes

Plains tribes were mostly nomadic, traveling after the buffalo herds, but over time, small villages did spring up where they planted for sustenance. They were dominant in the Plains areas from the mid–18th century to the late 19th century. Here's a list of some of the Plains tribes:

- ✔ Arapaho
- ✔ Arikara
- ✔ Assiniboine
- ✔ Atsina (Gros Ventre)
- ✔ Blackfeet
- ✔ Blood
- ✔ Brule
- ✔ Caddo
- ✔ Cheyenne
- ✔ Comanche
- ✔ Crow
- ✔ Dakota
- ✔ Hidatsa
- ✔ Iowa
- ✔ Kansa
- ✔ Kichai
- ✔ Kiowa
- ✔ Mandan
- ✔ Missouri
- ✔ Omaha
- ✔ Osage
- ✔ Oto
- ✔ Pawnee
- ✔ Piegan
- ✔ Ponca
- ✔ Quapaw
- ✔ Sarsi
- ✔ Siksika
- ✔ Sioux
- ✔ Stoney
- ✔ Tejas
- ✔ Teton
- ✔ Tonkawa
- ✔ Wichita
- ✔ Yankton

The Southwest

The American Southwest is mystical, man. There's a reason New Mexico is known as the Land of Enchantment. The endless deserts and spooky caves, the red and yellow landscapes, the mountains that, if you look at them at just the right angle, and in just the right light, might seem to show the face of a long-dead chief or warriors.

The Southwestern tribes paid attention to their dreams, if you know what we mean.

The land and its location

The Southwest culture area includes

- Arizona
- New Mexico
- Southern Utah
- Colorado

This is a desert area, so rainfall is light in most areas, with cold winters and hot summers. There are some forested areas, mainly in the mountain areas. There are only two major rivers here, the Rio Grande and the Colorado River.

Housing came in a wide variety of forms, and other types of structures included wickiups, hogans, tipis, and subterranean houses. (See Chapter 15 for more on the various types of domiciles of the American Indians). The following list gives you an idea of what some of these structures were like:

- **Adobe house:** A structure built from a special type of dried mud brick. The brick is made from clay, sand, and straw. These types of structures are often found in desert areas because they are very durable and can handle extremely hot weather quite well.

- **Wickiups:** A round, domed structure. It usually has flexible wooden poles that are either completely arched or gathered together at the top. It is usually covered in thatch. It is similar to the wigwam.

- **Hogans:** A special structure among the Navajo. There are a variety of designs depending on their purpose. Modern hogans are often round or multi-sided and only have one room inside. Many hogans are used only for ceremonial purposes. Traditionally, the door faces east.

Surviving the desert

The early settlers were hunters. The Clovis and Folsom societies were the earliest historical Southwest culture inhabitants. Later, various groups lived here, including the groups identified by archaeologists as the Ancestral Puebloans, Hohokam, and Mogollon. Each of these groups became quite good at growing corn, beans, and squash. Later Pueblo/Hopi groups would develop dry land farming methods, which were well suited to the low rainfalls here.

After contact with Europeans, raising cattle, horses, and sheep became quite common. The Navajo are particularly known for raising sheep. Baskets, weaving, jewelry-making and pottery are highly developed art forms for many of the Southwestern tribes.

Seed gathering is an important activity for many of these groups. Special pottery was even developed to hold the seeds.

Leadership among these groups often rested in a specific leader, but today tribal councils exist to run the show. Bows and arrows were common fighting and hunting tools. Intertribal conflicts seemed to develop in certain areas, especially among the Apache, River Yuma, and the Pima. There are nuclear, matriarchal, and patriarchal families and clans in this area. Pueblo societies became very distinct among themselves. Each Pueblo has certain different practices, events, or customs from each other.

The tribes in the Southwest have religious practices that are specific to their community. Today, there has been some blending of practices with Catholicism, due to the extensive presence of Catholic missions. Dances are held by some of the Pueblos on specific saints' days.

There are six major language groups in this culture area:

- Athabascan
- Hokan
- Kiowa-Tanoan
- Penutian
- Uto-Aztecan
- Zuni

Some Southwest tribes

Many of the Southwestern tribes are gone with the wind now. But their names still resonate in the annals of Native American history.

Some Southwest tribes, including the Apache, Hopi, and Navajo, are still going strong, though, and many live on reservations in ancient Southwestern lands. Here's a list of some Southwest tribes:

- Acoma
- Apache
- Cochiti
- Cocopah
- Hano
- Havasupai
- Hopi
- Hualapai (Walapai)
- Isleta
- Jemez
- Laguna
- Maricopa
- Mojave
- Nambe
- Navajo
- Pecos
- Picuris

- Pima (Akimel O'odham)
- San Ildefonso
- San Juan
- San Felipe
- Sandia
- Santa Ana
- Santa Clara
- Santo Domingo
- Taos
- Tesuque
- Tohono O'odham (Papago)
- Yavapai
- Yuma (Quechan)
- Zia
- Zuni

Lost in translation

There are countless stories about Italian immigrants coming to Ellis Island and having their real last name changed from whatever it was to the name of their hometown in Italy, simply because the name of the town was on their "papers" — which they couldn't read. Mario Puzo used this common occurrence in *The Godfather* when Vito Andolini ended up named Vito Corleone, because his hometown in Sicily was named Corleone.

Many Indian tribes throughout the centuries faced similar "lost in translation" moments, and many tribal groups also changed their names to accurately reflect what they call themselves.

As the (funny but true) story goes, a missionary once asked a local Indian if he knew the name for a certain tribe. His answer (in his language) was "Pima." In his language Pima roughly translates as "I don't know." The Pima are now known as the Akimel O'odham (river people).

The Papagos (which means "bean eaters") changed their names to Tohono O'odham ("desert people").

The Great Basin and Plateau

The Great Basin and Plateau area is a broad expanse that's just southwest of Washington State and spreads across several states. It's something of a hybrid of terrain and climate, including forests and deserts, and it's called a "basin" because it's almost completely surrounded by mountains, which makes it appear like it's, well, a basin!

Taking a look at the terrain

The Great Basin and Plateau culture areas are often lumped together. The Great Basin culture area includes Nevada and parts of California, Colorado, Idaho, Oregon, Utah, and Wyoming. The Plateau culture area includes parts of Idaho, Montana, Oregon, and Washington. The Plateau culture area is centered around the higher elevations of the Columbia River watershed and is between the Cascades and Rocky Mountains.

The area has very cold winters and hot summers. There are some forested areas, mainly in the mountain areas. There are three major rivers here, the Columbia, Fraser (in British Columbia), and the Snake. There are some very large forests in the Plateau area. Some of the tallest trees in the world grow here. The trees grow so tall because of the plentiful rainfall. Conversely, the Great Basin has some of the lowest rainfalls on the continent.

Traditional housing came in a wide variety of forms. The adobe house was very common and is still in use among both tribal and non-tribal people in the Southwest. They are very durable and can handle extremely hot weather quite well. Other types of structures included wickiups, hogans, tipis, and subterranean houses. (See Chapter 15 for more on the various types of domiciles of the American Indians.)

Fishing and foraging plus

The early settlers were

- **Hunters:** Small game was often hunted.
- **Gatherers:** The camas root grows wild in many areas here. Camas root is a flowering plant that grows wild in the intermountain region of the United States. The baked root is very similar to the sweet potato.
- **Anglers:** Fish were often found in many of the rivers and streams.

The area was sparsely populated and many groups were nomadic. Many tribes had a group of leaders, and politics were usually grounded in the local village. Generally speaking, intertribal conflicts were fairly rare.

Bows, arrows, spears (digging sticks), and nets were common fighting, hunting, and fishing tools. Baskets were a highly developed craft, but there was little pottery.

Tribes in this region have traditional stories that explain many of the geographic features. Some of these involve the actions of spirit beings or of distinguished ancestors.

There are six major language groups in these culture areas:

- ✔ Cayuse
- ✔ Hokan
- ✔ Klamath-Modoc
- ✔ Sahaptin
- ✔ Salish
- ✔ Uto-Aztecan

Some Great Basin and Plateau tribes

The Great Basin and Plateau tribes were influenced by interactions with the Plains Indians and many today still exist, the most famous being the Shoshoni and the Ute.

Here are some Great Basin tribes:

- ✔ Bannock
- ✔ Goshiute
- ✔ Lemhi
- ✔ Mono
- ✔ Paiute
- ✔ Panamint
- ✔ Shoshoni
- ✔ Ute
- ✔ Washo

Here are some Plateau tribes:

- Cayuse
- Chelan
- Coeur d'Alene
- Columbia
- Colville
- Flathead (Salish)
- Kalispel
- Klamath
- Klikitat
- Kutenai
- Lake
- Lillooet
- Modoc
- Nespelem

- Nez Perce
- Nicola
- Okanagan
- Palus
- Sanpoil
- Shuswap
- Spokan
- Tenino
- Thompson
- Umatilla
- Wallawalla
- Wishram
- Yakama

The Pacific Northwest

The Pacific Northwest is known for having its own rain forest and for its array of climatological "styles," if you will. Ocean winds, enormous rivers, and even volcanoes and earthquakes all comprise this area stretching down the western coast of the U.S.

Home sweet (and rainy) home

The Pacific Northwest culture area includes the coastal areas for about 150 miles inland from Oregon to southern Alaska.

The area has cold winters and warm summers. The area is mostly forested. With rainfall averaging over 100 inches a year, the area is often considered a temperate rain forest. There are many islands, rivers, and lakes in the region. Much of the area is mountainous.

Traditional housing was primarily large wooden houses. They were often long and wide, with peaked roofs. The sides and roofs were made from wooden planks, often cedar. They are very durable and withstood the rain quite well. Totem poles are often found in many villages in this area. A *totem* is commonly a being which watches over a group of people. A *totem pole* is not always related to a totem. It is a large carving, usually made of wood. It features a group of figures, one on top of another. The meaning was often the recounting of a family history. It could also be religious, symbolic, or for any of a few other reasons. (See Chapter 19 for complete details on the totem pole.)

Traditional stories from some Northwest tribes involve supernatural beings or trickster figures such as Raven. Raven is a troublesome character sometimes, but at other times allows good things to happen in the world, such as the return of the Sun.

Sustaining life in the Pacific Northwest

The early settlers were gatherers, anglers, and hunters. With an abundance of seafood and wild agricultural products available, extensive farming was not needed. Hunting of deer and elk was also practiced here. Fishing was highly developed. From salmon on the rivers to long trips on the ocean, fishing (including whales) was a major operation. Basketry and wooden box manufacturing were developed. Trade was highly developed with a market-based, capitalistic economy being common.

Many villages had a specific leader, but there was little recognition of tribal nations. Kinship and the local village were the most important factors. Bows, arrows, knives, and harpoons were common fighting and hunting tools. Some intertribal conflicts seemed to develop in certain areas. There are nuclear, matriarchal, and patriarchal families and clans (Haida: Raven and Eagle) in this area.

Family status within the community was often very important. A family wanting to raise or establish their social status would often participate in a giving of gifts called a potlatch. This practice was severely restricted by the government in historical times, and many potlatch items were removed from the community and taken to museums. Tribes are only now getting these returned. In the Chinook language, *Potlatch* roughly translates as *to give*. A Potlatch is one of many community ceremonies, often held in a large hall. The events can be religious, civic, a wedding, performances, or a formal exchanging of gifts for social status. In several matriarchal tribes, such as the Haida and Tlingit, girl children were preferred over boys.

There are three major language groups in this culture area and some considerable diversity in the number of languages within these three major groups:

- ✔ Chinookan
- ✔ Na-Dene
- ✔ Penutian

Some Pacific Northwest tribes

- Alsea
- Bella Bella
- Bella Coola
- Chehalis
- Chetco
- Chilliwack
- Chinook
- Clackamas
- Comox
- Coos
- Cowlitz
- Gitskan
- Haida
- Heiltsuk
- Kathlemet
- Klallam (S'kallam)
- Klatsop
- Kwakiutl
- Lummi

- Makah
- Nooksack
- Nootka
- Pentlatch
- Puget (Lushootseed)
- Puyallup
- Quileute
- Quinalt
- Salish
- Sooke
- Squamish
- Tillamook
- Tlingit
- Tolowa
- Tsimshain
- Twana
- Umpqua
- Wishram
- Wasco

California

California's name came from a 16th-century novel, and its history is, to put it mildly, *diverse*. The state boasts an array of varied climates and geographical terrains, and four flags have flown over it since its earliest days.

California and its climate

The California culture area includes all but the east edge of the state of California.

The climate in the culture area varies widely from north to south. In the north, winters can be very cold and the summers warm. The southern summer area has a moderate climate with cold winters and hot summers. There were large forests covering much of the region. There are also desert areas. There are several mountain ranges, wide valleys, rolling hills, and long beaches. There are a wide variety of trees and natural vegetation in this area. Lakes and rivers were abundant. Rain ranges from heavy in the north to sparse in the south. Some areas had sunshine almost every day of the year. Other areas were constantly overcast from coastal clouds to Tule fog.

Housing varied with the terrain and weather. The Pomo utilized wooden tipi-like buildings in the winter. Others used grass huts, subterranean structures, sweathouses, and plank houses.

Nice, but not 90210

The early settlers were hunters, gatherers, and anglers. This is one of the few southern culture areas where corn, beans, and squash were not major crops for early farmers. Women often saw to the planting and manufacture of skins into clothing. Seeds, acorns, grasshoppers, and yucca were part of the diet for many California tribes.

Fish and all kinds of wild game were caught. Men often did the hunting and fishing. Fishing included small catches from ocean-going boats.

There were a wide variety of societies in California. Decisions were made by an array of bureaucratic "systems," including single tribal leaders, council groups, clans, and family groups. Intertribal fighting was not that common in this area. Many conflicts could be settled by a payment arranged by dispute negotiators. (The first lawyers!) Bows, arrows, nets, traps, and harpoons were common fighting, hunting, and fishing tools. Baskets and pottery were common in many areas.

American Indian tribes have long used Tule plants, which grow in central California, to make mats, boats, and even houses. Tule fog is a thick fog that forms in the long central valley of California. It usually happens after the fall and winter rains and is named after the Tule plants.

There are five major language groups in this culture area:

- ✔ Algonquian
- ✔ Athabascan
- ✔ Hokan
- ✔ Penutian
- ✔ Uto-Aztecan

Some California tribes

California tribes adapted to their locales, and several different culture areas developed in the state. Some of the more memorable tribes include the fishing Chumash and California's largest tribe, the Yurok. Here are some California tribes:

- Achomawi
- Atsugewi
- Cahuilla
- Chumash
- Costoan
- Cupeno
- Diegueno
- Esselen
- Fernandeno
- Gabrielino
- Hupa
- Kamia
- Karok
- Kato
- Luiseno
- Maidu
- Miwok
- Numa
- Patwin
- Pomo
- Oolone
- Salinan
- Serrano
- Shasta
- Tolowa
- Tubatulabal
- Wailaki
- Wappo
- Wintun
- Wiyot
- Yahi
- Yana
- Yokut
- Yuki
- Yurok

Present-day subsistence practices

Many tribes strive to maintain a connection to the way that their ancestors lived, even if this is not the main means of subsistence. Farming, hunting, gathering plants, and fishing are all ways in which tribal people provide food and clothing for themselves, even as they jump in their SUVs to head off to work as doctors or lawyers. From the Abenaki to the Zuni, many tribal people still see this as an important means of maintaining identity.

Some groups have updated their tools, but their activities are similar to those of their ancestors. For example, in many Inuit communities, snowmobiles have replaced dog sleds, but hunting remains the main source of food.

Chapter 6

The Five Civilized Tribes

*T*here are over 500 federally recognized tribes in the United States, and there are many more tribes who have not received federal recognition, some of whom have applied for recognition and many who have not. The population of these tribes ranges from just a few dozen to hundreds of thousands. In this chapter, we give you a more detailed look at some of these groups.

Among all of the tribes along the southeastern part of the United States, five tribes made a marked impression upon the English colonists. In the minds of many of the English, these five tribes were far above other tribes in their intelligence, work ethic, and character. The tribes also made some effort to acquire some of the culture of the Europeans. These tribes were

 ✔ The Choctaw

 ✔ The Cherokee

 ✔ The Chickasaw

 ✔ The Creek (Muscogee)

 ✔ The Seminole

Collectively, they were known as the Five Civilized Tribes.

Religious practices are only briefly mentioned here. Many American Indians still practice these religions or hold them in high esteem. Within any given tribe, there may be variations as to what the proper ceremony or function of an event is. The descriptions here are only intended as generalizations for educational purposes, and are offered in a respectful manner.

What's in a Name — a Tribal Name

Tribal names have changed through the years depending on who's getting to do the labeling. In a lot of cases, the names of the tribes are not what the people actually call themselves. The Europeans might have misheard the tribal name, or misunderstood what their translators were saying.

A funny example of this is that the Caddo peoples were identified for many years by the Spaniards as the Tejas, when they heard people referring to Caddoan groups as "taysha," or friends. Many early Spanish maps label East Texas as the Kingdom of the Tejas. Over time, they realized their error and the Caddo today take their name from one of the groups in their early confederacy, the Kadohadacho. The state of Texas got something out of the deal, though — its name and motto — two debts owed to the Caddo. Well, that along with the lands in the eastern portion of the state.

Today, many tribes are returning to their original names. For example, the Tohono O'odam are people who were formerly known as Papago. Some tribes maintain the names that they were given by outsiders, such as Creek or Chippewa in their legal names, but in reality, are known as Muscogee or Anishinabe.

Choctaw: The First Code Talkers

The Choctaw people, one of the largest tribal nations in the United States, originally lived mainly in Alabama, Mississippi, and Louisiana.

Their language is Muskogean and is similar to other Southeastern tribes. Choctaw is similar to the Mobilean trade language, a dialect used among groups in the Southeast to facilitate interaction and trade.

The Choctaw origin traditions center on a large mound in Mississippi called Nanih Waiya. In one version of the creation, people emerged from the mound and went in different directions to eventually become Southeastern tribes like the Cherokee and Chickasaw. The Choctaw emerged last from the mound and remained in the vicinity. Another version says that the people followed two brothers, Chahta and Chikasa, who held a sacred pole that would lean in the direction they were meant to travel. When it finally stood upright, the Chahta stayed in the area and raised a mound over it, surrounding the pole with the bones of their ancestors. Both stories indicate the importance of that particular land to the Choctaw. After being held by the State of Mississippi, the site of Nanih Waiya was finally returned to the Choctaw in 2006. The 2000 census counted 158,744 Choctaws.

The official seal of the Choctaw Nation in Oklahoma can tell you a lot about the Choctaw. The seal has an unstrung bow, three arrows, and a smoking pipe-hatchet. The pipe-hatchet represents discussion and deliberation. The three arrows represent three major figures in Choctaw history, Apukshunnubbee, Pushmataha, and Mosholatubbee.

The following sections explain a little about who they are and how they lived and still live today.

How they lived

Around the time of European contact, the Choctaw had two major groupings, or what anthropologists call *moieties*. Within these, there were a number of clans or iksas. The social organization governed things like marriage and authority over children. The Choctaw were *matrilineal* in nature. This meant the family was organized along the woman's bloodline. Women and men each had their own set of rights and responsibilities, though.

Mound sites are important to Choctaw people because of the traditions involving Nanih Waiya. Archaeologists believe that the Choctaw incorporate the descendants of the people who constructed sites like Moundville, in Alabama.

A Choctaw game that is still played today is stickball. It was first described by a Jesuit priest around 1729, and he must have been alarmed at what he saw. This game was justifiably known as the Little Brother of War. Stickball was played by teams of as few as 20 or as many as 300 players. Using sticks with nets at the end, the precursors to modern lacrosse sticks, players tried to move a leather ball to the goal post. The games were sometimes used to settle differences between Choctaw towns. Today, it's played by both men and women and remains a large part of Choctaw identity.

Politically, the Choctaw were divided into three major districts. Each of their districts had a leader. This leader often went by the title of *mingo*. The three mingos would come together in general council to discuss matters of importance to the entire tribe. These councils were usually open to anyone who wanted to attend, or to speak.

European contact and loss of lands

The first confirmed contact between the Choctaw and Europeans was with De Soto's expedition in 1540. Word of De Soto's brutality against other tribes and his desire for riches reached the Choctaw in advance of his soldiers. De Soto's men clashed with the Choctaw near Mobile, Alabama. The reason for the battle is in dispute. Some say the Spanish were led into an ambush after taking Chief Tuscaloosa hostage. Others say the fighting started after the Spaniards beat a Choctaw who was forced into being one of their porters. The well-armed and armored Spaniards won the battle, but they suffered significant losses.

The Choctaw continued to have contact with Spanish, French, English, and American explorers and settlers in their homelands from around 1700 until the early 1800s. From 1776 to 1830, the Choctaw signed a series of treaties which slowly whittled away at the lands they claimed. They would eventually give up over 32,000,000 acres of land.

The Choctaw population at this time was estimated to be around 19,000 people. The Treaty of Dancing Rabbit Creek was signed in September 1830. It required them to give up their remaining lands east of the Mississippi. The majority of the tribe moved to Indian Territory, which is modern-day Oklahoma. Those who went to Indian Territory became the Choctaw Nation of Oklahoma.

Indian Territory was a large piece of land that the American government set up to be the new homeland for American Indians. It was north of Texas, south of Kansas, and west of the Mississippi River. Today, it is called Oklahoma. Curiously enough, Oklahoma comes from two Choctaw words: Okla, meaning people and homa, meaning red.

A provision of the treaty allowed for a small group to remain in Mississippi. This group eventually became known as the Mississippi Band of Choctaw Indians. Today, the Mississippi Band of Choctaw numbers about 8,900.

Some Choctaw in Louisiana refused to be removed and were federally recognized in 1995 as the Jena Band of Choctaw. Today, they are still a small group, with 241 enrolled members.

Of the tribes that would be removed from their old homelands to Indian Territory, the Choctaws were among the first to go. The first major group to leave numbered 4,000 and they set forth in 1831.

Charity-minded Choctaws

In 1847, the Choctaws heard about the potato famine in Ireland. Despite going through hard times themselves, a group of Choctaws collected money and sent it to help feed the starving Irish.

In gratitude, a group of Irish people walked the Choctaw route of the Trail of Tears in 1997, and in doing so, raised more than $100,000 for famine relief for Somalia.

The "other" code talkers

While you may have heard of the Navajo code talkers of World War II, did you know that several Choctaws served the same function in World War I? A small number of Choctaws served in the army's 36th Division. They participated in the Argonne-Meuse campaign as messengers or handling radio communications. They translated military orders or scouting reports into Choctaw. The Germans were never able to decipher any messages they managed to capture. Many Choctaw repeated these efforts in World War II, along with other American Indians from the Chippewa, Comanche, Cree, Crow, Hopi, Menominee, Mississauga, Oneida, Sac and Fox, and Sioux nations, as well.

Cherokees and the Trail of Tears

The Cherokee is one of the largest tribal nations in the United States. They originally lived in an area of over 81,000,000 acres covering Tennessee, Kentucky, North and South Carolina, Georgia, West Virginia, and Virginia. Their language is Cherokee, which is distantly related to the Iroquois languages. The word "Cherokee" is not native to the Cherokee language. Its origin is not known. It is often thought to be a Choctaw word meaning "cave people." The Cherokee used two main names to describe themselves:

- *Ani-yun-wiya* (principle people)
- *Keetoowah* (the name of one of their original towns)

"Cherokee" in their language was pronounced as "Tsa-la-gi." English settlers called them Cherokee for so long that the name stuck. There are now two Cherokee dialects, eastern and western.

The official seal of the Cherokee Nation can tell you a lot about the Cherokee. The seal has a seven-pointed star. The points represent each of the seven clans and seven of the characters of the Cherokee language as designed by Sequoyah. The wreath is made of oak leaves. This is the wood which was burned in the tribe's sacred fire.

You can find out more about the Cherokee and their past and present in the sections that follow.

Clans

Cherokee society was originally matrilineal, with emphasis centered around the woman's bloodline. Over time, changes in the Constitution affected the role of clans and matrilineality, but clans are still identified by Cherokee people. Today, traditionalists refer to the clans when deciding on appropriate marriages. Children take on the clan of their mother. A boy's mentor is his mother's brother (uncle), rather than his father.

Cherokee society has seven clans: Long Hair, Blue, Wolf, Wild Potato, Deer, Bird, and Paint.

Clan members are considered brothers and sisters:

- The **Long Hair Clan** (also called **Twister** or **Wind**) usually produced Peace Chiefs. Orphans and prisoners of war were made members of this clan. They were at the eastern side of ceremonies.

- The **Blue Clan** (also called **Bear, Panther,** or **Wildcat**) often produced healers for children. They were to the left of the Long Hair clan at ceremonies.

- The **Wolf Clan** often produced War Chiefs or protectors. It has often been the largest clan. They are usually to the left of the Blue Clan at ceremonies.

- The **Wild Potato Clan** (also called **Blind Savannah**) were the gatherers or farmers. The Wild Potato is usually to the left of the Wolf arbor.

- **Deer Clan** members were usually the best hunters and runners. The Deer Clan is often to the left of the Wild Potato at ceremonies.

- The **Bird Clan** (also called **Raven**, **Turtle Dove,** and **Eagle**) often produced people who could deliver messages between heaven and earth. They were also responsible for the birds. At ceremonies, they were usually to the left of the Deer Clan.

- Medicine People usually came from the **Paint Clan.** They were usually to the left at the Bird Clan at ceremonies.

How they lived

The Cherokee used bows and arrows, spears, blowguns, stone weapons, tomahawks, and battle hammers for hunting and warfare. The Cherokee could be fierce warriors. They often fought with the Creeks. They also engaged in a practice called *blood feud*. Simply stated, assaults against a member of one clan by another clan could be revenged against any member of the instigating clan. The responsibility for blood feuds was given to the Cherokee nation, in changes to the Cherokee constitution that were made around 1810.

The Cherokee also played the ball game the Choctaw played (see "Choctaw: The First Code Talkers" earlier in the chapter for more), but with different rules than the Choctaw. Another game involved marbles, which were originally made from stone, but today it is common for people to use billiard balls.

Rivers were sacred to the Cherokee. Rivers were considered to be the "Long Man."

Medicine persons

Cherokees looked to medicine men and women to help them with illnesses. The knowledge of which plants or materials to use to practice medicine was passed along from one person to another. Medicine people were not allowed to "advertise" their services. Patients came to them by word of mouth. Traditional Cherokees still seek them out today. You can imagine how difficult it would be to preserve knowledge of medicines after having been uprooted from your homeland. The traditional healers today are impressive for having maintained this knowledge.

Lucky number seven

The number seven played a major role in Cherokee society:

- ✔ There were the seven clans.
- ✔ Unlike many other North American tribes, Cherokees recognized seven cardinal directions, rather than the traditional four. There were the standard north, south, east, and west. There was also up, down, and within or center.
- ✔ There were seven levels of purity, with the seventh level being the hardest to achieve. The Cougar was believed to have attained this level, along with the cedar, holly, and laurel.

Encountering Europeans

Along with many of the other Five Civilized Tribes, the Cherokee's first encounter with Europeans was with De Soto in 1540. De Soto did not spend much time in Cherokee country, though. During the late 1600s, the Cherokee came into regular contact with Europeans, especially the British. Contact with the European world led to many advances and tragedies.

In the 1730s, the Cherokee signed a treaty with England. They agreed that King George was their sovereign. The king acknowledged them as a nation. In fact, the Cherokees were recognized as a nation by England before the United States became a nation.

No good deed . . .

The Cherokee also were involved in several wars in the 1700s, including the French and Indian War, and the Revolutionary War. Despite problems with English settlers, the Cherokees allied with England in both of these wars.

When the United States won the Revolutionary War, the Cherokees faced a gloomy future. The United States wanted land for its citizens. The Cherokee had one of the biggest pieces of land of any tribes in the area.

The Cherokees signed their first treaty ceding some land in 1721. This was with South Carolina. Over the next 110 years, they would lose all of their lands east of the Mississippi River. Some of these treaties were signed under duress. When Andrew Jackson was elected president, he saw American Indians in the Southeast as a true impediment to the United States. He wanted all of the Southeastern Indians to move west of the Mississippi, and especially to Indian Territory.

Removal

The Indian Removal Act was passed in 1830. This law all but demanded that the remaining tribes in the southeastern U.S. (especially the Five Civilized Tribes) move west of the Mississippi. (See Chapter 12 for more info on Indian Removal.)

The Cherokee fought these efforts. Their own laws eventually made it a capital crime for any Cherokee to sell, or give away, any Cherokee lands. The final blow to the Cherokee's desire to remain in what was left of their original homeland was the discovery of gold in their Georgia territory. Georgia passed a series of laws to deprive the Cherokees of all their rights, even those granted under federal treaties and laws. The Cherokees took some of the matters to court. Two cases went as far as the United States Supreme Court. In both cases, the court ruled in the Cherokee's favor. However, President Jackson refused to enforce the ruling.

Several Cherokee leaders had been educated New England colleges. Cherokees Elias Boudinot and John Ridge went to Connecticut for their schooling. They became familiar with the thinking of the American people. They traveled across the country speaking to anyone who would listen. They explained how the Cherokee had adopted many of the European ways of life, as they had been asked. The Cherokees had a formal government. They had their own written language. A greater percentage of Cherokees were literate than Americans. Some Americans had sympathy for the Cherokees, others did not.

In 1821, a member of the Cherokee Nation named Sequoyah invented a written alphabet for the Cherokee language. This is the only time in the history of the world that an illiterate individual would create an alphabet for his or her own language. It is actually a syllabary. Each of the 86 characters represents a syllable in the Cherokee language. The system was so simple that the vast majority of the Cherokees were able to become literate with just a few weeks of study. The syllabary is still in use today among the Cherokee.

The New Echota Treaty

Eventually, Boudinot and Ridge realized that the Cherokees would have to move. So, they decided to try to get the best deal they could before there were no options left. Boudinot and Ridge were the nucleus of what was called the Treaty Party. Contrary to the wishes of the elected Chief John Ross and the majority of the Cherokee people, a few hundred members of the Treaty Party initiated a treaty with the United States at New Echota, Georgia, in 1836.

The New Echota Treaty gave up all of the Cherokee's land east of the Mississippi, and required their removal to Indian Territory. When the treaty was announced, the Cherokee people were furious. Not a single member of the tribe's elected council had signed the treaty. Over 16,000 of the 18,000 members of the tribe signed a petition stating that the treaty was a sham and did not represent the true wishes of the nation. Despite the obvious illegalities involved, the U.S. Senate ratified the treaty by a one-vote margin.

A deadline for moving to Indian Territory was established as a part of the New Echota Treaty. Most of the Treaty Party members moved immediately. Believing that the U.S. government would not enforce such an obvious fraud, and that some accommodation could be worked out, most Cherokees stayed where they were. Unfortunately for the Cherokees, the government wanted the land and did enforce the treaty. When the deadline arrived, the Cherokees were forcibly taken from their homes, many of which were superior to those of the white settlers.

A terrible, tearful trip

The trip from the Cherokee lands to Indian Territory was approximately 1,000 miles. Between 15,000 and 17,000 Cherokees made the trip. Often, they had little more than the clothes on their backs. Much of the trip was made overland. A drought had lowered the levels of many of the rivers in the area. This delayed some of the trip into the winter months. As many as 4,000 Cherokees died during the trip due to sickness, fatigue, or exposure. Many of the dead were the young and the old. Many more would die in the next few years in Indian Territory since they had been ill-prepared to move to a new land.

This forced march was called "the place where they cried," or as it is better known, "The Trail of Tears." Both Elias Boudinot and John Ridge would eventually be killed for their part in the New Echota Treaty.

Surviving against all odds

The Cherokees would survive and eventually become successful in their new lands. One of the first institutes of higher learning west of the Mississippi River was created by the Cherokee Nation.

The Civil War also wreaked havoc among the Cherokee. The tribe was divided on whom they should back, if either side. Some Cherokees fought for the North, others for the South. As many as 25 percent of the male Cherokee population would be killed in the conflict. The last Confederate general to surrender was a Cherokee named Stand Waite.

Today, the Cherokee Nation is the largest Indian tribe in the United States. There are more than 200,000 tribal members. In the 2000 census, almost 750,000 people claimed to have some Cherokee ancestry. During the Trail of Tears time, a small group of Cherokees were able to hide in the mountains of western North Carolina. They were eventually given a small reservation by that state. There are three federally recognized Cherokee Nations:

- **The Cherokee Nation,** 200,000-plus members in Oklahoma
- **The United Keetoowah Band of Cherokee Indians,** 10,000-plus members in Oklahoma
- **The Eastern Band of Cherokee Indians,** 13,400 members in North Carolina

Chickasaw: They Were Called Warriors

The Chickasaw lived primarily in northern Mississippi and Alabama, and in western Kentucky and Tennessee. They appeared to be related to the Choctaw. The Chickasaw language is another version of the Muskogean language. The Chickasaw people are perhaps the least known of the Five Civilized Tribes. The following sections give you a glimpse of who they were and are today.

The upright stick

There may have been as many as 15,000 Chickasaws at the time of the European contacts. Like the Choctaw, their ancient beliefs are that they migrated into their homelands from the west at God's request.

As is often the case, the official seal of the Chickasaw Nation in Oklahoma can tell you a lot about them. Known for their great courage and ability as warriors, the seal features Tishomingo, the last war chief of the Chickasaw, who died in 1841. The two arrows represent the two parts of Chickasaw culture. One group lived within the towns. The other division lived in areas surrounding the towns as security. The towns were often fortified. A unique sign of an honored warrior was the wearing of swan feathers. The warrior on the seal wears a mantle made from swan feathers.

Like many of the other Southeastern tribes, the Chickasaw had a reverence for fire. They kept a sacred fire burning. Fire was such a special part of their life that it was considered evil to put out even a household fire with water.

At the hands of a friend

The Chickasaw had an interesting form of execution, and it was a practice shared with other Southeastern tribes. If a tribe member was condemned to die, they were given up to a year to tie up their affairs and obligations. During that time, they were free to come and go. No later than at the end of the year, they had to go to the place of execution. Normally a friend would be the one to put them to death. It is a point of Chickasaw honor and pride that of the few people who received this punishment, all of them completed their duty within the allotted year.

In the early historical period, Chickasaw towns would often stretch along both sides of a river valley for many miles. This helped to not overwork a small area. A family would often have both a summer and winter house, and a "woman's time" hut. The crop growing was usually communal. As with most tribes of the Southeast, the Chickasaw grew a range of crops, but most important were the "three sisters": corn, beans, and squash.

The Chickasaw also encountered De Soto in 1540. After his battles with the Choctaws, and noting the ferocious nature of the Chickasaw, De Soto did not openly confront the Chickasaw. He lived near them over the winter. Come spring, De Soto made too many demands of the Chickasaws and a battle ensued. The conquistadors soon left the area.

It was 1673 before the Chickasaws saw other Europeans. This was Father Jacques Marquette and Louis Joliet. They were exploring the Mississippi River, coming from the north. Knowing of the might of the Chickasaw, Marquette and Joliet did not linger in their territory for long.

Family feuds

Like feuding family members, the Chickasaw and the Choctaw were often fighting. The Chickasaw often raided other tribes to get slaves. They soon became allied with British traders from the Carolinas. This led them into many skirmishes with the French over the next 100 years.

The Chickasaw's political situation was similar to the Choctaw. They had a council and several leaders called minkos. The *High Minko* was their official leader, but his position was more for advice than for orders.

The Choctaw's first land cession was in 1801. The deal provided land to build a road through their area. The road would become the famed Natchez Trace. This "small trickle" of land surrender led to a torrent in the next 30 years.

Although they aided Andrew Jackson in defeating the "Red Stick" Creeks in 1813, Jackson soon persuaded the Choctaw to sign a treaty ceding a large part of their lands to the United States government. When Mississippi became a state in 1817, there was even more pressure for the Chickasaw's land. In 1818, they were only able to keep their lands in Mississippi by giving up their claims to land in Kentucky and Tennessee.

After the Indian Removal Act was passed in 1830, the Chickasaw's days in Mississippi were numbered. When they did sell their lands in 1832, they only received money. Many of the other Southeastern tribes were given land in Indian Territory and a cash payment. It was 1837 before the Chickasaw could find suitable land to purchase. Thus they entered their own Trail of Tears.

On the wrong side

With the onset of the Civil War, the Chickasaws decided to join the Confederacy. This would be their first loss in a war. In fact, their government was the last one to surrender to federal authority in the Civil War. After the war, any tribe that had sided with the Confederacy lost more of their lands, as well as their prized slaves.

With the passage of the Dawes Act and other legislation, by 1901 the Chickasaw Nation had lost all of their communal lands. Tribal members were given individual allotments of land, and the tribal government was disbanded. The tribe reorganized in 1963. They remain today one of the largest tribes in the United States.

In the 1700s, a group of about 50 Chickasaws moved into South Carolina at the state's request. The community still exists in Hemingway. It is called the "Chaloklowas Chickasaw Indian People." They are a state-recognized tribe.

According to the 2000 census, there are a little over 21,000 Chickasaw in the United States.

Creek

The Creek people originally lived mainly in Alabama, Florida, Georgia, and Tennessee. There are two Creek languages, Muscogee, which is one of the Muskogean languages, and Hitchiti. One old story tells that the Creeks came out of a mountain in the west. They lived there until the earth opened up and ate their children. So, they began a long march to the east to find a new home.

The Creek were not one tribe, but a confederacy of many different towns. Over time, the towns united with each other and were identified based on geography as Upper and Lower Creek towns. While known by most people as the Creek, the name they use for themselves is *Muscogee* (or *Muskogee*). English colonists from the Carolinas called one member of the confederacy the "Ochese Creek Indians" (or Ocmulgee Creek) after the creek of the same name. Eventually, they shortened the name to just "Creek Indians."

The center of the circle

In the early historical period, Creek communities often had a large, permanent town surrounded by smaller villages. The larger towns often had a large open area in the center of the town. Similar to many of the other Southeastern tribes, this is where many of the major ceremonies and games were held, and the sacred fire burned. The central town often had a large, round building where the council met. Each of the larger towns had a leader called the *Mico*. Each of these towns could have as many as 500 people. Individual houses were often covered in thatch. The Creek were good farmers, had extensive corn fields, and cultivated many other crops, too.

The Upper Creeks lived near the Coosa and Tallapoosa rivers. The Lower Creeks lived near the lower part of the Chattahoochee and Ocmulgee rivers.

The Creeks had several encounters with Spanish explorers in the late 1500s; however, they managed to avoid any major battles with them. The Creek sided with the English of South Carolina and Georgia during the Apalachee War in the early 1700s. They were also known to be antagonistic to the Spanish in Florida. They established a significant trade in deer skins with the British. The Creeks would sell over 100,000 skins a year, for some time.

Eventually, the deer all but vanished from the area, and the Creek's prospects were not good. More and more colonists came into Creek territories looking for land. In 1790, led by Mico Alexander McGillivray, the Creek negotiated a treaty with the U.S. government. It was called the Treaty of New York and it ceded all of the Creek lands in eastern Georgia. The Creeks were acknowledged to be the rightful owners of large parts of western Georgia and Alabama.

Red Sticks, White Sticks

Further incursions by American settlers led to a major split among the Creek towns. Some of the Creeks wanted to resist the incursion of American settlers. Inspired by the Shawnee leader, Tecumseh, they wanted to join in a revolt against the Americans. Creeks in the Lower towns were friendly with the Americans and resisted calls to join the revolt. This led to a Creek civil war.

In 1813, at the **Battle of Burnt Corn,** the Red Sticks had a run-in with American forces. Later, the Red Sticks attacked Fort Mims, where many mixed-blood Creeks had sought protection with the Americans. The Red Sticks killed as many as 500 people in the fort. This caused a general panic in the area. General Andrew Jackson led an army into the region. Along with his American soldiers were many Cherokees and White Stick Creeks. At the Battle of Horseshoe Bend, Jackson's forces were victorious over a large Red Stick force. Further battles left the Red Sticks defeated. The remaining Creeks signed a treaty which gave up much of their lands in southern Alabama and Georgia.

Forced out

It was only two dozen years later that most of the Creeks were forced to move to Indian Territory (Oklahoma) with most of the other American Indians of the Southeast. One small group of Creeks managed to stay in Alabama. Known as the Poarch Band of Creek Indians, this group of is now over 2,000 people. They have a small federally recognized reservation in Poarch, Alabama.

The Muscogee (Creek) Nation in Oklahoma has about 40,000 citizens, according to the U.S. census in 2000. In partnership with the Oklahoma State University system, the Muskogee Nation operates the College of the Muscogee Nation in Okmulgee, Oklahoma.

Some Creek people have returned to their traditional style of political organization and have become federally recognized as Creek Tribal Towns. These include the Alabama Qassarte, the Kilagee, and the Thlopthlocco.

Seminole: The Unconquered People

The Seminole people are the descendants of many Southeastern tribes who joined together in Florida. Many Creek people were forced out of Alabama and Georgia and mixed with the local Apalachee, among other groups. The formation of this tribe occurred over many decades. There were several significant waves of immigrations, especially after the Creek War. Runaway African slaves also became part of the tribe.

The name Seminole has been translated as "one who has camped out from the regular towns" and "runaway." Some experts say it is a variation of the Spanish word *cimmaron* which means "wild." While the name Seminole has it own variations because it emerged from so many groups, the Seminole Indians had two languages: Muskogee and Hitchiti.

By the 1800s, their population was estimated at around 5,000 people. As with many of the other Southeastern tribes, they had a Green Corn Dance. Various ceremonies were performed at this time. Individual houses were called *chickees*. It had a cypress log frame, which was raised above the ground. The roof was usually a thatch made from palmetto. (See Chapter 15.)

Problems aplenty

The Seminoles soon faced the same problems most tribes faced: American and Spanish settlers wanted their lands. Southern plantation owners also wanted the slaves who had taken refuge with the tribe. There were numerous disagreements over these issues.

A series of small violent encounters led to the First Seminole War. The starting date of this war is a matter of debate. Historians say it started somewhere between 1814 and 1818. It ended in 1818. Many of the battles were with American forces led by General Andrew Jackson. The army bested the Seminoles in most of the pitched battles. The fighting eventually led Spain to sell Florida to the United States.

In 1823, the United States signed a treaty with the Seminole at Moultrie Creek. This treaty established a Seminole reservation in central Florida. It took several years, and much prodding by the army, before most of the Seminoles had moved to the reservation in 1827. By the 1830s, the Indian Relocation Act called for all Southeastern tribes to move to Indian Territory (Oklahoma). Some of the Seminole signed the Treaty of Payne's Landing in 1834, which gave them three years to move. The conflict between the Seminoles who did not sign the treaty led to the Second Seminole War.

The Second Seminole War

In 1835, the fighting began in earnest. By 1837, a treaty was signed by several of the remaining Seminole leaders. Seminole chiefs Osceola and Sam Jones refused to surrender. They led a mission to Fort Brooks to help release over 700 Seminoles awaiting removal to Indian Territory. When Osceola and other leaders later met with the army at a peace conference under a white flag, they were seized and put in prison. The war continued.

According to the Seminole Nation's Web site, "by May 10, 1842, when a frustrated President John Tyler ordered the end of military actions against the Seminoles, over $20 million had been spent, 1500 American soldiers had died and still no formal peace treaty had been signed." The few surviving Seminoles were given a reservation in southwestern Florida. The rest were sent to Indian Territory.

The Third Seminole War

In 1849, more skirmishes took place among the Americans and the remaining Seminoles in Florida. More efforts were made to get the Seminoles to go to Indian Territory. A few of them left. Others stayed on their reservation. This led to the Third Seminole War in 1855.

While the army was actively involved in the Third Seminole War, much of the fighting involved militia. Chief Billy Bowlegs led many of the Seminoles. By May 1858, Bowlegs and most of the remaining Seminoles had surrendered. Most were shipped west. Chief Sam Jones and a few others remained in south-central Florida.

In all three wars, there was never a formal peace treaty. Often, the Seminoles were just left alone because it was too hard to find them in their inland Florida holdings. This is the reason the Seminoles are often called the "Unconquered."

According to the 2000 census, the Seminole now number around 13,000 people. They are located in Florida and Oklahoma.

Chapter 7

A Tally of Important Tribes

*T*here were, and still are, many more tribes than just the Five Civilized Tribes. These tribes all played — and continue to play — a role in the history of the American Indian, and their heritage informs their modern-day lives, cultures, and religious practices. Even the smallest tribes manifest great pride in their name, their ancestors, their past, and their achievements. Throughout this book, we have made every attempt to cite specific tribes when speaking about types of housing, or religious practices, or other culture-specific characteristics.

This is because, simply put, a tribe's identity is the sum total of their past, their present, and their future. And their name is their honor.

In this chapter, we'll look at some of the largest and most well-known American Indian tribes and discuss their past and their present.

Navajo: "The People"

The Navajo Nation is the second-largest tribal group in the United States. Their name for themselves is *Ni'hookaa Diyan Diné*. This translates as "Lords of the Earth" or "Holy Earth People." They also use the shorter form of "Diné" which means "the people."

"Navajo" comes from a Tewa Pueblo word which means "an area of cultivated land" or "strangers from a cultivated land."

The Navajo originally lived in the Subarctic as part of the Na-Dene people. Along with the Apache, they slowly migrated to the south. The exact date they arrived in the Four Corners area of the American Southwest is not known. Most experts say they reached this region between the years 1000 and 1400. Their language is Navajo, which is one of the Athabascan languages.

The Four Corners area is the only spot in the United States where four states share a common point. Arizona, Colorado, New Mexico, and Utah make up the four states. The Navajo reservation covers a large part of the Four Corners area.

The Navajo have a very detailed creation story. It says they rose up out of three underworlds before they reached this world, which is called the "Glittering World." There are four sacred mountains which mark the edges of their land:

- Mt. Hesperus to the north, in Colorado
- Mt. Taylor to the south, in New Mexico
- Mt. Blanca to the east, in Colorado
- San Francisco Peak to the west, in Arizona

There are four directions with a color for each of them:

- Jet Black, the north
- Turquoise, the south
- White Shell, the east
- Abalone and Coral, the west

Navajo life

As with many other tribes, the Navajo families are clan oriented. A child belongs to its mother's clan. Tradition states that a person should only marry a person from another clan. There are dozens of clans in the Navajo Nation.

When two Navajos meet for the first time, it is considered proper for them to introduce themselves. Part of this introduction is to mention their clans. This custom is not practiced by all tribes. Among the Cherokee, it is considered impolite to mention your clan, except under unusual circumstances.

The Navajo were originally hunters and farmers, but also fought with tribes in the area and conducted raids upon them. The Navajo took up sheep and goat herding once those animals had been introduced by the Spanish. Today, many Navajo people continue to be ranchers.

War and peace

With the invasion of the Spanish into the Southwest, the Navajos often had conflict with the conquistadors. Spanish settlers and the Navajo would go through periods of calm and conflict. The worst encounter was a punitive expedition by the Spanish in 1805 that tracked down some Navajos in the

Canyon de Chelly. The Navajos fled into one of the ancient cliff dwellings expecting it to protect them. However, the Spanish had firearms that could reach them. Over a hundred men, women, and children were killed.

Many of the Navajos in this era were living in small communities. While they were a people with a common heritage, they had no tribal government that covered the entire tribe. Efforts by the Spanish, the Mexican, and later the American government to find a central government to deal with were unsuccessful. Peace accords reached with one group would be unknown to another.

In 1863, American forces, under famed scout Kit Carson, entered Navajo territory. They were there to punish the Navajo for their continuing raids. Several of the tribes who had been the victims of the Navajo's raids volunteered to join the expedition. With the Navajo's ability to hide themselves in their canyons, the expedition's most effective tool became fire. Carson's people burned the crops and the homes of the Navajos whenever they could find them. This had a drastic effect in this arid region.

The Long Walk

During this campaign, the army had captured about 6,000 Navajos. Along with about 2,000 other Indians under their control, they would eventually be marched 300 miles from eastern Arizona to a "resettlement" camp in New Mexico. The army called the camp Bosque Redondo. The Navajos called their forced march "The Long Walk." Many of the Navajos were in bad shape because of Carson's "burnt earth" policy. Hundreds of Navajos died during the march. Life in Bosque Redondo was hard. The land was poor, and the conditions were unforgiving. The surviving Navajos were allowed to return to their homelands in 1868.

Navajo craftspeople are especially known for their skills in working with silver and weaving. Navajo blankets, rugs, and silverworks are some of the most prized crafts in the world.

A genuine Navajo rug will often have one minor flaw in its construction. This is something that is practiced by many Navajo weavers. By the old traditions, only the Great Spirit is perfect. Humanity should not try to be perfect.

Today, the Navajo are the second-largest tribal group in America today in population. According to the 2000 census, there were 270,000 Navajos. They have the largest reservation in the United States. It covers 27,000 square miles and is larger than 10 of the 50 states in America.

Lakotas, Nakotas, and Santee

These tribes are, perhaps, the best known of all American Indian tribes.

Once a large group of Indians, they split into three main groups. They are known by the different dialects of the language they speak: Dakota, Lakota, and Nakota. You may know them as the Santee, Yankton, and Teton Sioux. In their own languages, Dakota, Lakota, and Nakota each can be translated as something similar to "allies." Whereas, "Sioux" is a French variation of an Algonquian language word which means "enemy" or "snake." Check out Figure 7-1 for a depiction of a Sioux chief.

The term *Sioux* is the term used by most of the tribes belonging to these groups in their legal names. People may refer to themselves as Sioux, or specifically as Oglala or as Lakota. For your ease in reading, we will use the term Sioux to refer to all of the three main groups.

Within each of these three main branches are several smaller groups:

✔ **Santee Tribes:**

- Mdewakantonwan

- Sisitonwan

- Wahpekute

- Wahpetonwan

✔ **Yankton Tribes:**

- Yankton

- Yanktonai

Figure 7-1:
A Sioux chief.

✔ **Teton Tribes:**

- Brule (Burnt Thighs)
- Hunkpapa
- Itazipco (Sans Arcs)
- Minneconjou
- Oglala
- Oohenumpa (Two Kettles)
- Sihasapa

According to many scholars, the Sioux once lived in the northeastern part of North America. They slowly moved toward the Great Plains. They were first documented by Europeans in Minnesota in the 1600s. Some bands would linger in an area, as others continued to move on. Some theories say that the Sioux started their migration because of pressure from other tribes such as the Ojibwa.

By around 1800, the Sioux had spread across much of the north central part of the United States including North and South Dakota, Iowa, Minnesota, Montana, Nebraska, Wisconsin, and Wyoming. The Santee were primarily in Wisconsin. The Yanktons had some of the Dakotas and Iowa. The Tetons ruled the rest of the area. The Indians of the Great Plains were able to stick to their traditions and their lands for much longer than the tribes of the southeastern United States. But, once the Southeastern tribes had been moved to Indian Territory, other lands became the target of American expansionism. It was in 1803, with the Louisiana Purchase, that the Sioux came under the jurisdiction of the United States.

The buffalo

Upon entering the Great Plains, much of the Sioux's life was centered on the buffalo, or the American Bison, as it is more properly called. The Sioux used the buffalo in almost every part of their life. American hunters saw the buffalo as a source of food, but they also saw it as sport. Between 1867 and 1883, tens of millions of buffalo were killed by American hunters. In one three-year period, almost 5,000,000 buffalos were killed. In many ways, the near extermination of the buffalo did more to remove the Indians from the Great Plains than all of the armies put together.

Below we list some uses of the buffalo:

✔ **Bones:** Tools such as awls and brushes

✔ **Brains:** Used to soften hides

✔ **Fat:** Food and paint

- ✔ **Hair:** Rope and thread
- ✔ **Hides:** Clothing, shelter, and containers
- ✔ **Hoofs:** Glue
- ✔ **Horns:** Arrows, cups, and spoons
- ✔ **Manure:** Fuel
- ✔ **Robes:** Extra warm clothing and bedding
- ✔ **Sinew:** Bow strings and thread

Just a short time after the Sioux entered the Great Plains, Americans also had a presence there. In 1804, the Lewis and Clark Expedition entered the region. In the 1840s, American settlers and prospectors heading for Oregon and California really started crossing Sioux lands in significant numbers. In the 1860s, gold was discovered in Montana, and the Dakota Territories were set up. 1868 saw the last of the treaties between the United States and Indian tribes. In 1869, the first transcontinental railroad was completed. 1874 saw the discovery of gold in the Black Hills. All of these events had a significant effect on the lives of the Sioux.

In 1851, the United States and many tribes agreed to the Fort Laramie Treaty. This designated over 60,000,000 acres as the Sioux Reservation. Through a process of wars and treaties, the Sioux's land was rapidly whittled down to less than 10 percent of that amount. The Sioux fought to keep their lands. Parts of it (the Black Hills, or the Paha Sapa, as they call it) were sacred to them. History books of the time usually labeled a victory by the army as a "battle." A victory by the Indians was often called a "massacre." (For a depiction of a Native American, see Figure 7-2.)

Figure 7-2:
A Native
American.

The Sioux fought the army in many of their lands. The Santee War of 1862 took place in Minnesota. It was instigated by the lack of promised food being delivered to the tribe. Many people died on both sides. For their part in the uprising, 38 Santee Indians were hanged in Mankato, Minnesota, on December 26, 1862. This was the largest mass execution in U.S. history.

The Sioux Wars

The Sioux Wars of 1866–1868 took place primarily in Wyoming. The Bozeman Trail was built through Sioux lands despite a treaty that prohibited it. The trail was to help prospectors get to the Montana mining areas. Forts were also established in the area. Sioux warriors fought under Chief Red Cloud. Battles such as the "Fetterman Massacre" and the "Wagon Box Fight" were fought. Red Cloud's forces won this war. The trail and nearby forts was abandoned for a period of time.

The Sioux War of 1876–1877 was the largest series of battles in Sioux–U.S. Army relations. This involved more violations of treaties, and Sioux warriors going off the reservation to live in their old ways. Mostly, it was because gold had been discovered in Sioux lands. This war featured such battles as the Battle of the Little Big Horn, Battle on the Powder River, Battle of the Rosebud, Battle of Wolf Mountain, and Battle of Slim Buttes. Some of the famous names in this war included Sitting Bull, Crazy Horse, and George Custer. (Figure 7-3 shows you Sioux Indians.)

Figure 7-3:
Sioux
Indians.

Wounded Knee

The final series of battles involving the Sioux was in 1890. A Northern Paiute by the name of Wovoka had a vision. His vision saw the return of the old American Indian way of life and the removal of the white man from their lands. His prophecy became a religion to some. It was called the Ghost Dance religion. In order for the prophecy to come true, the Indians would have to dance the ghost dance, and to live in a righteous manner. While he also talked of this being a peaceful process, Indian agents became fearful of the numbers of Indians who began to believe in the message.

This all led to a confrontation on the Pine Ridge reservation in South Dakota. The army attacked a group of Miniconjou and Hunkpapa Sioux at a place called Wounded Knee. Most of the Indians were unarmed. Shooting broke out, and when it was all over, 25 soldiers and over 150 Lakota men, women, and children were dead. For all practical purposes, this was the last significant fight between American Indians and the U.S. Army. (See Chapter 11 for more on the Wounded Knee massacre.)

At 108,000 people, according to the U.S. census of 2000, the Sioux are the third-largest tribal group in America, and the Pine Ridge Reservation in South Dakota — a 2-million-acre expanse the size of Connecticut — is the second-largest reservation in the country.

Chippewa: We are Anishinabe

The Chippewa are the fourth-largest tribal nation today and live mainly in Minnesota, Wisconsin, and Michigan (as well as in Canada). *Chippewa* is the term most used in the United States for this tribe; in Canada, they're known as Ojibwa. Interestingly, if you add an "O" in front of Chippewa, it does sound a little like Ojibwa. Their traditional name is Anishinabe. They are closely related to the Ottawa and the Potawatomi.

"Chippewa" is said to mean "puckered." This refers to the seams on the Anishinabe moccasins. There are around 150 individual Chippewa bands or tribes in the U.S. and Canada.

Their language is Anishinaabemowin, which is one of the Algonquian languages. According to their old stories, they originally lived on the Atlantic coast. They began moving to the west about 500 years ago. One of their creation stories is of a series of prophecies. It says they will have seven great fires. Each of these fires will be a special time in their history.

As delivered by the prophets, the final fire is said to mean "New people will emerge. They will find the old ways and the old traditions. The nation will be reborn."

The Chippewa traditionally would fish, hunt, and farm corn and squash. They are especially known for their use of wild rice, which grows on the water. They go out in their canoes and gather it together. Today, as in the past, one person steers the canoe, while the other uses a stick to knock the rice into the boat. Wild rice harvesting is a very important part of Chippewa tradition. The right to harvest the rice is cherished.

In different parts of their history, the Chippewa had great trading networks. They traded all of the normal food and tools. They were also known for finding copper that could be used to make many things.

The Midewiwin was their medicine society. It had a very powerful influence on the lives of the Chippewa. They were shamans who used a variety of methods to help the sick. This included using Migiis shells, which were normally only found in the Pacific.

The Chippewa are one of the few tribes who were able to beat the Sioux in battle. Experts have suggested the reason the Sioux moved from the Great Lakes area is that the Chippewa continued to press them out of the region.

Around the middle 1700s, there were as many as 25,000 Chippewas, according to reports made at the time. According to the United States census there were an estimated 105,000 Chippewas in the year 2000.

Pueblo: The First Apartment Buildings

There was no single tribe called the Pueblo. This term is cultural and describes how some of the tribes in the Southwest lived. The Pueblos are mainly in Arizona, New Mexico, and Texas. The word *Pueblo* is Spanish for village.

The languages of the Puebloan tribes belong to different language families. (See Chapter 2 for more details about the earliest times in Pueblo history.)

Some of these tribes are believed to be the descendants of the people formerly known as Anasazi. There's a good reason that the Anasazi are now known as the Ancestral Puebloans.

The two oldest continuously inhabited settlements in the United States are in this area. Oraibi, on the Hopi Reservation in Arizona, and Acoma (Sky City) in New Mexico, date back to around 1150. St.Augustine, Florida, is the oldest European-founded continuously inhabited city in the United States and was founded over 400 years later.

The western Pueblos tend toward matrilineal societies. The eastern Pueblos are more often patrilineal. Within each of these groups, traditional roles, customs, and religious practices vary. While some Pueblos have adopted various forms of Christianity, many also still follow old traditional practices.

Almost all Pueblos share the creation story that says they entered this world through a hole in the roof of the world below. They were able to reach the hole by using a ladder. Kivas (usually underground ceremonial chambers) will sometimes have a ceremonial hole in the floor to symbolize this entrance place. There are often ladders in Pueblos that represent the ladder used to exit the underworld.

The first Spanish expedition into Pueblo areas was that of Francisco Vasquez de Coronado in 1540. When he did not find the fabled "Seven Cities of Gold," he left the area. In 1598, Spanish conquistador Juan de Oñate Salazar began a major expedition into the lands north of the Rio Grande. Oñate claimed most of modern New Mexico for Spain. He then established a capital city in Santa Fe.

Many of the domesticated animals (cattle, goats, horses, and sheep) introduced by the Spanish were adopted by the Pueblos. While cotton was used for textiles, wool from their sheep and goats soon became the predominant fiber.

Spanish efforts to dominate the daily life of the Pueblos, including religious conversions, led to considerable resistance by the Pueblos. In 1680, a Tewa Pueblo Indian named Popé led a revolution against the Spanish. Starting in the Taos pueblo, the revolt was successful. The Pueblos managed to rid much of New Mexico of Spanish forces.

Twelve years later, the Spanish, under Diego de Vargas, returned with a vengeance. They reconquered the area, and destroyed many of the villages. Other than a few other incidents, the Pueblo remained at peace with their Spanish, Mexican, and American neighbors. During much of this time, the Hopi had little contact with the Spanish or the Mexican governments.

In 1821, Mexico gained its independence from Spain and ruled New Mexico and Arizona. In 1848, The United States took possession of New Mexico and Arizona, and thereby had control over the Pueblos. Today, each of the major Pueblo villages is treated as a separate entity. According to the 2000 U.S. census, there are 60,000 Pueblo Indians.

Apache: Uncertain Origins

The Apache people are one of the larger tribal nations in the United States. Their language is one of the Athabascan languages. There are several different dialects. There is debate on the meaning of the Apache. The most accepted theory is that it is a Zuni or Tewa word meaning "enemy." Their name for themselves is Indé. According to the U.S. census of 2000, there were 57,000 Apaches.

There are six major Apache groups. They are:

- ✔ Chiricahua (Chíshínin in their language)
- ✔ Jicarilla (Tinde in their language)
- ✔ Lipan
- ✔ Mescalero
- ✔ Plains Apache (Kiowa-Apache)
- ✔ Western Apache

Within each of these tribes are many communities. Each has some differences, so it is a bit hard to make generalized statements about the Apache. So, let's look at the Jicarilla Apache as an example.

The Jicarilla

Jicarilla society is matrilineal. Often, the authority in the family was at the grandparents' generation. Grandparents were usually responsible for educating the children. Jicarilla custom says it is disrespectful to stand while an elder is in the room.

For puberty-aged children, young girls had the Adolescence Ceremonial Feast (Keesda); young boys had the Ceremonial Relay Race (Go-jii-ya).

Red Clan, White Clan

In the 18th century, the Jicarilla moved throughout their traditional territory. Two groups split apart from each other and took up residence in specific areas. Over time, they came to be known as different communities. The Llaneros (Red Clan) ranged the plains. The Olleros (White Clan) stayed near the mountain valleys. The plains Jicarilla lived a semi-nomadic life. They would hunt the buffalo on the plains in southern Colorado, northern New Mexico, and small parts of western Oklahoma and Texas. This was a good life for them until the Comanche moved into the area in the early 1700s. Conflicts with the well-armed Comanches forced the Jicarilla to move closer to the mountains. Here, some of them took up a more settled, agrarian lifestyle. They raised such crops as corn, beans, squashes, and melons. They picked berries and grew tobacco. Still, they hunted game in the area as well.

They often wore clothes made from buckskins. Their homes were most frequently wickiups. They were constructed into a domed frame made from young saplings. The sides and top were mostly thatch made frombuffalo grasses.

Jicarilla is Spanish for "little basket." The Jicarilla were well known for their ability to weave small baskets. These baskets could be used as cups or to carry small objects.

Politics

The Jicarilla practice democracy. Each adult is allowed to have his or her say in a matter. Other than in hunting or war parties, the group consensus was how decisions were made. War or hunting leaders often made decisions for a group, but they could easily be replaced.

The Jicarilla generally faired well under Spanish and Mexican rule. They were far enough away from the populated areas to have much contact. Their lands were considered unsuitable by the Spanish. When the United States took over New Mexico in 1848, this would change. With much of New Mexico under Spanish or Mexican land grants, which the Americans were legally required to honor, Apache "traditional" lands suddenly looked good to settlers. Additionally, lands that had been used by the Jicarilla for many years were land-granted to settlers by the Mexican government.

Encroaching settlers and hunters began to take their toll on the wildlife in the area. The Jicarilla began to engage in raids on American settlers and wagon trains. While they were few in number, they were very resourceful. Their horses were some of the best in the Southwest. They could often easily outrun army pursuers.

War

In the 1850s, the Jicarilla signed a treaty with the United States, and one with the territorial governor. They were to be given title to some land and material so they could take up farming. For their part, they agreed to stop their raids and to stay out of certain territories. Neither treaty was ratified by the U.S. Senate. However, the Jicarilla had already moved to the lands they were offered. When the supplies did not arrive, many of the Jicarilla moved away and started raiding again. On April 10, 1854, the territorial governor declared war. The war ended the next year, but the Jicarillas still had no homeland. This began a series of councils to give the Jicarilla their own land and to have them stop raiding. For various reasons, no land could be found.

By the late 1870s, some estimates placed the Jicarilla population between 400 and 1,000 people. Northern New Mexico settlers did not want the Jicarilla anywhere near them. But Americans from the eastern part of the country were more sympathetic to the Jicarilla's situation. In 1883, the Jicarilla were placed in the Mescalero Apache reservation in southern New Mexico. The two Apache groups did not get along very well. Still lacking a title to their land, many Jicarilla left the reservation and moved to an area near Santa Fe and in northern New Mexico. This led to renewed protests from the local settlers.

In 1887, President Grover Cleveland established a Jicarilla reservation by executive order. They were given 415,000 acres northwest of Santa Fe, along the Colorado border. Despite finally having some dedicated land, the Jicarilla continued to have problems. Disease, especially tuberculosis, and other hardships reduced their numbers to about 600 people in 1920. An additional piece of land was added to the reservation when it was determined that the Jicarilla needed more fertile land to adequately support themselves.

Around 1930, oil was discovered in parts of the reservation. This has added another resource which has improved the Jicarilla's economic security.

Iroquois: Call Us Haudenosaunee

As with many American Indian tribes, the name by which they are known was given to them by another group. *Iroquois* is a French variation of the Algonquian word for rattlesnake or real adders. They call themselves Haudenosaunee. This can be translated as people of the long house, or people of the extended lodge. Their traditional lands stretched from Lake Erie to the Hudson River. This included both the United States and Canada.

There are many variations on how the various names of the Iroquois should be spelled. Each tribe had its own dialect, early historians recorded the names as they heard them, and there are disagreements within some tribes themselves.

There's a reason that the Haudenosaunee are known as the Six Nations; they are composed of, you guessed it, six nations. They were originally five, until the Tuscarora joined:

- Cayuga
- Mohawk
- Oneida
- Onondaga
- Seneca
- Tuscarora

From west to east, the tribes were the Seneca, Cayuga, Onondaga, Oneida, and the Mohawk. The Tuscarora joined the Iroquois Confederacy in 1722 after they were forced out of North Carolina by English settlers. There is considerable disagreement as to how long the Confederacy has been around. Many scientists have dated the beginnings of the Confederacy to the year 1451. Others say it was organized in 1142, or in the 1500s.

Iroquois creation stories often feature Sky Mother and her twin sons. The earth upon which we live is an island on the back of a turtle. It is this story which led some people to call the world "Turtle Island." Another aspect of Iroquois faith was the False Face Society. They were the Iroquois medicine people. They used masks as an intricate part of their healing process.

The Iroquois way of life

Generally, the Iroquois were matriarchal in nature. The woman had the home, and her children became part of her family and clan. Men were expected to marry someone from another clan. The three clans present in all six nations were

- Bear
- Turtle
- Wolf

Some tribes had other clans as well. Early on the Iroquois hunted the game of the region, they fished, and they raised the standard corn, beans, and squash.

Iroquois traditional homes were their namesakes, the long house. They could be up to 200 feet long. A few were even longer. They were an arching framework of interwoven branches, which were usually covered in birch bark. The Iroquois would usually stay in one area until the fields and the animal had been exhausted. This means a village could be in one place for as many as 20 or30 years. (See Chapter 15 for more on Indian dwellings.)

The women ran the homes and worked the fields. The men did the hunting. They were also warriors. Warfare was a constant situation among the Iroquois and their neighbors. Villages were fortified. Iroquois warriors are noted for their distinctive way of cutting their hair. The Mohawk style was named after them. This usually featured most of their head being shaved, except for a thin ridge running down the middle.

Inspiring the founders

The Iroquois are particularly known for their political structure. Tribal leaders were called *sachems*. While the sachems were men, they were usually chosen

The meaning of names

The Cayuga (Gweugwehono) were called the "people of the mucky land," or "those of the great pipe."

The Mohawk (Kahniakehaka) were the "keepers of the eastern door," or "people of the flint."

The Oneida (Onyotaaka or Onayotekaono) were the "people of the standing stone."

The Onondaga (Onundagaono) were the "keepers of the fire," "people of the hill," or the "wampum keepers."

The Seneca (Nundawaono) were the "keepers of the western door," or the "great hill people."

The Tuscarora were the "shirt wearing people."

by the clan mothers. The Great Iroquois Council (or Iroquois League) is often thought to have been formed in the middle 1500s. It was a council with 50 of these sachems. They led the Confederacy during peace times. There were usually 10 Cayuga, 9 Mohawk, 9 Oneida, 14 Onondaga, and 8 Seneca. The leader of the Council was usually an Onondaga. Another group of men led the Confederacy during war.

While the Council had many laws, the main one was called the Kainerekowa, or the Great Law of Peace. Each tribe was free to make its own laws, but one of the main principles of the Great Law was that the member tribes should not fight each other. After they stopped fighting each other, they became a powerful force in the area between the Great Lakes and the Atlantic.

The Iroquois would often use diplomacy or force to overpower their neighboring tribes. For example, The Iroquois often had problems with the Lenni Lenape (Delaware) tribe. To insure that the Lenape followed their wishes, the Iroquois sent some of their tribe to live with the Lenape. This group of Iroquois eventually became known by the name Mingo.

The Iroquois Council's complex system of self-rule was used as a model by the founders of the United States. America's founding fathers borrowed from the Iroquois Council's various forms of governmental responsibility to establish the different branches of the American government and the separation of powers.

Choosing sides

During the Revolutionary War, the Iroquois had to decide who they would support. They remained neutral for some time. Generally speaking, the Mohawk and Cayuga were pro-British. The Oneida were pro-American. Many of the Iroquois sided with the British after some of their towns were attacked by American forces. After the war, many Iroquois moved to Canada in hopes of receiving better treatment from the British government there.

The Iroquois would sign many treaties with the United States, including:

- Fort Stanwix Treaty, 1784
- Treaty of Fort Harmar, 1789
- Agreement With The Five Nations, 1792
- Treaty of Canandaigua, 1794
- Treaty With The Indians Living In The Country of The Oneidas, 1794
- Treaty of Amity, Commerce, and Navigation, 1794
- Treaty With The New York Indians, 1838

Today, the six separate tribes are still extant and live in the U.S. mainly in New York, Wisconsin, and Oklahoma. There are also Iroquois in Ontario and Quebec. According to the 2000 United States census, there are 45,000 Iroquois living in the United States.

Alaska: The Tlingit

The Tlingit people live mainly in the northern part of the panhandle of lower Alaska (near Juneau, Sitka, Ketchikan, and so on). Their language is Tlingit, which is one of the Athabascan languages. Raven is an important figure in Tlingit culture. He was there for the creation of the world, on the Nass River in interior Canada. Traditional stories say the Tlingit traveled under the glaciers in boats to come out on the rivers nears the coast. Some estimates place the Tlingit on the Pacific coast as far back as 8,000 years ago.

Traditionally, the Tlingit are matrilineal. Families are built along the mother's bloodline. Fathers play a relatively minor role in the lives of their children. As is common in most matriarchal societies, a child's maternal uncle is his or her mentor. A son-in-law would almost never even speak to his mother-in-law.

Two moities

Well, really there are three, but two of them, Wolf and Eagle, are actually combined:

- Raven
- Wolf
- Eagle

The Wolf and Eagle clans are usually listed together as one group. Within the clans are houses. The family house is one of the main areas of Tlingit culture. As many as 50 people could live in one of these large plank board houses. Even though the clans are matrilineal, the oldest male is the head of the house, or "house leader." A person would usually identify more with their house than their clan.

Usually, the house leader (*hít s'aatí*, in their language) with the highest status was also the local clan leader. Often, villages did not have an individual leader, this rested in the clan system. When Europeans first encountered the Tlingit, they often found it difficult to deal with a village where each household had a leader.

Dinner's served

Tribes along the northern Pacific coast enjoyed an abundance of food. A commonly heard local expression is "when the tide goes out the table is set." There were two basic settings for the Tlingits, the winter village and the summer village. Summer camp was along the many rivers of the Pacific coastline. Each stream is "owned" by a specific clan or family. Fishing was a primary occupation among the Tlingit. Salmon was their most important, and abundant, catch. The Tlingit would also go fishing in the ocean in their large dugout canoes. The canoes could be over 35 feet long. Unlike many other coast tribes, they did not hunt whales. The Tlingit also hunted many of the animals who lived in their forests.

Storytelling was a favorite pastime for the Tlingit. Raven and his exploits as a creator-trickster-teacher make up the bulk of their tales. Some stories were told by all of the Tlingit; others were considered the exclusive property of a specific clan or house. The "Raven Cycle" is the name for many of these stories. Songs could also be "owned" by a specific clan or house.

Potlatches (*Koo.éex'* in their language) are a large part of their society as well. The potlatch has many complicated meanings. Potlatches could be held for a variety of different reasons, but they were often ceremonies honoring a significant person who had died. They were used both to honor the dead and to add a certain balance to the community. They often take place a year after a person died. Gifts are given out by the clan or the house of the deceased. Some potlatches could last over a week.

The Tlingit owed slaves. This was considered fairly common for people along the upper Pacific coast. Capitalism (for lack of a better term) was practiced by the Tlingit, and slaves were considered part of a person's wealth. This practice stopped in the late 1860s.

The Russians

Their first encounters with Europeans were in the middle 1700s. They mostly had encounters with Russians. The Russians set up trading and fishing centers along the coast lines. This led to both beneficial trading and armed conflicts. The last of these conflicts in Alaska was the Battle of Sitka in 1804. Members of the Russian America Company had set up a post near Sitka. The legality of this post was challenged by the Tlingit. Tlingit structures were built in such a way that some cannon fire would bounce off. The Tlingit were outnumbered and outgunned. Despite this, they managed to escape annihilation. Their flight across some mountains to safety is called the "Kiks.ádi Survival March of 1804." It is considered one of their finest moments.

The Brotherhood

The Alaska Native Brotherhood was the first major organization to try to represent Alaska Natives in the society of the time. Founded in 1912 by two Tlingits, it was designed to make sure that all people were treated equally, and to help preserve Native cultures. A similar group called the Alaska Native Sisterhood was established soon after. These and other groups, along with individuals such as Tlingit Elizabeth Peratrovich, were instrumental in eliminating discrimination against Alaska Natives by European and American governments.

The Tlingits have managed to retain much of their culture and traditions. Interaction with the modern world has changed them as well. As with most American Indian and Alaska Native groups, retaining their language and culture has been a high priority for them. According to the 2000 census, there are an estimated 15,000 Tlingits.

Part II
Interacting with Others

The 5th Wave   By Rich Tennant

In this part . . .

Once Columbus "found" the Caribbean islands and then the mainland, the exploration — and exploitation — began in earnest.

The Spanish and French sent explorers and claimed huge areas for their monarchs back home. Tribes had to contend with Europeans who wanted . . . well, they pretty much wanted everything. Explorers and settlers wanted the land, the resources, the animal furs, the gold, the waterways, and all the other riches in what they essentially considered "for the taking" wilderness.

This part looks at Columbus's exploits and influence, some of the explorers who left their mark, and notable Indian chiefs, leaders, warriors, and women whose entire world changed with the arrival of the white man. It also looks at some of the violent conflicts between Indians and white folks, and also between tribes. U.S-Indian relations over the years are covered as well, with details on some of the more important legislation passed relating to Indians.

Chapter 8

"Columbus Sailed the Ocean Blue"

. . . .

In This Chapter

▶ Detailing fact and fiction

▶ Looking for the new route to Asia

▶ Exploiting the Arawaks

▶ Checking out his later voyages

▶ Looking over what Columbus wrought

. . . .

C hristopher Columbus a divisive figure? The great Italian explorer who discovered America? How can that be? Who could have a problem with Columbus?

Well, the truth is some people do, some people don't. In this chapter, we look at not only what Columbus did, but the impact of his actions and the opinions and views of both Columbus lovers and Columbus bashers.

It's "equal opportunity" criticism and praise time, folks!

Sifting through Fact and Fiction

Christopher Columbus — also known as Christophorus Columbus, Cristoforo Colombo, and Cristóbal Colón — was born in Genoa, Italy, in 1451.

There's been ongoing controversy (maybe "ongoing discussion" is a better way of putting it) about Christopher Columbus's birthplace, even though Columbus himself wrote that he was born in Genoa. Case closed?

The "falling off the edge of the world" is a joke. Very few people in Columbus's circle believed the world was flat, and it isn't true that Columbus's assignment was to prove the world was round. That's a myth perpetuated by biographers of Christopher Columbus who, um, *made stuff up*. Washington Irving, in particular, in his *Life and Voyages of Christopher Columbus*, is egregiously responsible for making grammar and high school students believe this myth as fact.

Another myth is that Queen Isabella had to pawn her jewels to come up with the cashola to send Columbus on his merry way. This is also not true and was, in fact, made up by Bartolemé de Las Casas in the 16th century.

Fiction is fiction; fact is fact.

Facts we're pretty sure of are that Columbus was the son of a wool weaver and merchant. In his early years, Christopher worked in his father's business, and also as a mapmaker and possibly a book merchant. He always had an interest in the sea and, beginning at the age of 14, he began serving as a sailor on a range of ships and voyages in the Portuguese merchant marine. He may have also served as a privateer — a pirate for hire.

When Columbus was in his 20s, he and his brother began soliciting funds for maritime expeditions of exploration. He wanted to find routes to China and India. He first tried King John II of Portugal in 1484, but that was a turndown.

It wasn't until 1486, when he was 35 years old, that Queen Isabella and King Ferdinand of Spain listened with attention to his proposal, and then placed his request — dubbed by Columbus the "Enterprise of the Indies" — under serious consideration.

Initially, they, too, also turned him down, but they were so intrigued by his idea of finding a route to the east — such a route would save time, which would save money — (the more things change, the more they stay the same) — that the monarchs ordered his idea be studied by "learned men and mariners."

Columbus's "Google Maps"

Columbus consulted several reference works and atlases to come up with his ideas regarding how far it was from here to there, how big the Earth was, how wide the seas, and so forth.

These books included:

✔ *Geography* by Ptolemy

✔ *Imago Mundi* by Pierre d'Ailly

✔ *The Travels of Marco Polo*

✔ *The Perpetual Almanac* by Abraham Zacuto

✔ *Ephemerides* by Johannes Müller

✔ *Prospettiva* and the *Meteorologia Agricola* by Paulo de Pozzo Toscanelli (possibly — Columbus may have simply corresponded with Toscanelli)

✔ Correspondence (possibly) with Antonio Gallo

This "studying" by said learned men and mariners took more time than Columbus had anticipated (see the later section, "Columbus's First Voyage (1492–1493)" for more information).

Columbus's First Voyage (1492–1493)

For six years, Columbus waited, and then finally his voyage proposal was approved. Why did the Spanish monarchy decide to back what was unquestionably a risky endeavor with little assurance of a happy outcome?

Deciding to back Columbus was a power play by Ferdinand and Isabel. If the adventurous navigator succeeded in finding a new route to China and the Far East, Ferdinand and Isabel's standing in the European Royals Club (there wasn't really a club) would skyrocket, and then the pope would gravitate to their side to go after the Muslims and convert them to Christianity. (Sound familiar? In more ways than one?)

The Capitulations of Santa Fe was the agreement between Queen Isabella and King Ferdinand of Spain and Christopher Columbus signed in Santa Fe on April 17, 1492. ("Capitulations" in Columbus's time meant "enumerated agreements," not "items of surrender.") Columbus was 41 years old, and his prior seagoing experience had been, to put it kindly, limited. He had apparently been on a few sea voyages prior to 1492, but nothing that was remembered as particularly significant.

The Capitulations stated that Columbus would embark on a voyage west in an attempt to find a new route to Asia. The mission would be funded by Spain, and the Capitulations spelled out the terms of the deal (and it was a pretty good all-around deal for Columbus, who hadn't really been all that successful prior to embarking on his voyage of discovery):

- Christopher Columbus would become the viceroy and governor general of any lands he discovered. He would be in charge of "all those islands and mainland in the Ocean Sea which by his hand and industry he would discover and acquire." He was also granted the authority to "hear and dispatch all civil and criminal proceedings pertaining to the said offices of the admiralty, viceroyalty, and governorship." He could also "punish" ne'er-do-wells.

- Columbus's compensation was 10 percent of, well, everything, but mainly gold and other precious metals and stones discovered in any of the lands he claimed.

- Trade with the new lands would be under his control.

All in all, it was a pretty good deal and Chris probably felt it was worth the six-year wait. Yet, the bottom line was that Columbus was promising to repay the funds expended on his trip with the bounty he'd discover and claim upon his arrival in "India." And notice that there was nothing said regarding people who might be living on "those islands . . . he would discover."

So, on August 2, 1492, Columbus set sail from Palos, Spain, with around 90 men in a fleet of three ships, the *Pinta*, the *Niña*, and the *Santa Maria*, which Columbus himself captained.

Here is where Columbus stopped on his voyage:

- Canary Islands
- San Salvador (October 12, 1492)
- Cuba (October 28, 1492)
- Haiti (December 6, 1492; he named it Hispaniola)

He made these stops on his return trip:

- Santa Maria, the Azores
- Lisbon, Spain

Wiping Out the Welcoming Arawaks

The Arawaks were the Native peoples Columbus first encountered upon his arrival on the island of Hispaniola (Haiti) in December 1492. The second group he came upon were known as the Caribs, on the Lesser Antilles islands.

In a report to his Spain backers, Columbus describes the people that he met and offers a few suggestions on how best to deal with them. (And there's a line about the Natives believing Columbus and his men came from Heaven, which, in hindsight, is irony at its most tragic, isn't it?)

Columbus told his Spanish backers that the Natives had no religion that he could identify, but that they were gentle people and seemed not to know how to be evil. He reported that they didn't kill each other, rob from each other, didn't have weapons, were very timid, and that they were certain that he and his men were divine visitors from Heaven. He recommended that Ferdinand and Isabella resolve to turn them all into Christians. He also commented on the fact that they were all naked, all the time. Guess he felt he ought to mention that, since it was probably a rather noticeable custom to him and his men. (Ahem.)

Considering this perception, it is no surprise that Columbus saw these Natives as ripe for two things: conversion and exploitation. And even though common custom in Europe dictated that only unoccupied lands could be claimed in the name of a monarchy, Columbus claimed his discovery for Spain, wrote it down, had it notarized, and delivered it to the Spanish Crown upon his return.

"We could subjugate them all"

There weren't any monsters, but there were cannibals!

Columbus also provided Spain with additional assessment of the island Natives, and reported back that making them slaves would be an easy thing to do, and that he thought this was a good idea.

He also wrote that he hadn't seen any monsters, but that there might be a chance that the Natives were cannibals. His bottom line was that he could take over the whole bunch of 'em with no more than 50 men.

It is now known that Columbus put forth his mistaken "cannibal" story to justify his exploitation of the Indians and bring the Spanish monarchy onboard for whatever he wanted to do to assure complete domination of the Natives and their natural wealth.

Columbus's mistake came from seeing gourds in the Natives' homes containing the bones of their ancestors. He leaped to the erroneous conclusion that because the Natives saved their family members' bones, they had thus eaten Grampa for dinner.

We know with certainty that Columbus enslaved, brutalized, raped, and slaughtered the Arawak people. He shipped Indians back to Spain to be sold as slaves. He gave young Indian girls to his crew members to be used as sex slaves. He put Indians to work as slaves in the gold mines.

The Requiremento and other bull (s)

In 1455, Pope Nicholas V issued a papal bull (a formal proclamation by the pope) called *Romanus Pontifex*. Catholics were urged to conquer all Saracens and pagans and make them their slaves. And guess what? The Indigenous people were considered pagans.

And then, in 1493, Pope Alexander VI, in a papal bull called *Inter Caetera*, gave the New World to Spain — much to the displeasure of Spain's rival Portugal.

It speaks volumes about the power of the Catholic Church and the politics of the time that a pope could issue a papal bull that awarded Columbus's discovery to Spain and that people acceded to it as indisputable!

France complained, but it did no good, and Spain assumed total control over the lands — and the people. (By the way, there was a proviso that protected the lands of Christians. How thoughtful.)

The Native population of the Caribbean dwindled from estimated millions to mere hundreds from illness (from Europeans and their animals), extermination, and suicide. Mothers killed their newborns rather than allow them to become slaves; pregnant women aborted themselves; Natives killed themselves en masse to escape the horrors of living in an enslaved society.

And then, in 1513, the pope issued the *Requiremento*, which was an official decree, a solemn edict from the Church that was read to the Indians so that the Spanish could state that the Natives had been fully informed of two things:

- The pope officially ruled the world.
- The Natives were now officially screwed.

The *Requiremento* was insane. That sounds harsh, but this document may be the quintessential example of what can happen when a theocracy is in charge. The *Requiremento* was read to the Indians in Spanish (which, of course, they didn't understand) and the bull stated that the Indigenous peoples had to acknowledge the Catholic Church as the ruler of the world. If they didn't comply, the Church promised to do as much harm and damage to them as it possibly could.

A quarter of a century later, in 1537, Pope Paul II issued a papal bull titled *Sublimis Deus*, which revoked in large part the slavery component of the *Requiremento* by stating unequivocally that Indians were human beings and were entitled to liberty and dignity. This bull was commonly ignored.

The Burning of the Bulls

Papal bulls were never anything but bad for Indigenous peoples. Over the past decade, groups of Native Americans have petitioned the Vatican to revoke the encroaching bulls, singling out especially the 1493 *Inter Caetera* bull.

Indigenous people meet every October 12 in Honolulu to symbolically burn the bulls. The first public Burning of the Bulls took place in Hawaii in 1997.

They pledge to continue until the pope formally revokes the edict.

Columbus's Three Other Voyages

Columbus's voyages began as journeys of exploration and devolved into missions of conquest, subjugation, and exploitation.

As the old saying goes, money changes everything, and the gold, gems, and, yes, human bounty in the Indies quickly led to the Spanish colonists doing everything in their power to control and sell the Natives, mine the mountains clear of gold, and establish dominance in an already-occupied land.

No wonder many Indians these days consider Columbus Day a day of mourning.

The following sections are about the voyages Columbus made to North America after his discovery became widely known, and after the New World's riches became a highly sought-after prize to the European powers.

Voyage two: The first slave roundup (1493–1496)

When Columbus went back to Isabella and Ferdinand for backing for a second trip to the newly discovered lands, he had no problem getting the money. They named him Admiral of the Ocean Sea, and he was made supreme commander of 17 ships and 1,500 men.

This time, Columbus's orders were clear:

- ✔ Set up a trading post.
- ✔ Convert the Natives to Christianity.
- ✔ Greatly expand the colony he had left behind in Hispaniola.
- ✔ Continue to look for a new route to Asia.

Columbus's second journey departed Spain on October 13, 1493, and made good use of the north Atlantic trade winds. He arrived in the West Indies in early November and later that month discovered that the small group he had left behind had been massacred by hostile Natives.

He then established a short-lived colony called La Isabela, and then traveled to Cuba and Jamaica.

During his three-year stay, he established colonies, fought with the Natives, and enslaved them to dig for gold. He headed back to Spain in March 1496 with 500 slaves for Spain.

Voyage three: Mutiny and insurgency (1498–1500)

In May 1498, Columbus left Spain for his third voyage to his discovered lands, this time with six ships. When they arrived at the Canary Islands in June, the fleet split into two groups of three, with one heading for Hispaniola, and the other, captained by Columbus, venturing to look for new lands.

After sighting the coast of South America, Columbus ordered his fleet back to Hispaniola where he discovered the colonists were very unhappy with him. And his crew wasn't in the best of moods either. Not to mention that the powers back in Spain were upset about the less-than-ample quantities of gold being sent back.

Columbus hung some of his rebellious crew, and tried to quash the resistance, but Ferdinand and Isabella had had enough. They appointed a new commissioner of the colonies, who arrived in 1500, arrested Columbus, and had him sent back to Spain, shackled and humiliated.

Voyage four: Stranded on Jamaica (1502–1504)

Columbus was imprisoned for about six weeks in Spain, and then freed by Ferdinand. The crown then agreed to fund a fourth voyage, which would be to find a water passage to Asia. Columbus set sail in May 1502 with four ships and about 140 men. His son, Ferdinand, then 14, accompanied his father and would later write a detailed account of the trip.

All in all, this trip, Columbus's last, was an abysmal failure. Storms resulted in his older ships being beached and Columbus and his crew ending up stranded on Jamaica for an entire year.

He and his crew (half of whom mutinied against Columbus, but were quickly overpowered), were rescued in June 1504 and he returned to Spain in November of that same year.

The Impact of Christopher Columbus

How the mighty have fallen! Every Columbus Day now, the blogosphere and newspaper Op-Ed pages explode with indignant, repulsed articles spelling out in detail the new and terrible image of the disgraced Italian explorer.

Today, even the most ardent defenders of the "Columbus as hero" school of thought have had to take a step back from their dogmatic praise of the master navigator and acknowledge the negative impact he and his voyages had on Native peoples.

So, was Columbus a genocidal invader or not? Perception is a funny thing. As is context.

To many Native Americans, Columbus is a symbol of the beginning of their end. To many Italian Americans, he is a brave Italian explorer.

The reality, and the truth, is that he is both, and that both sides of the argument make a valid point.

Thanks to Columbus, a country that many consider the greatest in all of human history was created. Columbus's discovery effectuated European expansion into an enormous, abundant New World, resulting in a nation that has defined "liberty" for the rest of the world since 1776. There is no argument that the United States of America changed the world.

Yet, in addition to claiming his discovery for Spain, Columbus also wanted to conquer Jerusalem with the gold he found in the Indies. His policies were genocidal, of this there is no doubt:

- He rounded up slaves and shipped them back to Spain to be marched naked through the streets and then sold at market.

- He enslaved island Natives and set them to work stripping the mountains of gold from top to bottom.

- His men treated the Natives like animals, often torturing them and beheading children for amusement, killing men, women, and children at will, chopping off their hands if they were deemed to be lazy, using their corpses as dog food, and even simply walking up to a Native and slicing off a thick piece of flesh from his body to check the sharpness of their knives.

Thus, the problem with the word *discovery* when talking about Columbus. Upon his arrival, there were civilizations with established societal structures, a thriving cultural life, and a healthy economy. The European guiding principle of colonization resulted in the devastation of Native populations.

Here is the good Columbus is remembered for:

- He opened up the Americas to European settlement.

- He created enormous profit for Spain, Portugal, Italy, and other European countries through the gold and precious stone mines he operated on the Caribbean islands.

- He successfully navigated seas that had never before been traversed, setting the stage for all future visits to the New World by Europeans.

But this is the evil Columbus is remembered for:

- ✔ He launched and grew the slave trade between the newly discovered lands and Europe.

- ✔ He and his men brought to the New World diseases to which the Natives had absolutely no immunity, resulting in mass epidemics and diminishment of the populations.

- ✔ The results of his exploitation of the Arawaks and other Native peoples was the genocidal destruction of millions of people.

Chapter 9

The Spanish and French Stake Their Claims

I n 1493, Columbus returned to Spain with word of his great discoveries. Columbus ultimately made four journeys to the New World, but he was not the only person in service to a crown heading out on voyages of exploration.

There were quite a few Europeans who would be among the explorers of North America after Columbus. Many of the earliest explorers were Spanish, but a few French and English would travel here, too. There were many motivating factors for these trips of exploration, and the majority of them can be summed up with the phrase: "Gold, Glory, and God."

In many European countries, only the oldest son could inherit the family fortune. So, many a younger son would decide to seek his fortunes elsewhere. Very few explorers were in it for the thrill of finding new lands. While this might have been true to some extent, most explorers were hoping for financial reward. This chapter explores just who these explorers were and what they found.

John Cabot: England's First Steps in the New World

Born in Italy around 1450 as Giovanni Caboto, he would become known by the name his English employers gave him: John Cabot. Like Columbus, Cabot was looking for a quick trade route to Asia. Several people had been unsuccessful trying at the middle latitudes, so Cabot thought he would find a "Northwest Passage."

Seeking seafarers

Some of the European explorers of North America were:

- John Cabot (an Italian sailing for England)

- Amerigo Vespucci (an Italian sailing for Spain and Portugal)

- Juán Pónce de León (a Spaniard sailing for Spain)

- Hernán Cortés (a Spaniard sailing for Spain)

- Jacques Cartier (a Frenchman sailing for France)

- Hernando De Soto (a Spaniard sailing for Spain)

- Francisco Vázquez de Coronado (aSpaniard sailing for Spain)

- Jacques Marquette (a Frenchman sailing for France)

- Louis Jolliet (a French Canadian sailing for France)

- René Robert Cavelier, Sieur de La Salle (a Frenchman sailing for France)

The French and English came to North America because they were not part of the pact between Spain and Portugal. The Spanish would explore the southern parts of the United States and North America. The French would claim much of Canada and the central part of the United States. The English would plant their flag along the Atlantic coast north of Florida.

Sailing for King Henry VII of England, Cabot's ship *Matthew* left England in 1497. He eventually landed somewhere in Maine or Newfoundland. He was the first explorer to actually land on the North American mainland. The early Spanish explorers only visited islands up to this point. Cabot would claim the area for England on June 24, 1497. He tried to go north, but ice blocked his path.

Cabot returned to England with reports that he had found Asia. He launched a second expedition with five ships in 1499. Only one ship would make it back to England. Little is known of what happened on that voyage, or to Cabot. However, Cabot did establish an English presence in North America.

Cabot's claim of the land for England meant that all of the American Indians of this region would be facing English colonists who thought they had the right to live on the Indians' land. Here's what his claims led to for some of the Native people:

- For the Abenaki, Cabot meant that fishing fleets would soon come to the Grand Banks area off of Maine and Newfoundland. This led to interactions with the Abenaki. These interactions led, inevitably, to exposure to European diseases. The Abenaki had no immunity to such illnesses. This led to many deaths. Disease may have led to the deaths of more American Indians than all of the armies put together.

> ✔ For the Mi'kmaq (Micmac), Cabot's visit with them had the same effect. It is said that Cabot took three Mi'kmaqs with him on the return voyage of his first expedition. These contacts would get the Mi'kmaqs into the fur trade with Europeans. Obtaining arms from the Europeans gave them a distinct advantage other nearby tribes.

> ✔ For the Beothuk tribe, Cabot's visit would prove to be the first steps toward annihilation. While it was not the case with Cabot, many of the Europeans who followed him would take Beothuks as slaves.

Amerigo Vespucci: America's Namesake

Amerigo Vespucci was born in 1454 in Florence, Italy. With Italy not being involved in the exploration business, Vespucci decided to try his luck in Spain. In the late 1490s, he was one of the captains of a fleet of four ships that reached the northern coast of South America. They then headed north into the Caribbean. The fleet had many of the sailors from Columbus' first trip. Vespucci's next trip landed in Guyana or Brazil. He sailed to the south and reached the mouth of the Amazon.

His next voyage, around 1501, was for Portugal. This trip again followed the coastline of Brazil. It is possible they went as far south as Argentina. These latitudes were much farther south than those which were known for Asia. As with many of these early trips, exact locations were hard to determine. When he returned, he told his sponsors that because the land was so far south, it might be a new continent. He was perhaps one of the first people to make this assertion.

For the Indians, Vespucci was a spreader of untruths (although probably not intentional on his part). He often wrote of entire tribes (Caribs) as cannibals. He also wrote that Indians did not have any religions.

Vespucci was the first European to contact the Arawak (Taino) of Bonaire Island. To the Arawak, Vespucci was the forerunner of slave traders. Many of the Arawak of the island were made into slaves after their island failed to impress the Spanish.

To the Arawak of Curacao, Vespucci was the strange man who left sick sailors on their island. To the Arawak and Caribs of this area, Vespucci is the man who gave their country the name it has today. When Vespucci arrived in Lake Maricaibo, he noticed the many Indian houses on stilts in the water. This led him to naming the place "Little Venice" or Venezuela.

The name game

There are a variety of stories as to how Vespucci's name became associated with North and South America. One says that he wrote two long letters to friends. These letters had great details about his trips. They also had explanations about how this had to be an unknown continent because the land went so far south. The letters also glorified his part in these trips. Many experts doubt that Vespucci wrote the letters. But they were widely copied and distributed throughout Europe.

In 1507, large map was created by German map-maker Martin Waldsseemüller. This map had the name America on the new continent. The reasoning was that he was the first person to think, and have some firsthand evidence, that it was a new continent.

Pónce de León: Conquering the Tainos

Juán Pónce de León was born in Spain. He traveled with Columbus on his second expedition in 1493. He decided to stay in the New World and settled in Hispaniola. The following sections describe his explorations.

The good people

There were two major Indigenous groups inhabiting the islands of the Indies at the time of the first contact with Europeans. One group was the Caribs, and the other was the Tainos. The Tainos occupied the island of Hispaniola. *Taino* is believed to be a name Columbus gave to the people. It is believed to mean "good" or "noble."

When de León arrived in Hispaniola, there were many thousands of Tainos living there (see Figure 9-1 for an example of an Indian gathering). Some estimates place their population well over 200,000. Using force, de León conquered the Taino on the eastern half of the island. For these efforts he was made governor of the region. As part of Spanish rule, the Taino were required to pay a regular tribute of gold. If they could not pay the tax, they faced torture, slavery, or death. It would not be long before the Taino were almost gone on Hispaniola and throughout the Caribbean.

Enslaving Puerto Rico

Searching for more gold, de León decided to go to Puerto Rico. In 1508, he tially welcomed the Spanish. Within a year, de León had established Spanish control over much of the island. He was then named governor. Under de León's leadership, many Tainos became little more than slaves. They worked in the mines and fields and built towns and Spanish fortifications. Many of the Tainos would die from the diseases they caught from the Spanish. To the Taino, de León was the typical conquistador. He would conqueror the people in order to get anything they had of value.

The search for the Fountain of Youth?

Around 1511 (after his father Christopher Columbus's death), Diego Columbus was named governor of Puerto Rico. Pónce de León decided to strike out on his own, again. Using his own money, he took three ships and sailed north.

Many stories say he was looking for the "Fountain of Youth." It was a Lucayo Indian (the Lucayo were a small tribe within the Taino) named Andres Barbudo who helped to spread the stories about the Fountain of Youth. Barbudo was taken as a slave and sent to Spain. After he learned Spanish, he told many people that his father had gone to Bimini Island and bathed in a special pool. He said that when his father returned home he was much stronger and healthier, and felt much younger.

Indians from other tribes, possibly the Timucua, also told of special curative waters that could be found in Florida.

On the other hand, some believe de León was looking for riches. In any case, his fleet landed on the mainland on April 2, 1513. It was most likely the Timucua Indians who saw de León and his shipmates come ashore. This would be the first of many contacts the Timucua Indians would have with the Spanish. Over the next three centuries, the Timucua would cease to exist.

Figure 9-1:
An Indian
gathering.

Seeking slaves?

Some experts believe it was not the search for a Fountain of Youth that led Pónce de León to Florida. His trip was really to find more slaves to work the Spanish mines and plantations. Barbudo's tribe, the Lucayo, were just wiped out by the slave trade. Pónce de León only used the story to generate interest among the soldiers he needed to take with him.

Most sources say he named this new land "Florida," which is Spanish for "flowery," because of its lush vegetation. Others speculate the name was because he landed during a Spanish celebration of Easter called "Pascua Florida." His exact landfall is disputed, but it was somewhere in northeastern Florida. He sailed south, went around the Keys, and then went along the west coast of Florida for a distance.

Pónce de León made trips to other islands, and he tried to colonize Florida with little success in 1521. In fact, his expedition was attacked by the local Indigenous tribes. Pónce de León was struck by an arrow, and died from his wound soon thereafter. If he did discover the Fountain of Youth, it obviously did not help.

Influenza, dysentery, and smallpox often followed in the footsteps of the first Spanish explorers. By 1520, smallpox had already reached the Mexican mainland and laid waste to a significant number of the Aztec, Maya, and other Indigenous inhabitants. Estimates are that over 1,000,000 Taino (Arawak) people had been killed either by disease, warfare, or being worked to death by this time.

Hernándo Cortés: Conquering the Aztecs

Hernán Cortés was born in Spain. He is also known as Hernándo Cortés. Seeking his fortune, he traveled to Hispaniola when he was 18. He quickly moved to Cuba, where he helped in the conquest of the island by Diego Velázquez. He was rewarded with land, Taino slaves, and a government position. Despite having several disputes with Velázquez, Cortés achieved considerable success in Cuba.

In 1519, under the authority of Cuban Governor Velázquez, Cortés organized and helped finance an expedition to the mainland. Their official purpose was to find captured Spaniards and to establish trade. Just before he was to leave, Velázquez decided to take command of the expedition away from Cortés. Cortés ignored the Governor's order, and left quickly with several ships, 16 horses, and approximately 500 men. So the sections that follow have Cortés pick up where Velázquez left off.

A tussle in Tabasco

Landing first on the Yucatán peninsula, Cortés found a Spaniard named Jerónimo de Aguilar who had been shipwrecked there for seven years and had learned some of the local Maya language. After winning a small battle against some of the local tribes in what is now Tabasco, Cortés was given a Native woman who was called Doña Marina or La Malinche.

La Malinche spoke both Maya and the Aztec language of Nahuatl. Cortés was able to talk to almost all of the tribes he met. He spoke Spanish to de Aguilar, de Aguilar spoke Maya to La Malinche, and La Malinche would translate that into the Aztec language. It has been speculated that La Malinche was the daughter of a minor Aztec chieftain. When La Malinche's father died, her mother remarried and had a son. The son became heir to the family name and fortune. La Malinche was cast off by the family and eventually became a slave. To some, she is a traitor who helped Cortés conquer Mexico. To others, she was someone who reasoned with Cortés and made things better than they might have been.

All fired up

Cortés moved on up the coastline and established the town of Vera Cruz. In Vera Cruz, he took the bold step of burning his boats. Now, his followers would have to succeed in Cortés's true plans, the conquest of Mexico.

The Aztecs ruled an empire that spread from the Atlantic to the Pacific and covered much of the central part of Mexico. They were the overlords of many tribes and demanded much of the tribes they ruled. This worked in Cortés's favor. He was able to find many tribes that hated the Aztecs. One of the tribes Cortés encountered was the Tlaxcala. Initially, the Tlaxcala fought with Cortés. The Tlaxcalans were somewhat successful in their battles with the Spanish. It suddenly occurred to them that they could use the Spaniards against their enemies, the Aztecs. They would both join forces to defeat the Aztecs.

In the halls of Montezuma

Moctezuma II (also known as Montezuma) was the Aztec emperor. He was born around 1480, and became emperor in 1502. His people knew of Cortés's arrival. Moctezuma was very concerned because of an Aztec prophecy that told of the return of the fair-skinned god Quetzalcoatl. Quetzalcoatl was supposed to return from the east. Cortés's arrival coincided when a very special year in the Aztec calendar similar to our millennium. Moctezuma was quite superstitious and he did not want to offend a god, if, indeed, Cortés was Quetzalcoatl. In case he was a man, Moctezuma tried to bribe Cortés to leave with gifts and gold. Instead of making him leave, this whetted Cortés's appetite even more.

As Cortés and the Tlaxcala marched to the Aztec capital, they reached the town of Cholula. Cholula is near modern-day Puebla, east of Mexico City. The people of Cholula were still allied to the Aztecs. They did not surrender to Cortés, and most of the village was killed in the subsequent fighting.

The largest pyramid in the world (by volume) is located in Cholula. It is over 200 feet high and almost 1,500 feet along each side. It is so large that most people mistake it for a hill. The Great Pyramid in Egypt is taller, but only half as wide.

Cortés arrived at the Aztec capital of Tenochtitlán (modern Mexico City) on November 8, 1519. At the time, the city had well over 100,000 residents. Some historians estimate the population could have been over 300,000. In either case, this made it one of the largest cities in the world. The city was in the middle of shallow Lake Texcoco. It could be reach by several causeways. The city is filled with many tall and ornate temples. It is by far the most amazing thing any of the Spaniards had even seen. When many Spaniards first saw the city, they wondered if it was a mirage.

Cortés and his Spaniards were welcomed into the city. Moctezuma, again, lavished them with gifts. This further enflamed the greed of the Spaniards. They soon took Moctezuma hostage with demands of more gold. Cortés forced Moctezuma to pass along his edicts to the Aztecs. A few months passed, and Cortés was notified that Pànfilo de Narvàez had arrived from Cuba with a small army. Narvàez was there as the representative of Cuba's Governor Velázquez. Cortés left and traveled to the coast to see if he could get Narvàez to join him, instead of arresting him.

Blood bath

While Cortés was gone, the Aztecs conducted one of their many religious rituals. What happened next depends on whose story you believe:

- ✔ According to the Spaniards, they were disgusted by the religious practices of the Aztecs, which involved human sacrifices. When the Aztecs refused to stop the sacrifices, they were killed.

- ✔ According to the Aztecs, however, the Spaniards saw all of the gold that the priests and rulers were wearing. This incited them to kill them all to take the gold.

Regardless of whose story you believe, many of the Aztec leaders and priests were killed in what amounts to a blood bath. Some estimates put the number of dead Aztecs around 500. This event raised the Aztec people's anger to a fever pitch.

By the time Cortés returned, his captains had barricaded themselves in the palace for their safety. Cortés got Montezuma to tell his people to stop their revolt. According to the many historians, Montezuma was killed while he was addressing his people. Historians disagree as to whether the Spaniards or the Aztecs killed him. In any case, the Aztecs rose up, and Cortés and his men fled for their lives. They tried to escape down one of the causeways through the lake. Many of the soldiers were loaded down with gold and drowned when they were pushed into the lake. This battle, on June 30, 1520, is known as *"La Noche Triste"* (the sad night).

Cortés, his surviving soldiers, and his Indian allies quickly left the area. Slowly, they built their forces back up. Eventually, they returned. This time, Cortés had many small ships and he attacked from the lake, as well as from the causeways. He destroyed the aqueduct that brought fresh water into the town. Slowly, but surely, Cortés fought his way into the city. He and his forces finally conquered the city in August 1521. Cortés went on to overthrow the entire Aztec empire.

Cortés destroyed many of the ornate temples of the Aztecs. He built Mexico City on top of the ruins. Eventually, he would be appointed governor and captain-general of what would come to be known as New Spain. Forces under Cortés and others eventually conquered all of modern Mexico.

Years later, after losing most of his official positions, Cortés was given a large land grant, and the title of Marquis, in Oaxaca (southwest of Mexico City). In his later years, he demonstrated a more benevolent attitude to the Native people of Mexico.

Contrary to a commonly held belief, there are many Aztecs living in Mexico. Their language is still spoken throughout much of central Mexico.

Jacques Cartier: Discovering Canada and the Great Lakes

Little is known of Cartier's early career. It has been suggested that he was with Verrazzano in 1524. Jacques Cartier went to Canada three times, in 1534, 1535, and 1541. He would be the first European to visit the St. Lawrence River and he even gave this land its present name.

A lot of the little details, as well as the *not* so little ones, are not known about many of the early explorers and the tribes they met. Even among historians, there are many disagreements about names, dates, and events.

Cartier's first voyage lasted from April 1534 to September 1534. The Mi'kmaqs were not the first American Indians he had encountered. In mid-June he had seen Indians in Labrador (called the "Land of Cain"). They appeared to be hunting seals and might have been Beothuks. Cartier soon learned that the St. Lawrence was not an entrance to China, as he had hoped. He did continue his explorations inland, though. These sections take you through his journeys and dealings with the Indigenous peoples and his exploration for riches.

Not so fast

On the July 6, 1534, the Mi'kmaq saw two ships in the nearby waters. Several hundred of them quickly gathered three or four dozen canoes and headed out to the ship. Having encountered Europeans before, they were interested in trade goods. To their surprise, the cannons on the ship began to fire over their heads. The Mi'kmaq quickly returned to shore. The next day, they returned. This time they made certain that the Europeans could see the beaver pelts they had to trade.

This was the Mi'kmaq's introduction to French explorer Jacques Cartier and his 61 men. In what some have called the first trading between the French and the Indigenous people of North America, Cartier traded the Mi'kmaqs beads and knives for their furs. Cartier reported that the Mi'kmaq "bargained away all they had." While the changes did not happen immediately, the Mi'kmaq's way of life would change from their choosing to adopt a more trade-based economy.

The Mi'kmaq (Micmac) Indians lived in southeastern Canada and hunted, fished, and gathered other foods for sustenance. Their lifestyle varied throughout the year to reflect the seasonal changes. They were known to be expert canoeists. Their light but very study canoes were made from birch bark.

The Mi'kmaq did not know that Cartier's mission came with instructions from the king of France that could be summed up as, "There are ginormous quantities of gold and riches in the New World, so go, seek, bring back!"

Meeting the Iroquois

Cartier continued on in his exploration. He soon encountered some 200 Iroquois Indians in a nearby village. He would misunderstand the Iroquois word for village *(kanata)* as what the entire area was called. The name later appeared in his journals and maps as Canada. Their leader was called Donnacona. Cartier spent some time here. Some historians have called Donnacona's tribe Hurons. Donnacona's normal home was farther inland in a village called Stadacona.

Donnacona was quite distressed when on July 24, 1534, Cartier erected a 30-foot cross on Penouille Point. In reality, the cross was placed as a monument for Cartier claiming these new lands for France. Donnacona seemed to grasp this concept quite well. Some historians quote Cartier as explaining to Donnacona the cross was only a landmark, and had no real significance.

As Cartier prepared to leave, he took Donnacona's sons Domagaia and Taignoagny with him. Some say they went voluntarily; others insist they were kidnapped. In either case, Cartier returned to France in September 1534. His expedition was not much of a success. He had not found a trading route to China. However, he did find some potential clients for France.

Rumors of gold = a ticket home

While in France, Domagaia and Taignoagny learned to speak French. They soon learned that the French were not only looking for China, but they were also looking for gold and jewels. It is an often-told story that the brothers then starting telling the French about the land of Saguenay, which was inland from where they lived. Saguenay was a land with plenty of gold. Gold there was nothing more than just rocks. The brothers then told the French they would take them there if they ever went back home. Some people say the brothers made up the story in order to go home. Others suggest the tale of Saguenay was one of the wild tales long told by the Natives of Canada. Even others said it was an old tale from the Norse who had visited Canada centuries before. Regardless, the brothers would be home within the year.

The second and third voyages

Cartier's second voyage to Canada would last from May 1535 to July 1536. This time he had three ships. He followed the St. Lawrence River inland to the Huron village of Stadacona. Stadacona would later become the modern-day city of Quebec. This was the village where Donnacona normally lived. Donnacona tried to convince Cartier not to go any farther west. He was not successful.

Cartier went west. Farther upstream was the village of Hochelaga. Over 1,000 Indians lived here. Cartier climbed a nearby peak to see the surrounding territory. It was here that he could see that there was no great ocean to the west. He called the peak Royal Mountain, or Mont Real. Thus the name of Montreal was born.

Cartier would travel a bit farther into the inlands. During the winter his men developed scurvy from a lack of vitamin C. The Indians knew that by drinking a tea made from the needles of the white cedar, this problem would be solved. When they realized that Cartier's men would not learn this on their own, they showed them how to do it.

Cartier continued to hear stories of lands of vast riches, but they were always somewhere over the horizon. Cartier was frustrated with the lack of help he had received from Donnacona. According to some historians, Cartier arranged to remove Donnacona so a more agreeable Indian could take over. While taking part in a special event on May 3, 1536, Cartier seized Donnacona and about a dozen other Indians. He took them back to France when he left in July. All of the Indians would die in France, except for one small girl.

Cartier's third expedition would last from May 1541 to September 1542. There would be five ships and over 1,000 French this time. When Cartier returned to Stadacona, they received a warm welcome. The Indians asked about Donnacona. Cartier told them that everyone but the small girl had decided to stay in France because they had become so rich there.

The relationship between the French and the Indians slowly began to deteriorate. Cartier tried to establish a couple of settlements, with only marginal results. The French would have a couple of skirmishes with distrustful Indians as the winter passed.

Cartier would have no great successes during his third voyage. He would eventually go back to France. Cartier's greatest overall success was in establishing a French presence in North America. Other explorers after him (Champlain and others) would open up more lands to French colonists. It was their initial efforts that account for French still being spoken in Quebec today.

Hernando De Soto: Creating Hostile Relations with Southeastern Natives

Hernando De Soto may have been one of the most traveled Spaniards of his era when it came to North and South America. Under Pedrarias Dávila, he participated in the conquest of Central America around 1514. In the 1530s, he was in South America against the Incas with Francisco Pizarro. It was the riches he gained there that helped him finance his most famous expedition, the exploration of the American Southeast. In this section, you can find out more about De Soto and his explorations.

Two views of De Soto

From the Indigenous point of view, De Soto was a cruel and harsh taskmaster. He demanded tribute and slaves. He used force to get his demands fulfilled. To the Spanish, on the other hand, De Soto was a very efficient administrator who knew how to keep the peace and keep his treasury full. He helped to spread Spanish rule, and the Spanish faith, across new worlds. De Soto was made governor of Cuba by the king of Spain. His mandate was simple; colonize North America within four years. For this, he would get a large share of the spoils.

Many of the exact dates, the path they traveled, and the names of the tribes who encountered the Hernando De Soto Expedition are not completely identified. Scholars have used all sorts of methods to understand the route, and there are different versions put forth. Two of these were proposed by John Reed Swanton and Charles Hudson.

On May 25, 1539, Hernando De Soto, 620 Spanish soldiers, over 200 horses, and many other animals landed in Florida in the vicinity of Tampa Bay.

This was not the first time this area had been explored. Pànfilo de Narvàez and 400 men landed here on April 12, 1528. His expedition went through central Florida looking for gold. Like many Spanish conquistadors, Narvàez ruled with an iron fist. This would cause problems for De Soto years later. Several months later, only a handful of his men (most notably Cabeza de Vaca) would still be alive. They were the victims of the insects, swamps, weather, and Native people of Florida.

Juan Ortiz was captured as a part of the Narvàez expedition by an Uzica Indian chief named Hirrihigua. The Uzica were a part of the Calusa tribe. Ortiz learned some of the local languages. He was able to help De Soto talk to some of the different Indians they would encounter.

"North America belongs to Spain"

Despite much of the land already belonging to the American Indians who already lived there, on June 3, 1539, De Soto formally claimed North America for Spain. Showing his fearless nature, De Soto pushed through the rugged territory. He was determined to find riches. Due to Narvàez's earlier encounters with the Florida Indians, De Soto did not always receive a warm welcome.

De Soto's journey may have taken him through these modern-day American states:

✔ Florida

✔ Georgia

- ✔ Alabama
- ✔ South Carolina
- ✔ North Carolina
- ✔ Tennessee
- ✔ Kentucky
- ✔ Mississippi
- ✔ Missouri
- ✔ Arkansas
- ✔ Texas
- ✔ Oklahoma

(See Chapter 6 for additional information about Hernando De Soto's encounters with the "Five Civilized" tribes.)

For many Indian tribes of the American Southeast, meeting De Soto's expedition would be their first encounter with a European. Many of these encounters would be at the point of a spear. De Soto's troops engaged in dozens of fights with different tribes. He would often take hostages in order to get the supplies, slaves, or treasures that he wanted.

Pearl plunder

De Soto went north through Florida into South Carolina. The "Lady of Cofitachique" was the ruler of a tribe near modern-day Columbus, South Carolina. When De Soto's troops approached, she greeted them in a friendly manner. She gave them pearls and other gifts. She also let the Spaniards stay in her town. The Spaniards stole a large cache of pearls from a burial area. They took these and decided to move on. As was often the case with De Soto, the Lady, or her niece, was taken as an unwilling guide to other lands. After reaching Cherokee lands to the west, the Lady managed to escape. She also took back many of the pearls De Soto's expedition had stolen. Some say she hid until De Soto was gone and then returned to her village. Others say she took refuge with the Cherokee fearing De Soto would return to her village and look for her.

De Soto's expedition continued west and had many battles with the local tribes as their demands for provisions, salves, and riches persisted. Finally, on May 21, 1542, De Soto died from a fever in what is now Arkansas. Some say he was buried in secret along the Mississippi River so the Indians would not desecrate his body. Others say De Soto had told some of the local tribes that he was an immortal god, so they would obey his demands. Seeing his dead body would have led to a massacre of the 300 remaining Spaniards. So, he was buried in secret. Luis de Moscoso led the remaining tired conquistadors back to Mexico.

De Soto's expedition encountered many different tribes, some of which no longer exist. For the American Indians, De Soto was a treacherous, spiteful bully. His expedition brought nothing but poverty, pain, disease, destruction, and death. For the Spanish, De Soto's expedition was only marginally successful. They found none of the expected gold and jewels that had been found in Mexico. While they covered lots of land, it was mostly considered to be too hard to farm, or too close to hostile Indians to be worth exploiting. The expedition did establish the Spanish as the dominant force in the southern part of the United States for the next 300 years.

Francisco Vasquez de Coronado: Exploring the Southwest

His name was Francisco Vasquez de Coronado; he was the governor of a northern state in New Spain called Mexico; and he was searching for gold.

Seven golden cities?

In 1536, Álvar Núñez Cabeza de Vaca tediously trod into Mexico City. He was one of only a handful of survivors of the Narvàez expedition to Florida in 1528. Cabeza de Vaca and three companions had struggled on foot across the American Gulf Coast, through Texas, and much of the American Southwest to make it back to Mexico City. During his travels, he — along with Coronado and the Viceroy of Mexico — had heard of the golden area called the "Seven Cities of Cibola."

Now Coronado and the viceroy of Mexico were not fools. They knew that many stories of golden cities in what is now the United States had all proven to be just legends. But, still they hungered for gold, so they sent a priest named Marcos de Niza to go north and see if it was true. Marcos de Niza returned and told them that Cibola was a real city.

Appointed by the viceroy, on April 22, 1540, Coronado left the northern Mexico town of Culiacán with 340 Spanish, 300 Indian allies (from central Mexico), a thousand American Indian and African slaves, and over a thousand horses and mules.

He set out on his mission traveling north for the greater glory of God, Spain . . . but mostly for gold.

Coronado's Expedition passed through the states of Arizona, New Mexico, Texas, Oklahoma, and Kansas. Some of the tribes Coronado's Expedition may have come in contact with in the United States included the Apache, Pima, Navajo, Hopi, Pueblo, Comanche, Ute, and others.

They initially stayed close to the eastern coastline of the Gulf of California (known as the Sea of Cortes). They then cut inland into "uncharted" Indian lands. *Uncharted* may be the correct term, but there were old Indian trading routes through northern Mexico and the American Southwest. The ancient inhabitants of Chaco Canyon were known to have traded goods from Mexico as much has 400 years earlier.

On July 7, 1540, an advance guard reached Cibola. Cibola, in reality, was a group of Zuni pueblos in northwestern New Mexico. The first village they reached was the modern-day ruins of Hawikuh. They were surprised to see the typical Zuni multi-storied adobe buildings. They had expected giant temples, and all they found was a small village made from mud bricks.

Hello — we're in charge

A few hundred Zunis approached Coronado's men. Coronado had the standard greeting read to them. He was there to protect them as a part of the Spanish Empire. They would face no harm as long as they acknowledged the king and the Holy Father, the pope. But the Indians never consented to submit to either.

Armed with shields, bows, and arrows, the Zunis attacked the advance guard. According to Coronado at his trial for mistreating Indians, the Spaniards refused to return fire on the Indians. The Zuni were doing them little harm, so they did not respond. It was only after the Zuni came within a few dozen feet that Coronado says he gave the order for the Spaniards to defend themselves.

Fighting for food

According to Coronado, as soon as the Spaniards started fighting, the Indians retreated into their homes. Not having enough food to feed themselves, the Spaniards realized the Zunis would probably not just give them food. So they carried the attack into the city. The Zuni soon surrendered. Coronado soon learned that the Zuni pueblos were no golden paradise that would make them all wealthy. Marcos de Niza was sent back to Mexico City, as he was no longer believed.

Coronado sent several small groups out in different directions in hope of finding something worth the cost of the expedition. One of these small groups of soldiers was sent to the northwest. They saw several of the Hopi villages in northeastern Arizona. Then they found something which they decided was totally worthless. Spaniards under García López de Cárdenas were the first non-Indigenous people to see the Grand Canyon from its rim. Contemplating its relative value, it appeared to them to be only an obstacle to overcome. Thus, downhearted, they left.

Coronado took his part of the expedition to the settlements to the east, which the Zunis described to him. They soon reached the area of present-day

Albuquerque. They settled here for the winter. While it does appear that Coronado did try to avoid any undue problems with the Pueblos, he still needed food. There not being an overabundance of food in the region, Coronado had to take it from people who did not want to give it.

While in the Albuquerque area, Coronado heard about another city of great riches called Quivira. Quivira did exist. It was many hundreds of miles to the northeast. Whether the Pueblos actually thought its streets were paved in gold, or whether they just overestimated its worth to get rid of the Spaniards, is not known today.

A-quiver over Quivira

They headed out again, this time looking for Quivira. One guide the Spaniards called the Turk seemed to be leading them in ways that did not make sense. Soon they found an Indian who had actually been to Quivira. The Turk was put in chains, and the Spaniards followed the new guide.

As with all of the other stories of massive, bejeweled cities in the United States, Quivira turned out to be just a Native village in eastern Kansas. It was probably a Wichita Indian village. While he did discover the vast (and one of the greatest granaries of the world) plains of North America, Coronado did not find gold so plentiful that it hung from the trees. His dreams shattered, Coronado followed his own trail back to Mexico. Through attrition from disease, warfare, starvation, desertion, and being assigned to other tasks, Coronado returned with only a little over 100 men. Coronado did establish a Spanish presence in the American Southwest. This would linger in the area until the Americans took over in the mid-1800s.

As with those of Narvàez and De Soto, Coronado's expedition was a financial failure. Spaniards had invested their gold and jewels in hopes of finding even more gold and jewels. Considering themselves to be the betters of the local inhabitants, they felt it was their right to reap the harvest of this golden land. It mattered little that what riches there were already belonged to someone. In the United States, no one ever found a fabled El Dorado. But, El Dorado is another city in another continent.

Marquette, Jolliet, and La Salle: Charting the Mississippi

As described earlier in the section on Jacques Cartier, France had a foothold in North America along the St. Lawrence River. The French called this area "New France." Over the next 100 years, they would expand into the area around the Great Lakes.

Marquette and Jolliet

In Sault Ste. Marie in June 1671, in the name King Louis XIV of France, the king's representative Simon Daumont de Saint-Lusson took possession of the lands west and south of the Great Lakes.

Representatives of 14 American Indian tribes witnessed the formal events. The area annexed included the town of Sainte Marie du Sault, Lake Huron, and Lake Superior, and all land and waterways to which these locales were adjacent. It also included areas that that may have been discovered in the region later, and set the boundaries as Hudson Bay to the north, the Pacific to the west, and the Gulf of Mexico to the south.

The deal also required that the Indians accept becoming "vassals" of the king, and that they promise to totally obey him. In exchange for this, they would be under the king's protection against all invaders, enemies, princes, and other state sovereigns.

Such a deal? Or not? Whether they knew it or not, tens of thousands of American Indians were now under the claim of France.

Still hoping to get to China

Through the efforts of missionaries, traders, and Indian allies, the French learned of a great river called the "Missispi," south of the Great Lakes. The governor of New France hoped this might be the route to China that Europeans had spent almost two centuries looking for. Born in Canada, Louis Jolliet (sometimes spelled *Joliet*) had done considerable exploring in the area around New France as a fur trader. He was one of the witnesses of the formal land claims made in Sainte Marie du Sault.

The New France governor arranged for him and a French missionary named Jacques Marquette to look for this river. Father Marquette had been a missionary to several American Indian tribes around the Great Lakes. Between them, they spoke many different American Indian languages.

Jolliet hoped to be able to establish trade relations with many of the tribes they encountered. Marquette was interested in converting the Indians to Christianity.

On May 17, 1672, Jacques Marquette, Louis Jolliet, and five others left St. Ignace on Lake Michigan in search of the great river (see Figure 9-2 for a picture of the two men). They traveled for most of their trip in two canoes. During their travels, Marquette and Jolliet would meet or see many different American Indian tribes. For some Indians, Marquette and Jolliet were the first Europeans they ever met.

Tribes Marquette and Jolliet may have encountered during this trip included the Chickasaw, Choctaw, Huron, Kickapoo, Menominee, Pawnee, Sioux, and others.

Figure 9-2:
Louis Jolliet
and
Jacques
Marquette.

Many of the local tribes warned them against going south. Menominee tribal elders advised them that there were many unfriendly tribes in that direction. Marquette and Jolliet told them the trip had to be made. So with the help of two Miami Indian guides, they decided to travel through Wisconsin. After some travel across land, they arrived at the enormous headwaters of the Mississippi on June 17 and quickly headed south along the river.

Marquette's mentioning of Wisconsin in his journal is the first time the name appears in a European-American document. Based on the Indian name for the river they were on, he spelled it "Meskousing." Eventually, the M would be dropped when explorer La Salle could not read Marquette's handwriting. It would evolve into "Wisconsin."

They encountered many different tribes, animals, and plants. The explorers were startled by the size of the buffalo herds and some of the fish in the river. They made maps of the river and the surrounding territories.

After a cautious start, many tribes, such as the Illinois and the Quapaw (or "Akansea" as they called them), would make them honored guests.

The first whites

Marquette and Jolliet were the first white men to be seen in their area in around 100 years. The explorers saw them as potential allies against the Spanish. They also learned that the Mississippi River did empty into the Gulf of Mexico.

The lands of the Quapaw were on what today is called the Arkansas River. Marquette and Jolliet noted the Indians had Spanish trade goods. The Quapaw also warned them of hostile tribes along the river to the south. Not wanting to lose the valuable information they had collected so far, Marquette and Jolliet decided to return to New France to make their report.

To their credit, Marquette and Jolliet evinced a respectful mien of dignity toward the Indians and often impressed many of the Natives they met.

No thievery allowed

Tribal leaders noticed that, unlike the Spanish, the French didn't try to steal from them. Marquette and Jolliet seemed to treat them as people. Marquette and Jolliet still saw most of the Indians as savages, but they were humans.

The French were to learn much about the interior of the United States from this expedition. They gained valuable insights into the lives of some of the tribes living there. Marquette estimates that the Illini tribe alone had over 8,000 members. And, in the long run, the French presence in the area would solidify their claim on these lands over Spain and the British.

Marquette would die in Michigan in 1675. Jolliet would continue in the fur trade. In 1679, Jolliet would discover a land route to Hudson Bay for the New France government. The presence of the English there would be a thorn in France's side for years to come.

La Salle — Claiming the Mississippi

Not long after Marquette and Jolliet, came another French explorer. This one had a patent of nobility. His name: Rene Robert Cavelier, Sieur de La Salle, or as he was commonly called, La Salle.

La Salle was given land not long after he arrived in Canada. He became the master of Fort Frontenac (modern Kingston, Ontario). Soon he was exploring the Great Lakes and building more forts there. He established some preliminary good relations with the Illinois (Peoria) and Miami Indians while he was in the Illinois River area. He tried to make them allies against the Iroquois. He left the area to return to the settled parts of New France for extra supplies. By the time he had returned in 1680, over 500 Iroquois had invaded the territory and destroyed his forts and many of the Indian allies as well. He once again returned to Fort Frontenac in 1681.

Chartered by King Louis XIV, La Salle traveled south from Montreal in late 1681, and reached the Mississippi River by 1682. With him were about two dozen French and almost as many of his Indian allies.

La Salle would build several forts as he traveled. Near modern Memphis, La Salle's armorer got lost while hunting. Being concerned about the nearby Chickasaw Indians, La Salle built a fort for protection while they looked for him. Fort Prudhomme, named after the armorer, would provide La Salle refuge on both parts of his voyage.

La Salle continued his travels down the Mississippi River to the Gulf of Mexico. He was the first European to travel the length of the Mississippi

River. On April 9, 1682, he claimed all of the Mississippi River basin in the name of King Louis XIV. In King Louis' honor, he named the area Louisiana. This was a message to British and Spanish settlers to not move into this area. La Salle was disappointed, though. He had hoped the river would eventually lead to a passage to China. La Salle went back up the river and eventually returned to Montreal.

Louisiana covered an area from the Great Lakes to the Gulf of Mexico. It stretched from the Rocky Mountains to the Appalachian Mountains. In essence, it was most of the central part of North America.

La Salle would return to France to set up a significant colonization effort for France in the Mississippi River valley. He left France in mid-1684. His fleet of four ships missed the Mississippi River entirely. They landed in a bay south of modern Houston, Texas. Two of his ships would be lost. One was captured by Spanish pirates. And one ship carried disgruntled colonists back to France.

La Salle would explore significant parts of southern and eastern Texas before he was murdered by his own followers. Most of the remaining French who tried to establish a colony were killed by a coastal Texas tribe called the Karankawas. One of the members of La Salle's party was deliberately sent to live with the Hasinai, a group of Caddo in East Texas. Pierre Talon learned the Caddo language and served later explorers as a translator.

La Salle did establish some positive relationships with some of the tribes in the area of the Mississippi River. His travels on the Mississippi cemented France's claim to this large section of North America. His expedition's chronicler recorded many details about the various tribes they encountered. These records would prove to be helpful for historians. One of the unexpected results of his various trips was to get the Spanish to be more interested in their northern holdings.

Leaving the Native People Reeling

Over the centuries from the late 1500s to the middle 1800s, American Indian tribes would face continual invasions of their lands and resources.

Each new explorer would start a trickle of other interested parties. These trickles would soon become torrents of explorers, traders, missionaries, and settlers. The bounty was irresistible, and the attitude was rampant that it was all free for the taking.

The escalating encounters between the French, British, and Spanish would seldom prove to be beneficial to the Indigenous people of North America. As each of these major European powers sough to outdo the others, American Indian tribes were inevitably brought into the conflict.

Playing one against the other

Every time one of the European powers would fight over an area, they would work very hard to persuade the local tribes to back them up. These requests would lead to internal strife for many tribes. Distrust was pervasive among the naysayers, yet there were always Natives who believed it was in the tribe's best interest to "take sides."

Promises of trade goods and protection would be given to the tribes who provided warriors. Soon, one tribe would be fighting another tribe in the name of their European backers. These conflicts would take their toll on the Indians.

The tribes also learned to play the Europeans off each other. The Caddo in East Texas were sensitive to their importance to the French. They preferred the French method of attempted conquest over the Spanish heavy-handed religious conversion.

Making them sick

Also following the explorers came the creeping tide of disease. Every wave of Europeans brought new illnesses for which the American Indians had no immunities. Common diseases which would harm, yet not destroy, an ordinary European village would devastate an American Indian town.

Some historians believe the total population of North America would be reduced by as much as 90 percent due to diseases spread by the Europeans.

There were many people who were concerned about the welfare of the Indigenous people of the Americas. Even among the Spanish, who were known for their brutality, voices spoke up for more gentle treatment of the Indians. Many of the greatest names in Spanish exploration would be tried in Spain for inhumane treatment of the Native people. A few would be found guilty, but others would not.

Sadly, "God, Glory, and Gold" would be a death knell for many of the original inhabitants of this land.

Chapter 10

Native American Chiefs and Notable Women

*T*heir names are now a part of American culture. As well they should be, considering that they were the first "Americans," and that their history is the pre-Columbian history of North America.

Even people who have little or no knowledge of the specific details of American history have heard of Geronimo, Sitting Bull, and Cochise.

In this chapter, we include the stories of a few of the more notable Native Americans — men and women who changed the way Indians interacted with the new U.S. and its government, and contributed to the legacy of the surviving Native tribes in our country. We discuss the ones who are most well known — breaking the men down by chronological order and including the women in a section all their own — but there are countless others who were an important part of Native American history.

Space prohibits including all of them, but for more information, we recommend that you check out *The Encyclopedia of Native American Biography: Six Hundred Life Stories of Important People, from Powhatan to Wilma Mankiller* by Bruce E. Johansen and Donald A. Grinde (Da Capo Press), which is available in paperback. Also, a good Web site for Native American biographies is the incredibly comprehensive Biographies page of NativeAmericans.com, www.nativeamericans.com/Biographies.htm.

Men of the 16th and 17th Centuries

In the 16th and 17th centuries, Europeans were usually met warmly by Native peoples when they began arriving in their enormous ships. The Indians' welcoming demeanor was indicative of a deep-seated respect for others. But conflicts were quick to blossom, and it wasn't long before many began to realize they needed to take a cautious, "big picture" view of these newcomers.

When the Euros arrived, Native Americans had long-established, entrenched "lifestyles" (to use a detestable word). Theirs was an intricate and respectful balancing act that, yes, exploited the natural resources around them, but only for survival, and always with a sense of gratitude to the Great Spirit for allowing them to "benefit from his beneficence," so to speak.

What's really interesting about these initial "meet and greets" is that the Native peoples, upon realizing that they had visitors, manifested a great many traits that were immediately recognizable and understandable to the English, including generosity, respect, kindness, and openness. What was missing? Fear and suspicion. And that speaks volumes, doesn't it? In the following sections, we outline some of the most notable men that exhibited these positive traits in the 16th and 17th centuries.

Powhatan (Powhatan, c. 1547–c. 1618)

Chief Powhatan, whose tribal name was *Wahunsunacoc,* was one of the earliest Native American leaders and is famous for being the first Indian chief to have contact with the English. Although John Cabot had met Abenakis and Mi'kmaqs in 1499 (see Chapter 9 for more on Cabot), Powhatan's interaction was a significant milestone in Native/European history, and his contributions to Native American history bespeak leadership, plus a far-reaching vision of a mutually beneficial (and peaceful) relationship between Anglos and Indians. He is also remembered for being the father of Pocahontas. (See the section "Pocahontas (Powhatan, c. 1595–1618)" later in this chapter for more on Powhatan's daughter.)

In the 16th century, Powhatan's father, an Algonquin chief, had established a confederacy in Virginia by wiping out rival tribes. After his father's death, Powhatan ascended to "the throne," and brought in more tribes to expand the confederacy.

Here are some of the achievements and highlights Powhatan (see Figure 10-1) might have listed on his resume (if they had resumes back then . . . and writing):

> ✔ **Powhatan was the leader of the Powhatan Confederacy.** This group was comprised of between 9,000 and 12,000 Indians from 30 tribes and 128 villages spread over 9,000 square miles along the south-central Atlantic seaboard, the area that now spans from Washington, D.C., to North Carolina (which, at the time, was designated by the English as Virginia).

✔ **In 1607, Powhatan opposed the English settlement at Jamestown.** As legend has it, he changed his mind when his daughter Pocahontas convinced him to free Englishman John Smith. (See the section "Pocahontas (Powhatan, c. 1595–1618)" later in this chapter for more on what's fact and what's fiction in the Pocahontas story.) Once Powhatan ceased opposing the Jamestown settlement, the English presented him with a crown and gifts to cement the relationship.

✔ **Powhatan's fellow tribesmen did not respect their chief's friendly relations with the English.** Why? Because the English continued to take all the best land, as well as steal Indian food stores. Bands of Indians attacked settlers and it was only after Pocahontas married the Englishman John Rolfe in 1609, the first tobacco planter on Powhatan's territory, that a solid peace was established by Powhatan, which survived his death.

Powhatan died in Virginia in 1618, probably from smallpox. Pocahontas died the same year in England, probably from tuberculosis or pneumonia.

Figure 10-1:
Chief
Powhatan.

Squanto (Pawtuxet, c. 1580s–1622)

In the 16th and 17th centuries in North America, transportation was, to say the least, difficult. Travel was done on foot and horse, and in boats and wagons. Yet Pawtuxet Indian Tisquantum (now known as Squanto) was a world traveler, and he was in England and Spain for years at a time, traveled on foot in Europe, and traversed the east coast of North America from Newfoundland to New England. Yet ironically his traveling was mostly forced, due to being kidnapped and held as a slave by both the English and the Spanish.

Squanto was born in the 1580s of the Pawtuxet tribe. It's unknown what the exact date of his birth is as well as where he was born, but the Pawtuxet tribe was settled near Plymouth, Massachusetts, so it's likely that that's around where Tisquantum was born.

Some historians believe that Squanto was one of five Indians kidnapped in 1605 by Captain John Weymouth and taken to England, although there are questions about the validity of this story.

What *is* known is that even if he was in England from 1605 or so, he was back in North America by 1614. It was that year that English Captain Thomas Hunt persuaded Squanto and other Indians to board his ship to, we suppose, "check it out." The invitation was a trap, however, and it wasn't long before Squanto was on his way to Malaga, Spain, to be sold as a slave.

Squanto was purchased from his Spanish slaveholder by monks who took him to live with them in a monastery. After three years there, he fled to England, and ended up on a boat back to America. By this time he spoke fluent English, which served him and Pilgrim settlers well a few years later when Squanto helped the settlers survive their first winter in the New World and taught them survival skills, including fishing and planting, that literally saved their lives.

Today, Squanto is remembered for his assistance to the first Pilgrims. He died of smallpox in 1622.

Men of the 18th Century

The British and the French dominated the 18th century in the New World, and their interactions with Natives were both amicable and contentious. Some of the most famous Indian chiefs are from this era.

Big issues for Natives during this period included:

- Choosing with whom to align
- Knowing who to trust
- Maintaining cultural and tribal unity and integrity in the face of ceaseless incursion by Europeans

All of these issues boil down to long-term survival. Treaties were drafted and then ignored, Indian encampments were attacked for no reason, and then, when the British and the French stopped fighting, Indians lost power. They could no longer play one against the other, and this made precarious their well-being. And colonists doing things like paying bounties for Indians (or their scalps) certainly did not give them an encouraging sense of their future. These sections detail the Indigenous men whose bravery and loyalty to their tribes make them notable Natives.

Pontiac (Ottawa, c. 1712/1725–1769)

Pontiac was a great Ottawa chief whose name is now mainly known to many Americans as an automobile. How many Pontiac drivers these days have any knowledge whatsoever of where the name of their car came from?

Pontiac's early years are lost to time, since neither the British nor the French have any records of the doings of his Ottawa tribe during his first three decades, and there exist no known written Native documents. Historians have speculated on these years, and the consensus is that his father was an Ottawa chief and his mother a Chippewa woman.

Pontiac's tribal name was *Obwandiyag*.

Pontiac's first appearance in the historical record dates from the mid-1740s. This is when he is believed to have defended Detroit against an attack by northern tribes.

Then, in 1755, Pontiac participated in the defeat of British General Edward Braddock during the early phases of the French and Indian War. (See Chapter 11 for more info.) He is most remembered, though for his leadership in what has come to be known as *Pontiac's War,* or *Pontiac's Rebellion.*

In 1763, the victorious British were in charge, and the French-friendly Indians weren't happy about it. At *all.*

Some of the reasons for their discontent included the following:

- The British physically abused the Indians.
- The British encouraged rampant drunkenness among the Indians.
- The British cheated the Indians when trading with them.
- The British refused to supply Indians with the ammunition they needed to hunt for food and skins.
- The British arrogantly sold off Indian land, without even so much as a "by your leave."
- The British treated the Natives more like worthless underlings than equals.
- The British refused to continue the French practice of bartering with the Indians for needed goods and supplies.

Using his persuasive leadership skills, Pontiac pulled together a Pan-Indian coalition to go after the British. Thirteen British forts were attacked at the same time by tribes united in their hatred of the British and, by the end of 1763, eight forts had fallen.

Unfortunately for Pontiac and his "troops," however, he received no assistance from his presumed allies, the French. Much to Pontiac's horror, he learned that the French had given up great tracts of their land along the Mississippi and, without a source for ammunition, he had no choice but to abandon the revolt and make peace with the British.

In 1766, Pontiac and 40 other chiefs acknowledged that they were now subjects of the Crown. Pontiac was murdered in 1769 by an Indian who had been hired by an English trader.

It was Pontiac *himself w*ho allowed the British to occupy the forts that the French had relinquished in defeat. His only conditions? That the British respect Indians and Indian lands and continue to supply them with ammo. The British agreed, "moved in," and then immediately ignored their agreements with the Natives. And then did even worse.

Tecumseh (Shawnee, c. 1768–1813)

Tecumseh, a Shawnee, had an understanding of the white man that both inspired and terrified him, and his passionate devotion to Indian sovereignty made him one of the most important Indian voices of the 18th century.

Tecumseh, whose tribal name was *Tecumtha* or *Tekamthi*, knew in his heart — regardless of the platitudes and reassurances Indian tribes were hearing from Washington and settler leaders — that the ultimate goal of the white man was clear:

- ✔ Ownership of all Indian lands
- ✔ The extermination of all Indian peoples

With the help of his brother Tenskwatawa, a visionary prophet, Tecumseh forged in his mind the idea of a line in North America beyond which the white man *would not be allowed to pass*: the Ohio River. He and his brother formed Prophetstown, a village that welcomed all Native peoples and which existed to further the rights and future survival of Indians. But he was never successful in implementing his dream of securing ancient Indian lands for Indian people. Tecumseh also traveled to many other tribes to try to persuade them to join him in a revolt he was planning against the Europeans.

Tecumseh's major contribution to Native American history was his unwillingness to simply surrender Native lands to the whites on their demand. He is remembered today for his impeccable resistance and ethnic pride.

Tecumseh was killed fighting for the British during the War of 1812.

Was there a Tecumseh curse?

After Tecumseh was killed, his brother Tenskwatawa, who claimed powers of clairvoyance, is alleged to have predicted that if the despised William Henry Harrison were ever elected president of the United States, he would get sick and die in office.

Tenskwatawa also stated that the U.S. presidents elected every 20 years following Harrison's death would also die in office.

Well, Harrison *was* elected president, and he *did* get sick in office, and he *did* die shortly thereafter.

And, just as Tenskwatawa had supposedly said, each president elected every 20 years after Harrison's demise *also* died in office. The string of 20-year presidential deaths in office stopped with Ronald Reagan.

Although there's no concrete evidence that Tenskwatawa actually placed a curse on U.S. presidents, it is certainly quite the bizarre coincidence that what he said would happen, actually did happen for every president until Reagan, who broke the curse when he survived the 1981 assassination attempt on his life.

Chief Seattle (Suquamish, c. 1786–1866)

Chief Seattle followed in the footsteps of his father Schweabe, a Suquamish chief, and showed bravery and leadership as a very young man when he rallied and organized local tribes to create a unified defense against Indian raiders. However, his later decisions, after a conversion to Roman Catholicism, were not met with acclaim by many of his fellow Natives. Seattle agreed to treaties that relinquished Indian lands to the white man, some of which led to his people ending up on reservations. But it is believed that his overarching purpose was to protect Indians, and he knew that treaties were better than war. Some would argue that point.

But Chief Seattle, also known as *Sealth,* is mostly remembered for a speech he may not have even made.

Oh, the Chief did make a speech in 1854 in downtown Seattle (the city named in his honor), but he made it in his native Salishan language, and the only record if it came from notes made during the speech by Henry A. Smith — who didn't understand Salishan!

It is believed that another attendee at the speech translated the chief's words into Chinook, which Smith *was* able to understand.

We've all heard of procrastinating writers, but Henry Smith may have set a record. He waited *30 years* to transcribe his notes and, frankly, the resulting speech sounds suspiciously English for an elderly, pure-blood Suquamish chief. Nonetheless, the sentiments expressed in the beloved speech certainly speak to the general feelings Indians were experiencing at the time. (Probably now, too, to some extent.)

The 19th Century

The 19th century was a time of great struggle and sorrow for Native peoples. Battles were frequent, resistance was met with annihilation, and there was a pervasive sense among Indians that they were a dying people. Some fought back, yet in the end, European domination was inexorable and crushing.

The strength of the colonial expansionist movement was relentless. And once gold was discovered out west, the move to the Pacific intensified. Tribal lands were routinely violated, treaties and boundaries were consistently ignored, and Native Americans were increasingly "rounded up" and shipped off to reservations. Out of sight, out of mind, right?

Some Indians refused to sit still for what they saw as genocide.

Cochise (Chiricahua Apache, c. 1812–1874)

One of Cochise's most striking traits was his patriotism.

Yes, Cochise, the fiercest of warriors and determined exactor of vengeance against whites, was a patriot — but he was an *Apache* patriot who loved his people and his people's lands.

Cochise was born in the area that is now southern Arizona. At the beginning of his second decade, all hell broke loose between the Apache people and the European settlers.

Unrest and fighting continued for almost 20 years until the U.S. annexed the area in 1850. For the next ten years or so, it was relatively peaceful, but then, in 1861, renegade Apaches raided John Ward's farm and kidnapped his son — and Cochise and five others got blamed for it.

How? During a conclave with an army officer named Bascom, who was assigned to investigate the raid and kidnapping, Cochise and his men were accused and arrested. Cochise managed to escape, but his men, mostly relatives of Cochise, ended up being held hostage and later hung.

Geronimo's bones?

In 1918, it is believed that Geronimo's skull and some bones were stolen from his grave and transported to New Haven, Connecticut, to be used in initiation rituals at the infamous Yale University secret society Skull and Bones.

A recently discovered letter written by then-member Winter Mead and published in the *Yale*

Alumni Magazine seems to confirm the truth of the story, and Geronimo's nephew Harlyn Geronimo has written to President George W. Bush requesting his assistance in the return of the relics to their proper resting place.

This seems to have been the incident that set Cochise on the warpath. For the next ten years, he fought battle after battle with the white man, until he was surrounded one day in the Dragoon Mountains and taken into custody.

Cochise escaped yet again, however, and battled whites until 1872 when a lasting peace was negotiated and he retired to a reservation where he died of natural causes in 1874.

Cochise's name was *A-da-tli-chi*. He was also known as *Cheis*. Cochise's name means "hardwood" in the Chiricahua Apache language.

Geronimo (Chiricahua Apache, 1829–1909)

Geronimo is one of the most remembered leaders of the warring Apaches of the Southwest during the 19th-century pioneer years. If the Apaches had been Scottish, Geronimo would have been their William Wallace (the subject of Mel Gibson's classic film, *Braveheart*).

According to Geronimo, he was made war chief of his tribe at the age of 16, reporting to tribal leader Cochise. When Cochise died, his son Natchez took over, but he was quickly displaced by Geronimo, who was much more skilled in Indian battle tactics.

In 1858, Mexicans slaughtered Geronimo's wife, mother, and children, and his hatred for whites was born.

For almost 30 years, Geronimo warred with the white settlers and soldiers, refusing to relinquish his tribal lands to those he considered interlopers and thieves. He fought, but not out of vengeance; he wanted peace. In his autobiography, Geronimo was very clear: "The Indians always tried to live peaceably with the white soldiers and settlers."

Good gun

General Leonard Woods was involved in the capture and guarding of Geronimo and wrote in his memoirs about one memorable interaction with the ornery chief:

"About 2 o'clock in the afternoon the old Indian came to me and asked to see my rifle. It was a Hotchkiss, and he said he had never seen its mechanism. When he asked me for the gun and some ammunition I must confess I felt a little nervous, for I thought it might be a device to get hold of one of our weapons. I made no objection, however, and let him have it, showing him how to use it. He fired at a mark, just missing one of his own men who was passing. This he regarded as a great joke, rolling on the ground and laughing heartily and shouting, 'Good gun.'"

But considering the seemingly insatiable hunger for land, and Geronimo's realization that whites would take what they wanted, peace with the Chiricahua was infrequent and short-lived.

In 1876, Geronimo and a band of a few hundred Apaches holed up in the mountains of Mexico and defended themselves against capture attempts by the U.S. military and raids by the Mexicans for almost a decade in what has long been considered a kind of "Apache's Last Stand."

But Geronimo's resistance, motivated by tribal loyalty, was doomed to fail and, on September 4, 1886, Geronimo surrendered to U.S. General Nelson Miles. Geronimo then lived on military facilities, became a farmer, appeared at the 1904 World's Fair, and even rode in President Theodore Roosevelt's inaugural parade.

Geronimo's name was *Goyaa_é*, commonly spelled *Goyathlay*. "Geronimo" was the name given to him by whites.

Geronimo died of pneumonia and tuberculosis on February 17, 1909, still officially a prisoner of war.

Sitting Bull (Sioux, Lakota, c. 1831–1890)

Sitting Bull was born around 1831 and died in 1890 when he was shot by a Lakota who was working with the U.S. government as a law officer.

Sitting Bull was one of the most passionate resisters of white domination and their exploitation of Indian lands and, throughout his life, he warned his people to be very careful about embracing white civilization and all that came with it. He did admit that there was much about America that was great, but he detested the U.S. government's efforts to "round up" Indians onto reservations, and he had no qualms about fighting back when threatened.

Sitting Bull is probably one of the two or three most famous Indians in history and is remembered mostly for his devastating defeat (with Crazy Horse and others) of General George Armstrong Custer at the Battle of Little Big Horn ("Custer's Last Stand") in 1876.

After defeating Custer and fleeing to Canada, he ultimately refused a U.S. offer of a pardon in agreement for relocating with his people to a reservation. Sitting Bull did eventually surrender in 1881, because his people were starving. He served time in a military prison, and, after rejoining his people upon his release, later performed in Buffalo Bill's Wild West show for $50 a week until his repulsion for whites grew so overwhelming he quit.

In 1890, it was learned by the U.S. government that Sitting Bull's people were regularly gathering to perform the stirring ghost dance, which they believed would summon their dead ancestors to earth and allow them to overthrow the white interlopers. Police were sent to Sitting Bull's cabin to arrest him in hopes that his removal would create fragmentation among the Lakota and destroy their sense of unity. Several of the police officers were Lakotas.

One word at a time

Ron His Horse Is Thunder is a descendant of Sitting Bull and lives on the Lakota Standing Rock Reservation, which is in North and South Dakota (although the largest concentrations of Lakotas are in South Dakota).

The Standing Rock Reservation is plagued with great poverty and a staggeringly high teenage suicide rate, but His Horse Is Thunder believes it is not unemployment causing young people to embrace hopelessness and choose to end their lives, but loss of identity and, thus, he is working to reinstill pride in his people's legacy.

His Horse Is Thunder's legendary ancestor did not garner him any special treatment growing up. On the contrary, he was told from childhood that his lineage placed extra responsibility to his people upon him. His Horse Is Thunder thus went to law school, earned his degree, and then returned to the reservation where he was elected Tribal Chief of the Lakota.

One of the first ideas His Horse Is Thunder began implementing is to make the Lakota language the official language of the reservation. He hopes to one day hold all tribal council meetings in the Lakota language, and he is encouraging adults to learn Lakota (only 25 percent of the reservation's18,000 Lakotans are fluent) and then teach it to their children.

His Horse Is Thunder puts his efforts where his mouth is, too. He has promised that if he is not fluent in Lakota by 2009 when he is up for re-election, he'll decline to run.

His Horse Is Thunder is the Chairman of the President's Board of Advisors on Tribal Colleges and Universities, and is a board member for the American Indian College Fund, American Indian Higher Education Consortium, and the North Dakota Tribal College Association. His great-great-great grandfather must be very proud.

"Sitting Bull" is the English version of the chief's Hunkpapa Lakota name *Tatanka-Iyotanka*, which translates as a buffalo sitting on its haunches.

Sitting Bull at first surrendered peaceably, but then began to resist after being taunted for a lack of bravery by his 17-year-old son Crow Foot. Sitting Bull then pleaded with his followers to rescue him and, when two Lakota burst through the crowd and fired on the police, a Lakota officer named Catch the Bear shot and killed Sitting Bull.

Sitting Bull, who many believed had the gift of prophecy, once had a vision that he would be killed by one of his own.

Crazy Horse (Sioux, Oglala Lakota, c. 1840–1877)

Crazy Horse was one of the most adamant opponents to the whites' plundering of their sacred hills and, from an early age, he became known as a brave and fearless warrior. He was given his father's name as a young man, and he ultimately had three wives and was revered as a gifted leader and spiritual guide.

Yet, looking back, there is an irony in the Native Americans' response to the discovery of gold in the Black Hills of South Dakota in the late 1870s and the subsequent influx of whites seeking the Hills' riches.

The Oglala Sioux and other tribes fought fiercely — and futilely — to stop the gold rush, which they saw as an exploitation of their sacred lands. The Black Hills were part of their heritage, and that meant more to the tribes than the wealth buried beneath them. Yet Natives routinely lived off the land and used its resources, so in all likelihood, their problem with the mining of gold was that it was being done by whites.

To this day, the Oglala Lakota have rejected the offer of monetary payments for the South Dakota lands (payments for the hundreds of billions of dollars of gold removed from the Black Hills), insisting instead on the return of their land.

In 1876, Crazy Horse and an army of 1,500 Lakota and Cheyenne successfully defeated General George Crook in the Battle of the Rosebud. This defeat prevented Crook from continuing on and reinforcing General George Armstrong Custer's troops, and it allowed Crazy Horse to join the battle of Little Big Horn and help Sitting Bull decisively defeat Custer.

A year later, however, Crazy Horse surrendered to U.S. forces. The reason? The same reason many Indian warriors gave up: hunger and the inability to feed his men.

While garrisoned/imprisoned at Fort Robinson, Crazy Horse's wife became ill and he left the fort without permission to take her to her parents' home. Upon his return to the fort, he was arrested and, when he resisted, was bayoneted in the stomach. (There is some question as to whether he was stabbed by a soldier, or killed himself as a last act of honor.) He died hours later, and his parents removed his body and buried it. To this day, his burial place is unknown.

Crazy Horse's tribal name was *T'a_unka Witko*, which translates in English to "his horse is crazy."

Chief Joseph (Nez Perce, 1840–1904)

Chief Joseph's father Joseph the Elder was an early Native American convert to Christianity and, shortly after his son was born in 1840, he had the boy baptized and later educated at a Christian school. Joseph the Elder was a supporter of peaceful relations with whites and, upon his death in 1871, his son became Chief Joseph at the age of 31 and sought to continue his father's ways.

Before his death, Joseph the Elder warned his son about the intentions of the white man, telling him to "stop his ears" when approached by whites to sign treaties giving away parts of their land, the land that held their ancestors' graves. Joseph swore he would abide by his father's guidance. "A man who would not defend his father's grave is worse than a wild animal," he said.

But Chief Joseph, worried about what the American military would do to his people, and with a dedicated spirit of wanting to protect them, ultimately made great concessions to the U.S. to keep peace.

In 1873, Chief Joseph signed a treaty with the U.S. that allowed the Nez Perce to stay on their land. And for four years, the tribe lived in relative peace. But then, in 1877, the U.S. informed Chief Joseph that they were rescinding the treaty and that he and his people had 30 days to leave their land. If they remained beyond 30 days, it would be interpreted as an act of war.

Chief Joseph met with U.S. General Oliver Otis Howard, who tried persistently to persuade the chief to move his people. At this meeting, Chief Joseph spoke of individual rights and personal freedom, telling the general that he did not believe that the "Great Spirit Chief gave one kind of men the right to tell another kind of men what they must do."

Shortly thereafter, a series of events occurred that would serve to emblazon Chief Joseph's name in the annals of Native American history:

- ✔ General Howard went out with Chief Joseph and some of his men to look for land onto which the Nez Perce could relocate.

- ✔ Ultimately, General Howard wanted Chief Joseph to move his people to an area already occupied by both whites and Indians, assuring him that the military would remove the people there and guarantee it safe for the Nez Perce.

- ✔ Chief Joseph refused all land offered. He would not take what was not his.

- ✔ During this period, some of his young braves killed a few whites and Chief Joseph knew that this would prompt military action against the Nez Perce.

- ✔ Chief Joseph and his fellow chiefs set off for Canada in an attempt to save the lives of the Nez Perce.

Thus began Chief Joseph's 1,500-mile trek to freedom. A band of 750 Nez Perce evaded and fought the U.S. military in what is considered to day one of the most brilliant military retreats of Native American history, which is still studied today. In the end, however, the Nez Perce gave up.

After many deaths and the deprivation that came from being on the run, Chief Joseph surrendered to General Nelson Miles on October 5, 1877. His surrender speech ("I will fight no more forever") is one of the most memorable speeches in Native American history.

Chief Joseph died in September of the year he met with his former enemy General Howard (see the sidebar, "Enemies meet," earlier), 1904, and was buried in Nepselem, Washington.

Chief Joseph's tribal name was *Hin-mah-too-yah-lat-kekt,* or *In- mut-too-yah-lat-lat,* which translates as Thunder Rolling Down the Mountain.

Enemies meet

In March 1904, 27 years after the Indian war between General O. O. Howard and Chief Joseph and the Nez Perce, the two former foes met as invited guests at the commencement ceremony of the Indian Industrial School in Carlisle, Pennsylvania.

Notable Indian Women: Not Stay-At-Wigwam Ladies

A powerful and important element of Native American tradition and culture is the concept of balance — balance in all things.

Thus, even though traditional Native American societies would seem at first glance to have been patriarchal and restrictive of women, the reality is that women always played critically important roles in the life of the tribe, and their contributions were not seen as master/servant, or dominant male/ submissive female roles, but rather as the balancing element needed for survival and a happy life.

Native women were invaluable components for Native American life:

- ✔ They gathered materials and built (and then maintained) the homes.
- ✔ They gathered firewood for cooking and heating.
- ✔ They located and gathered herbs for medicinal purposes.
- ✔ They tended crops.
- ✔ They made tools from bones.
- ✔ They weaved blankets.
- ✔ They crafted pottery.
- ✔ They raised the children.

Medicine women treated ailments, and it was believed that women, as the source of all new life, had a greater connection to the spirit world than the men of the tribe.

The women discussed in this section are examples of the strong, independent female Native Americans who, to the tribe, were analogous to their venerated and beloved Earth Mother.

Pocahontas (Powhatan, c. 1595–1618)

Pocahontas was born in Virginia around 1595, the daughter of the great Indian Chief Powhatan. It is believed she was around 10 when she saw her first white man at the Jamestown settlement. Over the next few years, she became a frequent visitor to the settlement, serving as a liaison between her father and her fellow tribe members and the English colonists. It is known she saw to it that the settlers always had food, and that she carried messages back and forth between her father and the Jamestown leaders.

In 1607, one of the English settlers, Captain John Smith (see Figure 10-2), was captured by Powhatan Indians and brought before the great Indian Chief Powhatan as a prisoner. It has long been believed that Smith was sentenced to be executed and, so the story goes, was saved when Powhatan's 12- or 13-year-old daughter Pocahontas threw herself across his body to prevent him being killed, and then later, persuaded her father to let him go, which he did.

This "Native princess rescue" story is in doubt these days (there's no such thing as a Native American "princess," for one thing), but we do know that Powhatan did meet with Smith and that Smith was released from his custody. It is more likely that the Pocahontas story was an adoption ritual, rather than the dramatic story that has survived.

Figure 10-2:
Captain John Smith checking his compass.

One day, Pocahontas was captured by the colonists and held for ransom. The English wanted all the English prisoners Powhatan was holding, as well as supplies and tools they claimed the Indians had stolen. Powhatan acceded to some of the demands, but Pocahontas ended up being held for a year, during which she converted to Christianity and, in 1614, when Pocahontas was around 19, married the Englishman John Rolfe. Rolfe ultimately took his Indian bride to England and, from all reports, she was what you might call the "belle of the ball," and known as Lady Rebecca Rolfe.

In 1617, Pocahontas and her husband boarded a ship for a trip to Virginia, but they had to turn back when Pocahontas became gravely ill. She died in 1618, probably from pneumonia or tuberculosis. Her last words were reported to be, "All must die. 'Tis enough that the child liveth." (She and Rolfe had had a son, Thomas, in Virginia before they left for England.)

Pocahontas's contributions to Native American history were her efforts to maintain peaceful relations between the English and her people, and her later embrace by London society, proving to the English that Indians were not "savages."

Sacagawea (Shoshone, 1787–1812)

Sacagawea was a Shoshone guide and translator for Meriwether Lewis and William Clark on their 28-month "Corps of Discovery" expedition across the western United States between 1804 and 1806.

Sacagawea had been kidnapped by the Hidatsa tribe at the age of 9, and later purchased by French trapper Toussaint Charboneau when she was 16 to be his wife. Shortly thereafter, Charbonneau was hired by Lewis and Clark to accompany them on their trek westward because of his skills as a guide, and also because of his wife's translation abilities.

Was Porivo really Sacagawea?

How old was Sacagawea when she died? Well, the answer to that question depends on who you ask.

The widely accepted story is that Charbonneau and Sacagawea returned to the Hidatsa people after the Lewis and Clark expedition and spent three years with the tribe, and then moved to St. Louis, Missouri. A surviving December 1812 log entry by trader John Luttig states that Charbonneau's wife of around 25 years of age died of putrid fever (typhus) and left behind a daughter. (Sacagawea had given birth to a daughter around 1811.) The log entry referred to the wife as a "Snake Squaw," meaning Shoshone.

So that's that, right? Sacagawea died in St. Louis in 1812 at the age of 25.

Not so fast.

Shoshone legend tells a different story. According to the myth believed by many, Sacagawea's husband Charbonneau was abusive and, after moving to St. Louis, she fled him and joined a group of Comanches, ultimately settling with the Shoshone in Wyoming.

She lived there as Porivo, wore a Jefferson Medal identical to the ones given out to the members of the Lewis and Clark expedition, and spoke about seeing the Pacific when she was young. Porivo died at the Wind River Indian Reservation on April 9, 1884. If Porivo was, in fact, Sacagawea, she would have been 97 years old at the time of her death.

In 1925, Dr. Charles Fletcher, a Sioux physician hired by the Bureau of Indian Affairs to investigate the Porivo story, did extensive research and ultimately concluded that Porivo was, in fact, Sacagawea. Porivo's grave is in the cemetery at Fort Washakie on the Wind River Indian Reservation. A monument there describes Sacagawea's life and her contributions to American history.

Lewis and Clark also knew that Sacagawea's presence (and her new baby born on the trail shortly after the team embarked) would be a clear signal to other Indians that theirs was a peaceful expedition.

During the trek, Sacagawea was invaluable. She identified herbs and plants that they could use for food and medicinal purposes, and she is even the person we can thank for the existence of the Lewis and Clark journals: She rescued them when a boat they were in flooded and the books fell into the water.

After the expedition, Sacagawea and Charbonneau lived first with the Hidatsa and then in St. Louis (on William Clark's invitation) where she had a daughter and her son was enrolled in a Christian school. She reportedly died of typhoid in 1812. In 2000, the U.S. minted a Sacagawea $1 coin in her honor.

Wilma Mankiller, Cherokee leader (1945–)

When Wilma Mankiller ran for the position of deputy chief of the Cherokee Nation in Oklahoma in 1983 with Ross Swimmer, her tires were slashed and she received death threats. They won handily.

Wilma Mankiller was born on November 18, 1945, in Tahlequah, Oklahoma. When Mankiller was 12, her father agreed to move the family to San Francisco, California, as part of the Bureau of Indian Affairs relocation program. He and all the other families who agreed to the relocation were promised "a better life." Today, Mankiller describes the housing project they ended up living in as "Harlem West."

When Ross Swimmer resigned as chief in 1985 to head the Bureau of Indian Affairs, Mankiller stepped into the position of chief and was then elected in 1987 and, in a landslide, in 1991. She resigned in 1995 for health reasons, but is still a vibrant voice in Native American affairs.

So what's with the name Mankiller? Assigned Indian tribal names are often descriptive (remember "Dances with Wolves"?) so a surname like "Mankiller," not surprisingly, has long raised eyebrows. The truth is that her lineage traces back to a Cherokee man who was assigned the task of protecting his home village. He was named in Cherokee "Mankiller," but Wilma Mankiller has explained that the more accurate rendering of the name meant "soldier." In honor of her ancestors, she retained the surname, even after marrying her husband Charlie Soap.

Ada Deer (Menominee, 1935–)

The Native American's struggle to retain — and in many cases, regain — their identity continued well into the 20th century, and is ongoing even today. One of the staunchest defenders of Native sovereignty is Menominee nation member Ada Deer. In fact, the very existence of the Menominee is due, in large part, to Ada Deer's efforts.

Ada Deer's life is a story of firsts. Born in Keshena, Wisconsin, in 1935, throughout her life she has achieved these notable firsts:

- ✔ She was the first Menominee to receive an undergraduate degree from the University of Wisconsin-Madison.

- ✔ She was the first Native American to receive a master's degree in social work from Columbia University.

- ✔ She was the first woman to serve as chief of the Menominee tribe in Wisconsin.

- ✔ She was the first Native American woman to serve as head of the Bureau of Indian Affairs.

- ✔ She created the first grassroots organization — Determination of Right and Unity for Menominee Shareholders (DRUMS) — specifically formed to counter the U.S. government's termination of Menominee rights. Her efforts led to President Nixon signing the Menominee Restoration Act of 1972, re-establishing tribal sovereignty.

- ✔ She created the first social work training program on Native American reservations.

The Wisconsin Historical Society has described her as a "nationally recognized social worker, community organizer, activist, and political leader, [and] a champion of Indian rights who led the successful campaign to restore federal recognition of the Menominee Tribe."

Today, Deer is the director of the American Indian Studies Program at the University of Wisconsin-Madison and a fellow at the Harvard Institute of Politics at the John F. Kennedy School of Government.

Chapter 11

Battle Cries and Peace Pipes

· ·

In This Chapter

▶ Fighting, hunting, and scalping

▶ Wielding weapons for food and foe

▶ Understanding the first Thanksgiving as it really happened

▶ Breaking out battles, conflicts, and a restless peace

· ·

*T*he first meetings between Native Americans and the Europeans generally occurred in an atmosphere of wary respect.

Writings of the times make mention of how accommodating they were to the "visitors," and how generous they were with their food and other supplies. The Europeans spoke of people who wore little clothing, were kind, and who treated each other with the utmost esteem.

They also treated the Europeans with the same respect, and there is no doubt that the majority of Natives did not see them as conquering invaders. And since the Anglos didn't arrive with cannons blasting and swords swinging, it is easy to see how the Natives assumed such felicitude.

They never expected they'd be sold into slavery or massacred. Or that their villages would be leveled and their livestock slaughtered. This historical reality does not, however, suggest that there was constant discord between settlers and Native Americans.

On the contrary: There was a great deal of peaceful intercourse and mutually beneficial trade between Europeans and Native Americans. But the overarching agenda of those who came to our shores in ships was to claim the land as their own. And they did. And those that got in the way were sometimes dealt with amicably, with treaties and compromises. But just as often, the result was battle.

This chapter looks at certain times in the history of Native Americans when hatchets were wielded and arrows were flung.

Weapons of Choice

Until Native Americans were introduced to that most useful of weapons (see the picture of an Apache warrior in Figure 11-1), the rifle, all of their weapons of choice were made using natural materials easily obtainable from their surroundings.

Figure 11-1:
An Apache
warrior.

Their principal weapons were the following:

- **Atlatl:** This was the precursor to the bow, and was in use beginning in the Paleoindian period, around A.D. 12,000. The word *atlatl* comes from the Aztec language.

  This weapon consisted of a thrown spear with a dart on the killing end and a cup or handle on the throwing end. The atlatl was designed to increase the power of the arm strength of the thrower and, since they were meticulously balanced, a well-aimed atlatl could puncture a Spanish conquistador's armor with no problem.

- **Bow and arrow:** The bow and arrow, along with the tomahawk, is the iconic weapon of the Native American, and a common misperception made is that Natives invented it. This is not true. The bow and arrow is ancient, and is estimated to have been invented and first used approximately 11,000 years ago (9,000 B.C.). The earliest bow found was dated to that time period and was found in Hamburg, Germany.

  The bow and arrow was used for both hunting and battle. The bow itself was made from a piece of flexible wood, commonly ash, hickory, or oak, and was strung with a piece of sinew or long plant fiber that was tightened until taut enough to pull and release an arrow with great force. Today, wire or nylon filament is used, and the body of the bow can be made of plastic as well as wood.

Arrows were made from wood or reeds and were cut to a length appropriate to the bow being used. The length of the bow was determined by the length of the archer's reach, their size, and gender. An arrow too short or too long would essentially be useless for either downing an enemy or killing prey. Today, arrows are pine or plastic.

The tip of the arrow — the *arrowhead* — was made from metal if available, flint, obsidian, or some other type of stone that was sharpened to a point. Today, they're mostly metal.

The rear end of the arrow had fins made of feathers (turkey or goose, usually). These are called *fletchings,* and they stabilize the arrow's direction in flight and provide balance when fired. Today, fletchings are made of plastic.

Native Americans used the bow and arrow for both battle and hunting.

Today, archery is a popular sport — it's in the Olympics — and the majority of archers enjoy *target* archery as a hobby. There are also some hunters who use a bow and arrow as their weapon of choice. The bow and arrow is rarely used as a self-defense weapon anymore, but there are some special ops undercover agents who use it for killings because of its total silence.

- ✔ **Knife:** Early Native American knives used animal teeth or worked (or knapped) stone for the blade, and wood or a short length of bone for its handle. Later, metal blades became commonplace after Natives were introduced to them by the Europeans.

  A sharp, sturdy knife was one of the Native Americans' most important tools and, as is the case with other weapons, knives were used for both battle and survival: Cut up a squirrel, cut into an enemy, as it were.

- ✔ **Lance and spear:** Spears were first used in the Paleoindian period. This weapon was basically a larger, heavier, and longer version of an arrow, but without the counterbalancing fletchings. It was made of wood, and either its tip was sharpened to a vicious point, or a sharpened bone or stone tip was attached.

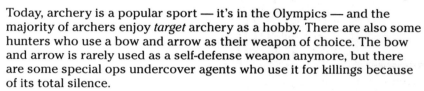

Prehistoric hunting in modern-day U.S.A.

Some U.S. states allow atlatl hunting and fishing, and there are companies today manufacturing exact replicas of the ancient weapon using modern materials. Most states that allow spears to be used for hunting allow the use of an atlatl, although, in many cases, restrictions and limited-use laws apply. Check with your local state fish and wildlife department if you have an interest in primitive hunting.

Atlatl hunting and fishing is not easy. As users say, it's easy to learn how to throw an atlatl, but it's extremely difficult to become an expert at throwing with an atlatl.

As with most Native American weapons, lances and spears (different terms for essentially the same weapon) were used for both fighting and feeding: An enemy could just as easily be downed by a hurled lance as a deer.

✔ **Tomahawk:** This light ax was used as both a tool and a weapon by Native Americans. In its earliest forms, the head was made of sharpened stone. Later, iron and other metals were used.

The term "tomahawk" comes from the Algonquian words "tamahak" or "tamahakan." In the beginning of the 17th century, these words described implements with stone heads that Natives used for chopping and carried for self-defense.

The Europeans quickly embraced the tomahawk as an all-purpose tool, and who can blame them? It was lightweight, could be used for a variety of uses, was relatively easy to make, and was a utilitarian implement.

It was a multi-use item like the other tools described and commonly employed by Natives both in villages and the wild. For combat, the tomahawk was effective within close range, unlike the spear or arrow. Plus, its heavy head lent itself beautifully for use as a hammer. A warrior could use his tomahawk to chop branches into the right length, sharpen their ends with the tomahawk's blade, and then use its heavy head to pound the stakes into the ground.

The tomahawk was an indispensable part of both the Native and settlers' gear, and what made it the item no one wanted to be without was the clever addition to the handle of the axe of a pipe bowl. When not being used for chopping wood or chopping heads, someone could sit back and smoke a bowl of tobacco from their tomahawk.

Today, tomahawks are popular for military use — soldiers in Iraq carry them — as well as for the sport of tomahawk throwing. The axe is now made with synthetic handles and steel blades and is available everywhere.

Scalping

Native Americans invented the practice of scalping, using knives to carve off the scalp and hair of a conquered foe, right?

Wrong.

The practice of scalping — either posthumously as a means of collecting a trophy, or while alive as a means of torture — goes back to the Scythians of Eurasia, c. 440 B.C.

It was also practiced in pre-Columbian North America, but the contentions that scalping was "invented" by Indigenous people, or that it was introduced to Natives by the Europeans, are false.

Scalping was employed for centuries before the first Native American scalped a vanquished enemy.

✔ **War club:** This tool was primarily a weapon, plain and simple, and its construction made it one of the deadliest.

The war club consisted of a thick length of wood that had at one end a head of wood or stone that was used as a bludgeon. Sometimes a log-like piece of wood was carved in one piece, making the grip end thinner, and leaving a heavy block-like projection at the end. A well-placed swing of a war club could easily shatter a skull, such was their impact.

Sometimes, war clubs had leather straps attached for ease of carrying and also so as not to lose the grip. They weighed as much as five pounds and could do a huge amount of damage.

Remember your physics class? Specifically, the formula, weight times speed equals force? A five-pound block of wood striking something at great speed was to be avoided, and a man on horseback wielding a war club was to be feared.

War Parties Weren't No Parties

A war party was a band of warriors (see Figure 11-2 to see what an Indian looked like in full battle mode) that carried out raids on enemies, or banded together to defend the tribe against invaders, both Native American and Anglo.

However, the term "war party" can be misleading, unless we want to define every raid during the period from the 17th century through the late 19th century — even Indian raids to do nothing but steal horses, for example — to be an act of war. "Raids" is probably closer to the reality in most cases.

Figure 11-2:
An Indian in full battle mode.

Counting coup

One practice, among Plains tribes in particular, that elevated a warrior's reputation was *counting coup*. This involved striking an enemy with either a lance, club, or stick without killing him. Striking with the bare hand was an even more honored act.

The Cheyenne, for example, would often mount war parties carrying weapons that could not be used from a distance. Stories are told of rival tribes facing off against each other and the battle not beginning until a single warrior broke rank, raced toward the enemy, and slammed one of them with a club or lance. This was a very brave act: The warrior had counted coup.

Coup could be counted against an enemy three times. This means that three individual warriors could each "take credit" for striking a single enemy.

There were attacks, though, by Indians, and during the early 18th century, their French allies, that resulted in death and destruction that can justifiably be called a war party. For example, in 1704 a group of Mohawks attacked Deerfield, Massachusetts, and killed 50 children and elderly, and then kidnapped 112 colonists, including a Puritan minister and his family.

Twenty more people were killed during a forced march to Canada. This was clearly an act of war and was much more than a simple raid. (The story of Reverend John Williams and the Deerfield massacre and kidnapping is told in the National Book Award–nominated book *Unredeemed Captive*. A twist to the story is that one of the Reverend's daughters refused "rescue" and instead, married an Indian and remained with his tribe until her death.)

The Colonial Era from 1621–1775

The earliest years of the European colonization of America, marked by the first arrivals of the English in the early 1600s along the Eastern seaboard, could be viewed as a microcosm of what was to come: periods of peace and treaties, boundary disputes and expansion efforts, bloodshed, raids, and battle after battle after battle.

Some historians consider the entire period from 1621 through the 1890 Wounded Knee massacre to be one long Indian War. (Obviously, this is not a popular viewpoint for those who emphasize the pro-European settler position.) This is a skewed view, when we consider the positive interactions between Indians and Anglos.

And as is often the case with dissimilar cultures who are "forced" (in a sense) to share common ground, trade was the catalyst for whatever peaceful dealings occurred. Trading in meat, fur, slaves, blankets, foodstuff, liquor, and other commodities often resulted in an uneasy alliance.

Early on, though, before the full-blown exploitation of the Natives' lands and resources, and before the Louisiana Purchase and the push westward, the intercourse between Indians and settlers could, in many cases, be described as warily amicable. (If you don't count Columbus's enslavement of the Arawaks, of course.)

What happened at the first Thanksgiving?

The first Thanksgiving — which took place in October 1621 (not November — President Lincoln moved the holiday there in 1863) — was a gathering to celebrate a treaty between the Native peoples and the Pilgrims, as well as express the Pilgrims' gratitude for help and guidance planting crops that helped them survive.

When the *Mayflower* (which Wampanaog Chief Massasoit had heard described as a "house floating on water") landed at Plymouth in December 1620, 102 settlers disembarked and staked out lots on which to build seven houses. However, their food supplies ran short, sickness became pervasive, and during that winter 50 settlers died from illness. Pilgrims were so desperate for food that they resorted to plundering burial grounds for any grain that had been buried with the deceased.

Chief Massasoit decided to help and sent Squanto, a man who spoke fluent English, to help the settlers survive in a land Indians had been thriving in for hundreds of years. Squanto taught the Pilgrims how to plant corn, build "winter-proof" shelters, and catch fish in the nearby streams.

A year after the Pilgrims landed, Massasoit himself (with 60 warriors as backup) visited the Plymouth settlement and saw firsthand the fruits of his benevolence. He then negotiated a treaty with English settlers, and a feast was held in celebration. The Natives contributed five deer for the three-day event, and the "guest list" is believed to have consisted of 90 Wampanaog Indians and 52 settlers.

In *Harvest Ceremony: Beyond the Thanksgiving Myth*, a pamphlet published by the Smithsonian Institute's National Museum of the American Indian, it's noted "Although there is nothing in this letter to suggest the giving of thanks, this is the celebration that has traditionally been associated with the contemporary holiday, Thanksgiving." Also, "Thanksgiving is a transplanted European harvest festival."

King Philip's War (1675–1676)

King Philip's War, which raged from 1675–1676, was one of the bloodiest wars in early American history. This war between the English and the Indians was the conflict that essentially cleared the way for massive English expansion.

As is still the case today, *personal* relationships can effect *peaceful* relationships.

The friendly and mutually cooperative relationships between Plymouth Colony Governor William Bradford and Wampanaog Chief Massasoit from the 1620s through their respective deaths in 1657 and 1660 (see Figure 11-3 for a depiction Chief Massasoit's death) had successfully kept the peace between English settlers and Native Americans for almost 50 years. Sure, there were outbreaks of violence and consistent disagreements (mostly about land, of course), but for the most part, it can be said that there had been an edgy alliance and a tense peace when Massasoit was alive (see Figure 11-4 for an example of a peace pipe).

Figure 11-3:
The death
of Chief
Massasoit.

After Massasoit's death, his son Wamsutta (named Alexander by the English), became the leader of the Wampanaogs. In 1662, Wamsutta was summoned to Plymouth by the Plymouth Court and taken there at gunpoint when he refused to recognize the court's authority over him. He was interrogated and released, but then died shortly thereafter. His brethren believed the English had poisoned him. And maybe they did.

His brother Metacom, whose English name was Philip, took over the leadership of the tribe and, after a decade of mistreatment, land grabs, and abuses imposed upon them by the English, decided that he and his people had had enough.

Figure 11-4:
An Indian
peace pipe.

In 1675, Philip launched an attack on Swansea, Massachusetts, and the battle
was on.

Even though the Wampanaogs were in alliance with the Nipmuck and
Narragansett, in the end, after one out of every ten Natives and English had
been killed, they lost the war. This effectively set the stage for the westward
expansion that would result in a sea-to-shining-sea United States.

The French and Indian War (1754–1763)

In England, the French and Indian War is considered just one phase of the
Seven Years War, the war which won Canada for Britain and in which Indians
fought against Indians.

The cause of the French and Indian War was fairly cut-and-dried: Both the
British and the French wanted as much of North America as they could grab.
And the fact that Indians originally owned the sought-after land didn't mean a
whole lot to either of the European countries.

One of the more memorable battles of the French and Indian War was the
Battle of Fort Necessity. It is remembered because it is the battle in which a
young George Washington surrendered the fort to the French. That was the
last time he'd make a mistake like that!

There were fish to catch, and beaver pelts to sell, and a huge parcel of land
that, if controlled by the British, would give them the entire eastern third of
the North American landmass.

The war began in 1754 and lasted nine years. Native Americans fighting for
the French included the Algonquin, Huron, Ojibwe, Ottawa, and Shawnee
tribes, a total of around 2,200 warriors. Fighting for the British were the
Iroquois. The war ended with the 1763 signing of the Treaty of Paris.

Pontiac's Rebellion (1763)

The British won the French and Indian War by defeating the French. The French had made allies of the Indians. The French lost their forts and many of them left, yet the Indians remained. This meant the Native Americans were perceived as a conquered people, subject to the rule of the British.

Makes sense, right? It did to the British. It most certainly did not to the Native Americans.

And so groups of Indians attacked British forts, deliberately maintaining a siege for three years until a treaty was signed with the British putting an end to hostilities. But the Indians still sorely missed the French. (See Chapter 10 for details on the causes of the war and a discussion of Pontiac's leadership.)

The American Revolution (1775–1783)

The mid- to late 1700s in North America was a complex time.

A new nation was aborning, and colonists were becoming increasingly riled over what they viewed as oppressive British laws and taxation policies. "No taxation without representation" was one of the rallying cries, and acts and laws passed by Britain rankled colonists who believed that only they could know what was best for them. Not British courts.

In fact, British domination of the colonies was rapidly becoming intolerable — and the Intolerable Acts had a lot to do with the burgeoning anger.

The Intolerable Acts were a series of laws passed by Britain in 1774 in response to the growing resistance against British control of the colonies. They were, in a nutshell, punishment. How dare the colonists challenge the sovereignty of the British Empire? The Boston Tea Party, in which colonists destroyed crates of tea in protest of new taxes, especially infuriated the Crown.

By 1775, the colonies had had enough:

- ✔ Too many laws
- ✔ Too many taxes
- ✔ Port closures
- ✔ Land "redistricting" (like the Quebec Act, which essentially voided the land rights of the Thirteen Colonies)
- ✔ A superior attitude on the part of the British rulers, who insisted on treating the colonists like children, rather than as fellow English citizens

All these factors combined to trigger what became one of the most important events in the history of civilization, resulting in a nation that stood for liberty and exemplified republicanism as government in its finest form.

So the colonists marshaled. They kicked out the British bigwigs, they started writing a Constitution, and they created the Continental Army. The battle was on.

The Indian View of the American Revolution

Most tribes wanted the British to win the War for Independence. Many of them saw a British victory and the subsequent total British control of the North American landmass as a way of stopping the relentless expansion into Indian lands by the colonists.

On July 13, 1775, the Second Continental Congress released a speech approved by all 65 of the delegates that addressed the Six Tribes and that essentially told them to remain neutral during the War for Independence. It was titled "A Speech to the Six Confederate Nations, Mohawks, Oneidas, Tusscaroras, Onondagas, Cayugas, Senekas, from the Twelve United Colonies, convened in Council at Philadelphia.

The speech given was a bit disingenuous, considering that the delegates were completely cognizant of the Indian's awareness of the impact a win by either side would have on their tribal land rights, their trading endeavors, and their ability to get needed supplies.

It was kind of like them saying, "We're going to wage war on lands on which you live, hunt, and farm, and you'll be smack dab in the middle of it all, but what we'd like you to do, if you don't mind, is ignore what's going on between us and Old England in this 'family quarrel' and go about your business."

Here's a look at how the Native Americans chose sides:

✔ **Pro-British:**

- Cherokees
- Shawnees
- Delawares
- Mohawks
- Cayugas
- Onondogas
- Senecas

> ✔ **Pro-American:**
>
> - Oneidas
>
> - Tuscaroras
>
> ✔ **Neutral:**
>
> - Creeks

The Treaty of Paris in 1783 marked the end of the Revolutionary War. The British recognized the 13 formerly British colonies as the new United States of America.

Although most Native Americans had sided with the British, there was no protection for them in the treaty and no mention of any rights they retained or lost; no mention of any land they would be allowed to keep; and no mention of any benefits granted them by the new government. Suddenly, with the war over, the British seemed to adopt a cavalier attitude toward their stalwart former allies.

The British did continue trading with the Indians, though, including guns, and the hope was that the Indians could stop further colonial expansion on their own.

Fat chance. Settlers piled into wagons and mounted horses and headed west. The thinking was obviously, "Well, we've got the coast, now let's take the rest."

And they did.

The Louisiana Purchase

In 1803, the United States purchased from France what ultimately became most of the middle of the country. When Spain ceded Louisiana to France in 1800, the New Orleans port was closed to U.S. traders. This posed a serious threat to America's fiscal solvency. So Jefferson sent negotiators to France and cut a deal to buy the entire region.

President Thomas Jefferson paid Napoleon Bonaparte $15 million for 800,000 square miles west of the Mississippi River. $11,250,000 was paid directly to France, and the remaining $3,750,000 was paid to U.S. citizens in settlement of claims against France.

The land purchased was approximately one-quarter of the U.S. landmass, along with a smidgen of what would ultimately become part of Canada.

Did Thomas Jefferson have the right to buy Louisiana?

Where in the United States Constitution does it say presidents can buy land from foreign countries? Answer: It doesn't.

And Thomas Jefferson knew this. Yet he also knew that the United States needed and wanted the land in the central of the continent. So the question Jefferson faced was, would the purchase have a long-term deleterious effect on states' rights and increase the power of the federal government — something Jefferson was four-square against?

In the end, Jefferson compromised his principles and his core beliefs for the good of the country. This was a tough call for him, considering his staunch anti-Federalism views. He couldn't wait for an amendment, and a lot was at stake. So he went for it, and the country was better off for his decision.

Westward Ho

The purchase of such an enormous parcel of land effectuated American westward expansion. Easily. It removed a foreign neighbor — France — from the mainland picture and guaranteed ease of the all-important Mississippi River trade.

The combined population of American, Spanish, French, and Indian in the Louisiana territory in 1803 at the time of the purchase was around 43,000. The population grew to around 76,000 by 1810 and, according to historians, Americans comprised the largest group.

Native Americans in the Louisiana Territory were now living in U.S.-controlled lands. It fell to Meriwether Lewis and his partner William Clark to explore the new territory and make it clear to the Western tribes what had occurred between the United States and France.

Lewis and Clark and the Corps of Discovery

Meriwether Lewis and William Clark spent more than two years exploring the new western Louisiana territory, and during their expedition interacted with many Native American tribes.

They carried "Jefferson Medals" with them, which they gave to Indian chiefs as a sign of friendship, and as an means of explaining what had happened with the Louisiana Purchase. The front of the medal showed President Thomas Jefferson, and the reverse showed two clasped hands, a universal sign of friendship.

Although Lewis and Clark and their team came in contact with tribes, both large and small, historians have agreed that there were a dozen-plus tribes with whom they had the most significant contact (states and regions mentioned are modern-day locales):

- **Arikaras** (South Dakota): Decimated by a smallpox epidemic, this farming tribe welcomed the Lewis and Clark expedition and was eager to hear about possible future trade possibilities with the United States. The children of this tribe were especially fascinated by Clark's black slave, York.

- **Assiniboine** (Montana): Things got testy with this tribe over trade practices and, when the expedition left them, there was fear of Indian attack, but it never happened.

- **Blackfeet** (Montana): The Blackfeet were big trouble for the expedition, mainly because the U.S. had aligned with their enemies, the Nez Perces, the Flatheads, and the Shoshones. (Meaning the U.S. had established peaceful relations with the tribes and would be providing them with supplies and, uh-oh, guns). When the Blackfeet heard this, they tried to plunder the expeditions' weapons stores (and then set loose their horses when they couldn't get the guns), and two Indians ended up dead. Later, the Blackfeet killed members of the Corps of Discovery, including John Potts.

- **Chinooks** (Northwest): This tribe gave the expedition problems by stealing from them. Overall, Lewis and Clark's journals express the sentiment that these Natives were lucky they didn't get killed by team members.

- **Clatsops** (Oregon): This tribe provided the expedition with food, and relations were amicable. But that didn't stop the Corps from stealing one of the tribe's canoes.

- **Hidatsas** (North Dakota): This tribe traded a lot, and fought a lot with neighboring tribes. A contentious bunch, you might say. Lewis met with the chief but both sides "kept their distance," so to speak. (See Chapter 10 for details on Lewis and Clark guide Sacagawea's involvement with the Hidatsas.)

- **Mandans** (North Dakota): These friendly and generous Indians were farmers and hunters, and the Lewis and Clark expedition stayed with them the winter of 1804–1805.

- **Missouris and Otos** (Missouri/Nebraska): Relations between the Corps of Discovery and the Missouris and the Otos were mostly peaceful, and the following year, the tribe sent a representative to Washington to meet with President Jefferson.

- **Nez Perces** (Pacific Northwest): The Nez Perces became friends of Lewis and Clark and fed them and stored their horses while the expedition crossed the Rocky Mountains.

✔ **Shoshones** (Montana): When the Corps of Discovery came into contact with the Shoshones, their guide Sacagawea recognized one of the tribesmen as her brother Cameahwait. (Sacagawea had been born a Shoshone but was kidnapped by the Hidatsas when she was a child. See Chapter 10.) This relationship encouraged the Shoshones to provide the expedition with horses they needed for their continuing journey. Family ties proved to be a great benefit for the expedition.

✔ **Teton Sioux and Yankton Sioux** (South Dakota): Bottom line? Teton, smooth sailing; Yankton, troubled relations. The relationship between the Teton Sioux and the Corps was tense, and basically, they just didn't get along with each other. The Yankton Sioux, on the other hand, were open to new relations with both the Corps and the United States, mainly because they were dirt-poor and believed Lewis and Clark could help. The Yankton Sioux later visited President Jefferson in Washington.

✔ **Walla Wallas** (Washington): Sacagawea's presence made relations between the Walla Wallas and the Corps friendly, and the expedition traded with them before heading off.

The War of 1812

After the Americans won the Revolutionary War, they continued their pursuit of Indian lands for the next several decades. This did not go over well with the tribes. Complicating matters was the fact that the British were helping many tribes fight off American land grabs.

Meanwhile, the British were also busy fighting Napoleon, and when they started running short of soldiers, they began taking American sailors off American ships at sea (without their consent, of course) and "impressing" them into the British military. And because England was warring with France, the sea lanes were often trouble spots, and this interfered with American trade.

So America declared war on Britain — two days after the Brits agreed not to swipe any more American sailors for their war effort. The mail was a little slower in those days and the U.S. didn't know that one of the reasons they declared war was no longer a reason to declare war.

Native Americans fought on both the British and the American sides during the War of 1812. And in the end, nobody won.

The Treaty of Ghent, signed on December 24, 1814, ended the war and — illustrating that war can be a totally mad endeavor — basically returned everything to its prewar state, including boundaries. Both sides let their prisoners go, and peace ensued.

Well, not really. And once again, it was the mail's fault. The Battle of New Orleans took place in January 1815 and the Americans won. But it was basically a meaningless victory, even though it was a huge battle involving 8,000 British troops and 4,000 U.S. troops.

Native Americans in the Civil War (1861–1865)

Approximately 17,000 Native Americans fought in the Civil War, the majority of them for the Confederacy. It is estimated from historical records that no more than 3,600 Indians fought for the North during the war.

The following are the only tribes that took part in the Civil War:

- ✔ Cherokee
- ✔ Chickasaw
- ✔ Choctaw
- ✔ Creek
- ✔ Seminole

These tribes were all part of the Five Civilized Nations, and their allegiance was split (unequally) between the North and the South. The Choctaw and Chickasaw mostly sided with the Confederacy. The other three tribes split their loyalty.

The Indians were given the designation "civilized tribes" because they had adopted many of the white man's practices, including owning slaves.

Why did the Native Americans get involved in a white man's war? Good question. And the answer is, to protect themselves.

The thinking among Indians (proven, unfortunately, by performance) was that the United States federal government in power was not going to honor treaties and fulfill promises made to Native American tribes.

So Natives, for the most part, took the side of the Confederacy, states comprised of Southerners who Indians believed would be more inclined to honor their land rights and customs if they either came into power as the head of government, or successfully seceded and became the United Confederate States of America. (Considering that slavery was one of the key issues the war was fought over, and the members of the Five Civilized Tribes owned black slaves, this reasoning made sense.)

Grant's Indian

On the northern side, the most famous Native American soldier was Colonel Ely Parker, an Iroquois of the Seneca tribe. He served under Ulysses S. Grant and was known as "Grant's Indian." Parker was the one who wrote out Confederate General Robert E. Lee's surrender terms at Appomattox.

Parker is most remembered for something he said to Lee at Appomattox. When Lee mistook Parker for a black man, he apologized and said, "I am glad to see one real American here." Parker's response? "We are all American, sir."

Stand Watie, a Cherokee born in Georgia in 1806, is the most remembered Native American to serve in the Confederate Army. He was fully supportive of the Confederate cause, and was the last Confederate general to surrender.

The Confederacy offered each of the tribes who joined them a representative in their Congress. This is something which the United States had also talked about, but never followed through on.

The Indian Wars

According to the U.S. Army Center of Military History, the series of conflicts known as the Indian Wars spanned from January 1790 through January 1891, comprising the wars (in chronological order) in Table 11-1.

Table 11-1	The Indian Wars
War	**Year(s)**
Miami	January 1790–August 1795
Tippecanoe	September 21, 1811–November 1811
Creeks	July 27, 1813–1819
	August 1814
	February 1836–July 1837

(continued)

Table 11-1 (continued)

War	Year(s)
Seminoles	November 20, 1817–1831
	October 1818
	December 28, 1835–August 14, 1842
	December 15, 1855–May 1858
Black Hawk	April 26–September 30, 1832
Comanches	1867–1875
Modocs	1872–1873
Apaches	1873
	1885–1886
Little Big Horn	1876–1877
Nez Perces	1877
Bannocks	1878
Cheyennes	1878–1879
Utes	September 1879–November 1880
Pine Ridge	November 1890–January 1891

Within these greater wars were memorable individual battles and skirmishes, but these are the official "Indian Wars" according to the U.S. Army.

The Sand Creek Massacre (1864)

Early on the morning of November 29, 1864, John Chivington, a Methodist elder turned U.S. military man and aspiring politician, launched an attack on a camp of Cheyenne and Arapaho Indians, killing an estimated 200 of them, with many of the victims being women and children.

The Indian camp near Sand Creek, Colorado, was under the protection of the nearby U.S. Fort Lyon, and the attack was unprovoked. A tribal chief, Black Kettle, upon seeing the 700 or so troops massing, raised both an American flag and a white flag of truce in front of his tipi, but to no avail (see Figure 11-5 for some typical Indian weapons that were used). Black Kettle survived, only to be killed four years later in another attack by troops under George Custer.

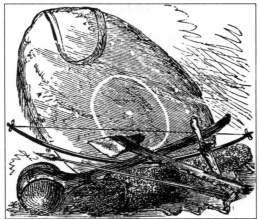

Figure 11-5:
Typical
Indian
weapons.

Chivington later testified before a Congressional committee that the Indians had been hostiles who had murdered whites and robbed farms, and denied some of his soldiers' reports that Indians had been slaughtered while surrendering. There were also widespread reports of atrocities being committed against the killed, including the scalping of men, women, and children, as well as the mutilation of bodies. Scalps were collected, and in later years, Chivington performed stage shows in which he displayed 100 scalps strung across a stage.

The Black Hills War (1876–1877)

There's gold in them thar hills! Remember that from almost every Western you saw when you were a kid?

We're not sure which hills the ubiquitous old-timer was talking about (Montana, maybe?) but his exhortation could have easily applied to the Black Hills, and serves to explain why the Black Hills Wars occurred.

From most estimates, Native Americans had lived in the Black Hills of South Dakota and Wyoming since around 7000 B.C. and they considered the Hills sacred land. The Lakota ultimately claimed final ownership (after kicking out all the other tribes) in the late 18th century, and the Treaty of Fort Laramie in 1868 sanctioned their possession.

But then gold was discovered in the Hills in 1874 (confirmed by an expedition led by General George Armstrong Custer) and all hell broke loose. Miners by the thousands began rushing to the Hills to stake their claim. As you can imagine, this did not go over too well with the Lakota, and adding to their anger was the U.S. Army's less-than-enthusiastic efforts to keep the trespassers away.

Chivington Condemned

A Joint Committee on the Conduct of the War was harsh and condemnatory regarding John Chivington's conduct during the Sand Creek Massacre. They described the massacre as "foul and dastardly" and said his cruelty was disgraceful.

They blasted him for taking advantage of friendly Indians, and excoriated him for betraying and murdering them, making the (accurate) point that they believed they were under the protection of the United States.

And the Commitee was also horrified by Chivington's behavior after the massacre: it seemed to bother them terribly that he actually had the temerity to boast of his actions upon his return to Denver.

How big was the move west? The town of Deadwood, South Dakota, grew to a reported 10,000 people in a few months. There's gold in them thar hills indeed.

The result of the discovery of gold and the U.S. government's inability (lack of desire?) to stop the encroachment onto Lakota land was a series of battles and skirmishes from 1876 through 1877 between the Lakota and whites, including what has come to be known as Custer's Last Stand. (See the section "Little Big Horn.")

Indians call it the Battle of the Greasy Grass. Most others call it the Battle of Little Big Horn, and remember it as one of the worst U.S. military defeats of all time. The beginning of the conflagration was the June 17, 1876, Battle of the Rosebud that took place between the Indians and troops under General Crook on the Rosebud River, about 30 miles southeast a little over a week before the Little Big Horn. Crook was coming up from the south and lost many troops at this battle and then went back to the south, away from the Little Big Horn, and Custer.

In the Black Hills, the Lakota Sioux and other allied tribes, including some Cheyenne and Arapaho, were furious about the constant invasion of whites, and in late 1875 and early 1876 they began leaving their reservations without permission, hoping to gather en masse in Montana under the leadership of Sitting Bull and mount a defense against the intruders.

Not so fast, the U.S. government said, and sent regiments to round 'em up and return them to the reservations where the U.S. said they were required to live. Custer led one of the regiments, and when he came upon an Indian encampment near the Rosebud River, he decided to attack.

Bad move. He had underestimated the number of Indians — by a factor of three — and his Seventh Cavalry was quickly annihilated. Some estimates put the Indian resistance at 4,000 warriors, although 1,200 or so is probably closer to the truth.

The victory for the Sioux was bittersweet. In the end, the killing of Custer and the defeat of the three regiments resulted in the U.S. government rewriting the 1868 treaty so that the Black Hills no longer were deeded to the Indians. And then the gold in them thar hills was fair game for all who wanted to stake their claim.

Wounded Knee (1890)

The buffalo would return, dead warriors would be resurrected, bullets would not pierce their shirts, and the white man would be swallowed up when the earth opened from great earthquakes.

In late 1890, the Lakotas on the Pine Ridge and Rosebud reservations in South Dakota believed that all these events would come to pass by performing the Ghost Dance, a sacred ritual encouraged by a Paiute shaman named Wovoka (who later adopted the white name, Jack Wilson). The Ghost Dance, however, made the U.S. military very nervous. Why? Because they misinterpreted it as a "prelude to battle" dance.

So the U.S. government did what governments often do when they're alarmed by something the "citizenry" is doing (even though Native Americans were not even considered citizens at the time): It banned the Ghost Dance from being performed.

The Lakota refused to obey the white man's order and continued the dance. Troops were sent in to confiscate weapons and, essentially, "shut down" the ritual. A shot was fired (allegedly when a Lakota resisted having his weapon removed from him) and, in less than an hour, more than 200 Lakota were killed or wounded, and an equal number fled, believed to have died later of exposure. The U.S. military lost 25 soldiers, and 39 men were wounded. The Lakota dead were left in the snow to be buried three days later in a mass grave.

Talking to God

Wovoka claimed that the Ghost Dance was given to him by God, and that he had stood before him in Heaven. He said God told him to guide his people and teach them to love one another and live in peace. God also told Wovoka that stealing was wrong, and that if Indians behaved morally, they would all be reunited with their loved ones for eternity after their death. The Ghost Dance was the means to this end, and Wovoka was taught it by God himself.

Beard Remembers Wounded Knee

A Lakota who went by the name of Beard and who survived the Wounded Knee Massacre recalled coming upon his mother during the onslaught. She was wounded, and swinging around a soldier's revolver as she walked slowly among the dead. She told him to pass her by because she was going to "fall down."

Beard watched as she continued walking and then saw her fall after soldiers on both sides of the ravine opened fire on her.

He bravely returned fire in an attempt to defend his mother, but it was too late, She had, indeed, fallen down.

The singing Beard heard was the death songs the mortally wounded were singing as they died.

The Wounded Knee Massacre is today considered the end of the Indian Wars of the 19th century. Colonel James Forsyth, acting under orders from General Nelson Miles, was later exonerated by an Army Court of Inquiry of culpability in the slaughter of innocents.

Native Americans in America's 20th-Century Wars

Native Americans have served in the United States military for over 200 years. George Washington himself, in 1778, said, "I think they can be made of excellent use, as scouts and light troops."

Our first president would certainly be pleased to learn that Native Americans have achieved much greater accomplishments than simply scouting and serving as "light troops."

Native Americans have served honorably in the U.S. military in all wars since the nation was formed.

For example:

✔ About 8,000 Native Americans served in World War I — but double that number had enlisted.

✔ In World War II, over 44,500 Native Americans, of which 800 were women, served in all theaters of the conflict.

✔ In the Vietnam War, approximately 86,000 Native Americans served, and the vast majority (almost 90 percent) of these soldiers voluntarily enlisted. This was the highest per capita number of any ethnic group who served during the war.

✔ The first Native American woman to be killed while serving with the U.S. forces was Lori Piestewa, serving in Iraq. She was killed in the incident in which Jessica Lynch was captured.

Native Americans have been awarded the military Medal of Honor, and many have achieved high ranks in their respective military branches.

Native Americans who have served, or continue to serve, in the U.S. armed forces are often asked how they can fight to defend a country that exploited them, stole their lands, and lied to them. A Native American soldier quoted in a March 16, 2003, article in the *Seattle Times* responded to that by saying, "That's old history. We have freedom. We have to fight for it."

The Navajo code talkers

The Navajo were used to transmit coded messages during World War II. These messages were based on their native tongue, and they were never broken, since no one but members of their own tribe could understand the language.

Although the Navajo World War II code talker program is the most famous, similar programs were used employing Native Americans during World War I, the Korean War, and the Vietnam War.

Interestingly, Hitler was aware of the code talker program and assigned German anthropologists to learn the Navajo languages and dialects, but the task proved too difficult for them.

Chapter 12

Delving into the Details of U.S.-Indian Relations

*U*pon their arrival, and for the next several centuries, Europeans had to contend with Natives who had been living on the North American continent for thousands of years. Such "contending" did not always go well.

Initially, tribes were treated like nations. Sort of.

There were seven stages of U.S.-Indian relations, beginning in 1608, and continuing through today:

✔ Treaties (1608–1830)

✔ Removal (1830–1850)

✔ Reservations (1850–1871)

✔ Assimilation (1871–1928)

✔ Reorganization (1928–1942)

✔ Termination (1943–1968)

✔ Self-determination (1968–present)

In this chapter, we begin by giving you an understanding of what tribal sovereignty is as well as give you an overview of each stage of U.S.-Indian relations, a discussion of its success or failure, and its important milestone moments that lead us to where Native Americans are today — self-determination.

Tribal Sovereignty

Tribal sovereignty consists of a tribe's governmental powers. This comprises powers usually exercised by the federal government, including the power to tax or not to tax, to enforce criminal laws, to adjudicate disputes within a court system, and so forth.

From the beginning, tribes have considered themselves to be sovereign nations, equivalent to the home countries of the European settlers (you can see an example of this idea in Figure 12-1). Today, the U.S. deals with tribes on a government-to-government basis.

In the 16th and 17th centuries, most Indian tribes were accorded tribal sovereignty and treated as legal equals by, first, the European countries the settlers hailed from, and later, by the new United States government.

Figure 12-1:
An Indian welcoming an Englishman and his family.

Britain, Spain, and France, for the most part, did not want to fight to acquire Indians lands. And contrary to common belief, most Indian lands changed hands through treaties, not conquest.

In the 18th and 19th centuries, huge tracts of land were ceded to the U.S. government, often for very little compensation. Like buying Manhattan Island from the Lenape Indians for around $24 worth of trade goods, for example.

Initially — Manifest Destiny and the Discovery Doctrine notwithstanding — tribal sovereignty meant that tribes were free to negotiate the sale of lands that they occupied and were considered the legal "owners" in treaties and negotiations. Land, natural resources, mining rights, and other lucrative goodies of the continent changed things in due course.

Treaties (1608–1830)

Treaties were the legal instrument of choice in the early years of European-Indian relations. A treaty is a formal contract in writing that spells out the terms of the agreement for both sides.

But how can one party to an agreement — in this case, a treaty — agree to anything if they can't read or write in the language of the other party to the treaty? Good question. And the answer is that the tribes were explained the terms of the treaty, as best possible, with the help of a translator if one was available, or through sign language and limited verbal exchanges, and that was that.

Chief Ouray of the Ute tribe said in 1879, "The agreement an Indian makes to a United States treaty is like the agreement a buffalo makes with the hunter when pierced with arrows. All he can do is lie down and give in."

Such a deal?

Looking back, it's no surprise many Native Americans feel like they haven't always gotten a fair shake from the United States.

In the 1802 **Treaty of Fort Confederation**, for example, the Choctaw nation ceded 50,000 acres of their land to the United States government for $1.

The prior year, in the **Treaty of Fort Adams**, the Choctaws received "care and protection," $2,000 "in goods and merchandise," and "three sets of black-smith's tools" for 2,641,920 acres of land.

Yes, you read that right — 2.6 million acres for two grand and some tools.

In the 1827 **Treaties of Buttes des Morts**, the U.S. government bought 500,000 acres of Menominee land in the Pacific Northwest for four and a half cents an acre.

These treaties were not atypical of the agreements signed between Indian tribes and the new U.S. government in the 19th century.

Here is a look at two of the more important U.S.-Indian treaties.

The Treaty with the Delaware Indians (1778)

This was a very important treaty and is considered by historians to be the first truly *official* treaty between the United States and Indians.

On September 17, 1778, at Fort Pitt, Pennsylvania, the treaty was signed by representatives of the U.S. government and John Kill Buck, The Pipe, and White Eyes of the Delaware Nation. The Indians could not sign their name, so they instead made their mark.

This significant treaty covered the following points:

✔ All prior offenses and hostilities between the U.S. and the Delawares were forgiven.

✔ The U.S. and the Delawares were friends forever and allies in time of war.

✔ The U.S. had free passage through Delaware lands.

✔ Delawares could join the U.S. military.

✔ Both sides had the right to a fair and impartial jury trial if charged with offenses.

✔ An agent was to be appointed to deal with the Delawares on trade issues.

✔ All the Delaware land rights previously agreed to were intact.

✔ The Delawares would be represented in Congress.

The Treaty of New Echota (1835)

This treaty, an agreement produced as a result of the 1830 Indian Removal Act, was never signed by elected members of the Cherokee tribe. It stated that the U.S. government would pay $5 million and land in Indian territory for the entire Cherokee nation's land holdings. A group of Cherokees who did not want to risk war with the U.S. signed the treaty.

It was renounced and rejected by a multitude of Cherokees, and even though a petition with thousands of names on it was sent to Washington to protest the treaty and the relocation, the Senate passed the treaty by one vote on May 23, 1836, and the decision was made to enforce it.

The petition (which is on display in the Smithsonian's National Museum of the American Indian) was signed by approximately 16,000 of the estimated 18,000 Cherokees (88 percent) who were alive at the time.

This treaty was the direct cause of the horrible 1838 Trail of Tears Cherokee removal march. (See Chapter 6 for more on the Trail of Tears.)

Indian treaties are equal to federal law.

Removal (1830–1850)

The Indian Removal Act was a bill passed by the U.S. Congress on April 24, 1830, that essentially made official a policy of removing Southeastern tribes from their lands.

This was considered necessary because the United States wanted to expand into lands owned by members of the Five Civilized Tribes, and they were, as many of the time put it, in the way. They were obstructing progress. They were holding back the growth of a nation that saw great tracts of southern lands and vast opportunities awaiting them.

There was cotton to be grown, and slaves to pick it. So the Indians had to go.

The Five Civilized Tribes were the Chickasaw, Choctaw, Creek, Seminole, and Cherokee. They were called this because they had adopted the ways of the whites: a European-style education, large farming enterprises, and the keeping of slaves.

Truth be told, this was not technically *forced* removal, contrary to some interpretations of the bill. Indians were offered money and land to "voluntarily" relocate. Members of the Five Civilized Tribes living in the South were asked to move to what is now Oklahoma.

In his Second Annual Message to Congress, delivered on December 6, 1830, President Andrew Jackson made it clear that Indians living on lands east of the Mississippi were to move to lands west of the Mississippi.

The Indian Removal Act provided funds for the government to facilitate their relocation. Jackson led off his statement with the following:

> "It gives me pleasure to announce to Congress that the benevolent policy of the Government, steadily pursued for nearly thirty years, in relation to the removal of the Indians beyond the white settlements is approaching to a happy consummation.

This is a disingenuous statement, since many would challenge the description of U.S. former policy as "benevolent," and there were many who would not describe the consummation of that policy as "happy."

Many Indians did, in fact, agree to move west. Very few were happy about it, but they went anyway. Many treaties were signed by tribal leaders in which they accepted cash in hand and land in Indian Territory for their lands in the U.S. South.

By 1847, the various removal treaties and removal wars (First, Second, and Third Seminole Wars, in particular) had resulted in 25 million acres of southern land being opened to white farmers, cotton growing, and slavery.

Reservations (1850–1871)

Contrary to popular belief, reservations weren't parcels of land the U.S. government paternalistically "gave" to Indians during the period of removal. In many cases, reservations were sections of Indian land the Indians "reserved" for themselves when signing treaties and agreeing to vacate and move west.

In 1850, Commissioner of Indian Affairs Orlando Brown painted a pretty picture of the whole sordid endeavor by stating that reservations should be "a country adapted to agriculture, of limited extent and well-defined boundaries; within which all, with occasional exceptions, should be compelled constantly to remain until such time as their general improvement and good conduct may supersede the necessity of such restrictions."

In 1851, the **Indian Appropriations Act** allocated federal money to move tribes onto reservations.

Reservations were "necessary" — but only until Indians displayed "good conduct."

Such admirable behavior would come after the Indians had been converted to Christianity, of course.

The reservation system was deemed a failure 20 years after it was implemented.

Assimilation (1871–1928)

When reservations didn't work to "civilize" the savages, the government decreed that the only solution to the Indian problem was to absorb them into mainstream American society and culture, to "assimilate" them.

This effort was undertaken by chopping up the reservations into smaller parcels for farming — 160 acres for a family and 80 acres for a single person — and removing Indian children from their families and educating them at boarding schools set up by the government.

At these schools, anything "Indian" was absolutely forbidden. Students speaking their native language would be severely punished. Parents were only allowed to visit once or twice a year, thereby completely eliminating their involvement in decisions regarding their children.

The assimilation plan didn't work either, and the Meriam Report of 1928, which looked at conditions on Indian reservations in 26 states, spelled out its failings in horrifying detail and sent shockwaves through the U.S. government and the tribal peoples.

Below are some of the more notable findings from the staggeringly important Meriam Report. Reading through this list powerfully illustrates just how difficult it was to be a Native American in America in the 19th and early 20th centuries:

- ✔ "An overwhelming majority of the Indians are poor, even extremely poor, and they are not adjusted to the economic and social system of the dominant white civilization."

- ✔ "The health of the Indians as compared with that of the general population is bad."

- ✔ "The prevailing living conditions among the great majority of the Indians are conducive to the development and spread of disease."

- ✔ "With comparatively few exceptions, the diet of the Indians is bad. It is generally insufficient in quantity, lacking in variety, and poorly prepared."

- ✔ "The housing conditions are likewise conducive to bad health."

- ✔ "Sanitary facilities are generally lacking. Except among the relatively few well-to-do Indians, the houses seldom have a private water supply or any toilet facilities whatever. Even privies are exceptional. Water is ordinarily carried considerable distances from natural springs or streams, or occasionally from wells."

- ✔ "The income of the typical Indian family is low and the earned income extremely low."

- ✔ "In justice to the Indians, it should be said that many of them are living on lands from which a trained and experienced white man could scarcely wrest a reasonable living. In some instances the land originally set apart for the Indians was of little value for agricultural operations other than grazing."

- ✔ "The survey staff found altogether too much evidence of real suffering and discontent to subscribe to the belief that the Indians are reasonably satisfied with their condition. The amount of serious illness and poverty is too great to permit of real contentment. The Indian is like the white man in his affection for his children, and he feels keenly the sickness and the loss of his offspring."

✔ "Several past policies adopted by the government in dealing with the Indians have been of a type which, if long continued, would tend to pauperize any race."

✔ "The work of the government directed toward the education and advancement of the Indian himself, as distinguished from the control and conservation of his property, is largely ineffective."

✔ "The survey staff finds itself obliged to say frankly and unequivocally that the provisions for the care of the Indian children in boarding schools are grossly inadequate."

✔ "The hospitals, sanatoria, and sanatorium schools maintained by the Service, despite a few exceptions, must be generally characterized as lacking in personnel, equipment, management, and design."

✔ "The exploitation of Indians in Oklahoma has been notorious, but this exploitation has taken place under the state courts and the guardians appointed by them."

The Meriam Report could not be ignored. Something had to be done — an Indian "New Deal" of sorts — and the Indian Reorganization Act was the next attempt by the U.S. government to come up with a fair, workable policy toward Native Americans.

Reorganization (1928–1942)

The Indian Reorganization Act (also known as the Wheeler-Howard Act), had noble intentions. Its defined purposes were

✔ To conserve and develop Indian lands and resources

✔ To extend to Indians the right to form business and other organizations

✔ To establish a credit system for Indians

✔ To grant certain rights of home rule to Indians

✔ To provide for vocational education for Indians

And, for the most part, the IRA worked to implement reforms called for by the Meriam Report.

Well over 150 tribes and Indian villages adopted constitutions; the credit system allowed economic improvements; and Indian kids went to public schools and their education improved drastically.

The Indian Reorganization Act was the basis for later Indian legislation and is considered a milestone toward achieving independence and self-determination for Indians in the United States.

The seven types of Indian lands

According to the U.S. Environmental Protection Agency, these are the seven types of Indian lands in the United States:

✔ **Reservations:** Lands set apart for the use of designated tribes.

✔ **Trust Lands:** Lands held in trust by the U.S. government for Indians, usually a tribe.

✔ **Checkerboard Lands:** Lands that are a combination of nonmember-owned parcels and tribal parcels, resulting in a checkerboard pattern.

✔ **Fee Lands:** Land owned by non-Indians within the boundaries of a reservation.

✔ **Dependent Indian Community:** Lands set apart for Indian use under the superintendence of the U.S. federal government.

✔ **Allotments:** Lands held in trust by the U.S. government for individual members of a tribe.

✔ **Ceded Territory:** Lands within a reservation or aboriginal area that have been sold by a tribe or taken by the U.S. government on which tribe members retains certain rights, like hunting and fishing.

Termination (1943–1968)

This policy dismantled tribes and took the official government position that Native Americans were subject to the same laws as applied to all American citizens. It severed the government-to-government policy that had been in effect, and allowed the U.S. to indulge in land grabs. And the U.S. was willing to litigate until doomsday to fight tribal resistance to this policy.

The termination policy essentially reversed many of the reforms that had been implemented during reorganization. Why'd the U.S. government do that, you're probably wondering, right? To save money, is why. The federal government wanted to cut the budget for Indian affairs and, in typical bureaucratic thinking, they figured fewer Indians, less money spent on them. The fact that the terminated tribes simply didn't fade away like frost in the morning sun seemed to have not occurred to them as being anything to worry about.

Also, it was about natural resources. There were valuable mineral resources on Indian land that proved irresistible, including:

✔ The Navajo lands had uranium and oil.

✔ The Crow lands had coal.

✔ The Hopi lands had oil.

✔ The Ute lands had oil, coal, and natural gas.

✔ The Apache lands had natural gas.

Due to the termination policy, the trust relationship that the U.S. government had previously established with the Indian population was now in tatters.

Self-Determination (1961–present)

It was President Richard Nixon who emphasized the critical importance of tribal self-rule after the failure of the Termination policies. His July 8, 1970, "Special Message on Indian Affairs" was a landmark admission by the U.S. government: Nixon stated that any and all U.S. policies concerning Indians should serve "to strengthen the Indian sense of autonomy without threatening his sense of community."

The trust relationship between Indians and the U.S. government was reaffirmed and financial support for tribes guaranteed.

The passage of the 1975 Indian Self-Determination Act was a milestone moment in U.S.-Indian relations, it gave Indians the power to contract with the government on their own, and it also allowed Indians to control how federal moneys were spent on Indian matters. This endorsed a simple, yet profound reality: Local knows best. Native Americans at the community level know best how to spend money in their own communities.

And the Indian Self-Determination Act allowed them to exercise their own discretion, for the benefits of their own people.

Sacred lands

On May 24, 1996, President Bill Clinton signed an executive order titled "Indian Sacred Sites" which ordered the appropriate federal agencies in charge of such "sacred lands" to do two things:

✔ Accommodate access to and ceremonial use of Indian sacred sites by Indian religious practitioners

✔ Avoid adversely affecting the physical integrity of such sacred sites

Sounds like a good thing, right? And at first glance, it does seem like an act of respect toward Indians, who do attach sacred import to ancient lands.

But what about the Constitution's "Establishment Clause?" That part of the First Amendment that reads, "Congress shall make no law respecting an establishment of religion"? An executive order is not technically a law enacted by the Congress, so that skirts that issue.

However, the accommodation of such sites needs only be carried out "to the extent practicable, permitted by law, and not clearly inconsistent with essential agency functions."

What this basically means is "we'll let you use lands for religious purposes as long as it doesn't inconvenience us."

Major Recent Acts of Congress Concerning Indians

The period of Native American self-determination began in 1968 with the **Indian Civil Rights Act** which, in a nutshell, guaranteed Bill of Rights protections — freedom of speech, religion, the press, the right of assembly, the right to petition for grievances, due process, equal protection, and so forth — to Indians.

Prior to this act, Native Americans were not legally guaranteed these rights.

Here are some of the other important recent Congressional acts pertaining to Indians.

The Indian Self-Determination and Education Assistance Act (1975)

This act essentially allowed tribes to create, with federal funds, their own schools, over which they had total jurisdiction. This was notable because, for the first time, Native Americans had complete control over their children's education.

The first schools to take advantage of the act were the Rock Point and Rough Rock schools in Arizona.

The Indian Health Care Improvement Act (1978)

This act provided healthcare for American Indians and Alaska Natives. It was overseen by the Indian Health Service under the auspices of the U.S. Department of Health and Human Services.

This act expired on September 30, 2000, and was extended through 2001. It has not yet been renewed.

The American Indian Religious Freedom Act (1978)

This act resolved certain conflicts between Indian religious beliefs and practices and federal laws that restricted the exercise of Indian beliefs, including the use of sacred lands and artifacts like eagle feathers. (See Chapter 14 for more on the legality of possessing eagle feathers.)

The Indian Child Welfare Act (1978)

This act gave tribal courts jurisdiction over Native American children living on reservations.

The Native American Graves and Repatriation Act (1990)

This act made it a government responsibility to return to culturally affiliated federally recognized tribes human remains, funerary objects, sacred objects, and objects of cultural patrimony that have been found on public lands, during activities that use federal funds, or that have been curated in facilities that receive federal funding.

Part III
Working for a Living

"They're showing 'Fort Apache,' 'Drums Along the Mohawk,' and 'Little Big Man' at the theater. The local paper calls it a retrospective of Native American culture and the cinema. The Shoshoni Review calls it a comedy festival."

In this part . . .

Food and shelter are the two most important needs of mankind. Without them, we're essentially dead in the water (to shamelessly mix metaphors!).

It was no different for the tribes who inhabited America, both before and after the European colonization efforts. In this part, you'll learn about how Indians fed their families and protected them from the elements. Hunting, fishing, trapping, farming, and trading are covered in detail. You'll also learn about the variety of Indian homes and gain knowledge of how Natives made their clothing and what they wore during the different seasons and in the various geographical areas with their wide range of climes.

Chapter 13

Mother Love

Mother Earth, Father Sky. It's a simple and elegant idea when you come right down to it: A mother feeds her children; a father watches over all.

Obligatory Political Correctness Disclaimer: Regarding the aforementioned "simple and elegant idea," add after it, "gender stereotyping notwithstanding, of course." We're talking about iconic models — models that state that mothers nurture, fathers support — and, yes, this is a generalization spanning eons of civilizations and societal constructs. And, yes, there are now, and always have been, *exceptions to this paradigm.* Offense is not intended. I'm only the messenger, reporting on cultural behaviors that literally go back eons.

A Mother Feeds Her Children

The Native American idea of the Earth being the mother of all living things is ancient, bespeaks a respect for the circle of life, and embodies the belief that our mother must be protected and, in exchange, she will provide the things we need to survive.

Native peoples formed relationships with the environment that mirrored more personal relationships among individuals. The concept of the earth as Mother indicates the human responsibility to give her respect. In return, the earth provides life for the people.

Tribes did not originally possess a separate concept of ecology, nor of resource management. Embedded in traditional lifestyle was a practice of working within the constraints of landscape and environment, and this emerged in tribal tradition as the practice of behaving with respect for the earth.

The traditional respect given to the earth should not be seen as representing the stereotypical one-with-nature Indians who cry at the first sign of a piece of litter. Indian tribes were and are like all human groups. Today, some people adhere more closely to traditional practices, while others seek to use resources in a less conservative manner.

It should be noted, however, that there is a backlash of sorts these days regarding this "one with nature" perception of Native Americans. In fact, the argument always seems to revolve around a perverted necessity to define Indians mythologically as either a "noble red man" or "bloodthirsty savage."

The reality is that both stereotypes are true, and both stereotypes are false. Indians were known to be savage in battle — as were the white Europeans. Nature *was* respected and worshipped.

But insisting on an "all or nothing" blanket definition of the American Indians as either this or that is incorrect, inaccurate, and demeaning.

Food on Four Legs

Whether or not you believe in killing and eating animals, Native Americans depended enormously on all living things for food, clothing, tools, and weapons.

Hunting for survival

Since food is life, Natives understood that their lives were sustained by the taking of the lives of animals. This profound realization resulted in animals being honored for their role in sustaining tribal people, with the resultant accompanying rituals and iconic representations.

Different animals became important to different tribes according to where people lived. A community of Inuit, for example, had no real interest in the bison, while caribou never made much of a dent in the traditional life of the Florida Seminole. However, it is possible to list some of the animals that were important to different tribes:

- Bear
- Beaver

- ✔ Buffalo, bison
- ✔ Deer, caribou
- ✔ Moose
- ✔ Muskrat
- ✔ Rabbit

The smaller animals like muskrat and squirrel were also trapped as well as hunted. (See Chapter 16 for more information on Native American trapping practices.)

Hunting practices today

Today, there are three types of hunting practiced in North America:

- ✔ Sport and trophy hunting
- ✔ Subsistence hunting
- ✔ Commercial hunting

Sport and trophy hunting

This is what it sounds like: hunting for fun. And it is an oftentimes volatile issue for both avid hunters and animal rights activists and environmentalists.

Over three-quarters of Americans support legal hunting as a sport, yet very few people actually go out and hunt.

Subsistence hunting

Subsistence hunting is hunting and fishing for food and other uses. It is an important part of the lives of people today (both Natives and non-Natives alike). For some tribes, hunting and fishing provides not just food, but also a tangible link to their ancestors. Conflicts sometimes arise when non-Natives misunderstand that tribes aren't simply hunting for food.

Subsistence hunting is a controversial topic in Alaska, mainly because of two reasons:

- ✔ It is necessary to define and regulate who are official subsistence hunters; that is, who specifically is allowed to hunt and fish as needed.

- ✔ It is necessary to differentiate between federal wildlife authority and management, and state authority and management, and in many instances, the twain don't meet. What happens when state wildlife regulations conflict with federal guidelines?

The state of Alaska has a bigger tent regarding who is eligible for subsistence hunting than does the federal government, which regulates federal lands and waterways and commonly limits hunting and fishing access to *rural* Alaskan natives who qualify based on a criteria of need and access to other sources for food and resources. Alaska allows *all* residents to be eligible for subsistence user status.

For the most part, subsistence use guidelines include using natural resources for:

- Food
- Shelter
- Fuel
- Clothing
- Tools
- Transportation
- Use in barter, sharing, and customary trade (United Fishermen of Alaska)

In 1978, the conflict between commercial hunting and subsistence hunting was decided by the Alaskan government. They stated that if an area becomes scarce of game, or a waterway of fish, subsistence hunters get priority. Commercial hunters were not happy about this, and fought the ruling at the polls, but were defeated.

The Alaska Supreme Court stepped into the fray and in 1989 ruled that giving rural hunters priority was a violation of the state's constitution. It was then that the feds took over and even now, there are no definitive standards regarding who's who, and who can hunt what in Alaska.

Many tribes have experienced significant backlash over the exercise of their traditional rights to hunt animals on land and in the sea. Some tribes have the right to hunt out of season according to treaties signed with the federal government. A tribe may have given up thousands of acres of land, but did so with the understanding that they would maintain the right to continue to interact with the environment according to cultural ways.

A famous case of backlash occurred with the Makah tribe's right to hunt whales. This was a right that they had reserved, but voluntarily not exercised during a time of low whale population. When the tribe decided that it was necessary to continue whaling as part of their traditional culture, non-Makah were outraged. Particularly disturbing were the protestors who believed that the Makah should not have the right to hunt with modern technology, as if only non-Indians should be allowed to participate in the 21st century!

Commercial hunting

Commercial hunting is practiced by both Native peoples and all other strata of society. In most cases, this type of hunting is state-regulated.

Making Good Use of Rich and Fertile Land

The seemingly boundless natural riches and resources of pre-industrialization America were breathtaking and awe-inspiring. They were also, in a sense, recognized as bounty for the taking.

Over two thousand years ago, the earliest Indian farmers were domesticating corn, beans, and squash. Later on, some tribes in the Southwest developed elaborate irrigation systems to carry water to their fields. Some of the earliest agricultural tribes included the Hohokum, the Pima, and the Maricopa Indians in Arizona and northern Mexico.

The first crops

If it weren't for Indians, we wouldn't have popcorn. And Italy would have never known about its now-hallowed tomato. And the importance of the potato (which originated among the Aymara Indians in Peru) to Ireland was so enormous that when the Potato Famine hit in 1845, by the time it was over, the population of the country declined from immigration and death by 12 percent.

Native Americans grew crops that are now disseminated all over the world, and important foods for countless cultures. Among many other foods, some of what we can thank Indian agriculture for include

- Avocado
- Corn
- Pecans
- Plums
- Potatoes
- Squash
- Sunflowers
- Tobacco (see Figure 13-1)

Figure 13-1:
A tobacco
plant.

 ✔ Tomatoes

 ✔ Walnuts

More than half of the world's different types of food have Native American origins.

Native American farming today

In 1991, a nonprofit seed conservation program in Arizona called Native Seed/SEARCH conducted a survey of Native American farmers in Arizona and New Mexico and learned one very salient fact about the state of farming as an occupation: young Native Americans didn't consider agriculture a viable profession. The organization described this lack of interest as "startling" and attributed many of the Native American woes — specifically poor health and social fragmentation within communities — to the decline in sustainable Indian agribusinesses.

In the past eighty or so years, the number of American Indians working in farming plummeted, but has shown signs of improvement. Today, according to the U.S. Department of Agriculture's 2002 Census of Agriculture, the number of Native American farm operators is around 24,000. This is up from 13,000 in 1997.

Seeking Seafood

Fishing has been a human endeavor for over 10,000 years.

When John Smith first arrived in Jamestown in 1607, he was absolutely astonished by the abundance of fish in America. The rivers, lakes, brooks, and coastal waterways were so rich with fish, he and his crew tried catching them with a frying pan! (True story.)

The Europeans quickly learned that the natives had been catching and living on fish for centuries, and to both the Indians and the colonists, fish stocks were considered inexhaustible.

Fish was an important component of the diet for tribes living within reach of sea or river, providing protein, while requiring little risk in obtaining. Killing and transporting a slain buffalo wasn't an easy job. Trapping or catching fish, on the other hand, often was.

Fish weirs

A fish weir is essentially an underwater cage in which large numbers of fish were trapped, and from which they could be harvested later at the tribe's convenience.

Fish weirs were constructed from stone or wooden stakes, and they were placed in rivers and in the sea.

Fish weirs were also used in the Midwest, although there were always, of course, riverine weirs. Archaeological evidence attests to the use of weirs by the Sac Indians across the St. Francis River to trap migrating sturgeon.

Other fishing methods

Native Americans also used other methods besides the very clever "trapping" method of the fish weir. The fishing methods varied according to the tribe and according to their environment. You wouldn't expect folks living along the rivers in the Southeast to get very far using a giant hook like that used by Northwest tribes when fishing for halibut!

These included:

- ✔ **Hand-and-line baited hook:** Carved bone fish hooks have been found in many archaeological sites near fishing sites. The lines were made from deer sinew and twisted bark.

- ✔ **Barbed harpoons:** The tips of these hurled sticks were usually made from carved bone or even metal, hardened by fire, and could pierce even the thick hide of a leviathan swordfish.

- ✔ **Nets:** Nets were used to capture huge quantities of fish. On some days, several hundred pounds of cod could be caught by net. Captain Smith, writing about the Powhatan, noted, "The women . . . make nets for fishing, for the quantities as formally braided as thread from the bark of trees and the sinew of deer."

Some tribes have signed treaties which allow them to fish in certain areas. These "treaty rights" allow them to fish in areas where non-Indians are not allowed to fish, or at times others are not allowed to fish. For example, the Makah are known for their annual whaling trip. They often take one gray whale as part of a ceremonial/religious/traditional event.

The Klamath Tribe originally had a treaty with the federal government that guaranteed the tribe a reservation of close to 2 million acres. The treaty also guaranteed other rights for the tribe, including the right to hunt and fish. Several subsequent federal actions shrunk and eventually eliminated the tribe's land reservation. However, the tribe's hunting and fishing rights survived the termination of the tribe's reservation because the tribe was not compensated for their hunting and fishing rights.

Do Indians get special advantages?

In most ways, Indians do not enjoy any of the special advantages many imagine they receive. Indian fishermen are regulated by tribal governments for protection of the fisheries, just as non-treaty fishermen are regulated by the state.

But unlike non-Indians, Indian fishermen have a treaty-guaranteed property right to fish that goes beyond any state or even federal law. For both moral and practical reasons, the first Europeans to arrive in America recognized the Indian's rights to their tribal lands and properties.

In 1778, the Continental Congress declared that Indian lands and property could never be taken without Indian consent. When the U.S. Constitution was drafted, Congress was given the power to make treaties — and the treaties were made "supreme law of the land." Thus, when Northwest Indians retained their fishing right and agreed to give up claim to this land, the agreement was, and still is, backed by the U.S. Constitution.

Skins: The Lucrative Fur Trade

The fur trade was an enormous fiscal engine that shaped the U.S. economy from almost the moment the first Europeans set foot on the North American continent. And it was a business that lived and breathed on the skills, experience, and knowledge of the American Indian.

Most of the time, men did the hunting, the women the skinning and preparation of the furs for shipping.

For 250 years — from 1600 to 1850 — the fur trade thrived.

The three periods of the North American fur trade

Historians divide the history of the fur trade into three periods:

- ✔ The French period, which included Dutch fur traders and ran from around 1600 to 1760
- ✔ The British period, which spanned the years 1760 through 1816
- ✔ The American period, which began when the British period ended in 1816 and continued through the end of the fur trade in 1850

The tribes traded furs for a wide range of items and materials that they otherwise would not have had available to them, including:

- ✔ Iron based products, such as axes, cooking pots, knives, and tools
- ✔ Utensils
- ✔ Cloth and other textiles
- ✔ Beads
- ✔ Guns
- ✔ Alcohol

The European clothing and hat industries were voracious consumers of North American furs. The beaver hat was big in Europe, as were expensive, luxury clothing items. The abundance of fur-bearing animals in the New World, combined with a skilled Native population able to consistently and dependably trap and skin fur-bearing animals and transport the furs to trading posts resulted in a thriving transatlantic business.

The demand for fur hats in Europe in 1668 was around 5 million hats. To put this number in perspective, think of it like this: that was more than one hat per person. *Every* person. (The only consumer item that comes close to that level of market penetration these days is probably the television.)

When you think of the North American fur trade, the Hudson's Bay Company stands front and center as the single most important and powerful trading company in the industry's history.

The impact of the fur trade on the Indians

The effect of the three-century fur trade on the native Indigenous population of North America is something of a mixed bag.

There were positive effects on tribes, including:

- The new availability of labor-saving tools
- The increased power over neighboring tribes that came from having guns
- The access to supplies like different types of food, as well as European medicines

The negative effects, on the other hand, included, of course, exposure to often devastating European diseases, plus:

- A rapid appearance of a new scourge, alcoholism
- The necessary and sometimes destructive interaction with more and more whites
- A willingness to go to war with other tribes
- A reconstruction of the way in which tribes related to their environments

Also, the fur trade depleted the environment of fur-bearing animals, and made the Indians change the way they lived to accommodate the insatiable needs of the European fur traders.

Tribes that participated in the fur trade altered how they behaved toward the animals that were a part of their cultural world. A hunter might thank an individual deer who provided food and clothing, but once the numbers of deer killed rose, it seems like it might be difficult to thank each one individually. In a cultural sense, this in turn might have angered the spirits of the animals who were not being properly thanked.

One study of the fur trade in eastern Canada has produced the intriguing idea that tribes participating in the fur trade deliberately broke with traditional ways in order to participate in a war against the animals who were blamed for bringing epidemic disease upon the people. In his book, *Keepers of the Game,* Calvin Martin explores the theory that tribes believed that the animals had broken their ancient pact and therefore people felt free to engage in the fur trade as a means of revenge. This theory, although not fully accepted, shows how tribal relationships to the earth were altered through the colonial process.

Today, furs and skins are an important part of traditional culture, particularly in traditional dress. Apache parents may talk about finding exactly the right deerskin to make clothing for their daughter's puberty ceremony. Young people go through the vendor tables at powwows looking for skins and furs to work into new and elaborate powwow outfits. It's no longer necessary that someone hunt the animal that provides the material for clothing, but it is important to many Native people that we know to whom we are indebted.

The lucrative fur trade resulted in Indians changing somewhat from their ecologically friendly lifestyle of only taking what they needed, to a more profit-based program.

Chapter 14

Dressing for Purpose and Pride

*O*ne of the ways we humans identify ourselves is by the clothes we wear.

Ethnic, national, cultural, religious, and social identity are all commonly displayed by specific garments worn, sometimes, as with many Native American groups, for cultural or social gatherings; and sometimes, as with clergy, all the time when in public.

And throughout history, garments have been made from materials available at the time and in the locations where the people lived. One of the main sources for Indian clothing was the deer as well as other animals. Every piece of the animal was used, out of both frugal practicality and respect. Nothing was discarded and, thus, the animal's spirit was honored.

Clothing differed from region to region according to climate and tribal traditions. After the arrival of Europeans, many tribes came to value cotton and wool cloth, and traditional clothing came to incorporate these as well as trade items like glass beads and metal buttons.

Native Garb

Feathers, fur, and hides were the common components of a wide range of Native garb. Tribes in Arctic regions wore heavier clothing that was insulated for warmth, using fur and thicker hides (like that of the caribou). Tribes in more temperate climes wore lighter garments that left more of the body exposed.

Loincloths

Loincloths were made from soft cloth or deerskin and were truly an ingenious item of clothing. A loincloth provided coverage and protection of the man's groin and buttocks, yet was easily made, put on, and removed.

The basic loincloth was a long rectangular piece of cloth or softened hide. The wearer would tie a leather belt around his waist, and then straddle the loincloth and pull it up close to his crotch. The front and back ends of the cloth would then be slipped under the belt and folded over, creating hanging flaps over his front and rear.

In warmer weather, men would wear the loincloth by itself and leave their legs and chest bare. In the chillier months, or when a hunting expedition involved moving through brush and bushes, men would add leather leggings that covered from mid-thigh to the ankles. Leggings were single pieces and were tied to the same belt that secured the loincloth.

Deerskin shirts

When the chest needed to be covered for protection, or due to colder weather, men would commonly don a deerskin shirt. These were usually pullover and often decorated with beads, feathers, and leather fringe.

To make a deerskin shirt, the deer hide had to be *tanned*, a process involving soaking it, removing the flesh and the hair (a tedious, time-consuming process), drying it out, smoking it, re-soaking it, and then finishing the surface with the slain animal's brains. (Sometimes urine was also used for the tanning process.) The final step was to buff the hide, which involved ringing it dry, and then stretching it and rubbing it until it was supple.

Sometimes strips of fur were added to the collar and around the wrists; drawstrings allowed flexibility.

The Native American's tanning rule of thumb — which has been proven to be almost always accurate — was that the brains of a killed animal were precisely enough to tan that particular animal's hide.

Deerskin leggings

The loincloth and deerskin shirt were simple garments that had a functionality and form that was a response to the outdoor environment and living needs — hunting, protection — of Native Americans.

The need for *more* warmth or protection resulted in the creation of leggings, which were, in a nutshell, single pants legs that were not attached to each other. They were also made of deerskin or some other animal hide, and were commonly worn with a garter or a belt around the waist from which they were suspended.

Leggings were not the same as pants, although some tribes did make what could be considered pants, mainly of fur.

Ceremonial Garb

Native American ceremonies were elaborate rituals involving special clothing (see Figure 14-1) and dancing. Like any cultural event, Native American ceremonies can be elaborate rituals involving specialized dress, dancing, music, and foods. They are used for healing, in reverence to the spirits of nature, or the Creator.

The clothing for such rites was designed to reflect the seriousness and importance of the ceremonies. Beautiful feathered headdresses, spirit masks, long robes, stone and metal jewelry, meticulously applied body paint, and beaded moccasins all spoke to the gravity of the ceremony, honored tribal traditions, and made clear the respect manifested by all participating.

Figure 14-1:
An Indian robe.

Plains war shirts

The Native American war shirt was not worn during battle but, instead, was put on for ceremonial rituals and served two specific purposes: to respect tribal honor and to recount the battle experiences of the brave wearing it.

These shirts were sometimes decorated with *scalp locks* — the tufts of human hair of vanquished foes or from family members — as well as with beads, sacred ornaments, feathers, and leather fringe. They were also commonly painted with designs symbolizing nature, battles, and patron animals.

War shirts had to be earned. A warrior had to perform certain acts of bravery and boldness in order to be granted the privilege of wearing a war shirt. Common requirements included counting coup, which meant physically laying a hand on an enemy and coming away from the act unharmed. Sometimes, a war shirt could also be earned by successfully stealing an enemy's horses.

Paint

Many Native Americans painted their faces before battle, or as part of a religious ceremony.

They used materials available to them from nature, including clay, plants ground up into a paste, and different color soils, berries, moss, and dung.

The most popular color for face adornment was red. Interestingly, even today, a red tie is perceived to be a "power tie." The color of fire was important and contributed to the image of strength and pride they wanted to manifest to enemies. War paint could be considered another form of "mask," except that instead of completely covering a warrior's features, it emphasized them.

Masks

Native American masks were made, carved, and worn for many purposes, according to tribal traditions.

Masks of animal faces were believed to imbue the wearer with the strengths and cunning of the particular beast worn. Masks were worn for prayer services and for tribal dances. Portrait masks depicted a particular individual, such as a revered leader, or a brave warrior. Some masks were worn as initiation into secret tribal societies.

Each tribe and culture area had their own masks and used them for their own purposes. The Northwest Indians, for example, made three types of mask:

- ✔ **Single face:** This is what it sounds like. A single face with no moving parts.
- ✔ **Mechanical:** This type of mask had moving parts like a hinged jaw, or eyelids that opened and closed.
- ✔ **Transformation:** This mask literally "transformed" when worn. A top mask would open to reveal a mask beneath.

Masks are still made today, and many artisans duplicate as best possible the original designs and styles of centuries-old masks. Masks are carved from wood and painted, and decorated with hair, fur, and feathers.

Many northwestern mask designs are considered to belong to a certain family. Anyone else making or using one would be in violation of what effectively could be called a copyright law.

Native American Accessories

Every culture and ethnic group has accouterments and appurtenances specific to them, and beloved by all its members.

From the Jewish Star of David and Irish claddaugh, to the Nepalese pashmina and the Russian ushanka, every nationality boasts its own decorative trappings. Truth be told, though, few cultural accessories can rival those of the Native Americans for splendor, color, and vibrancy.

Wampum belts

Wampum, short for *wampumpeag*, is the term for small beads that are polished, drilled, and strung together to make belts and sometimes bracelets and collars.

In the historic days of the Algonquin and Iroquoian tribes, wampum belts were often made from quahog (and sometimes other) shells. Today, plastic, acrylic, or stones are used since the quahog is an endangered species and, even if it wasn't, it would take thousands of shells to craft the purple beads needed for a belt or bracelet, and the work involved is cost and time prohibitive.

Interestingly, the transformation (or *evolution* might be a better word) of strings of wampum into items that were worn occurred as a matter of convenience.

When quantities of wampum were strung onto long fibers and used as currency and in barter transactions, it was a natural tendency for a Native to simply wrap the long strand around his waist or wrist for convenience of transportation.

Wampum belts had three distinct traditional uses among Northeastern tribes:

- **Currency:** Wampum was used as money, and the standard length of a strung strand of wampum beads was around 6 feet. In the 1600s and 1700s, this strand was worth around ten shillings in Anglo funds.

- **History:** Belts were woven with different color stones and beads to signify historical events in the history of the tribe. Whenever something significant occurred, the belt would be added to. Different-color beads meant different things, and a member of a tribe could "read" a belt and provide a complete history of his people. The lack of a written language made such artistic chronicling necessary for survival of the tribe's legends.

- **Communication:** Wampum belts and bracelets were woven for particular purposes. For example, if a tribe wanted to declare war on another tribe, they would weave a wampum belt in primarily red beads and have it delivered by an emissary to their enemy. Or if a young brave wanted to propose marriage to a young girl, he would have a bracelet woven and send it to her home where her family would accept it, but only to consider the proposal. If it was ultimately retained, the young man had a wife. If it was returned, it was a "Thanks, but no thanks."

Wampum (see Figure 14-2) was in existence from approximately A.D. 200. through the American Revolution. The English often traded wampum with Natives for goods and to finalize treaties.

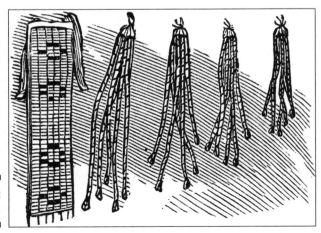

Figure 14-2:
Wampum.

Today, reproduction wampum belts are available for purchase through dealers who specialize in Native American crafts, clothing, and artworks. Also available are replicas of the wampum beads that one can use to make their own native belts or bracelets.

Feathers

The feather is a magnificent evolutionary achievement and is found only on birds. (Although it should be noted that there is evidence that there once existed feathered dinosaurs, but they are believed to have been the transitional genetic ancestors of the modern bird.)

Feathers act as insulation against cold and water. They aid in navigation during flight. For some birds, they act as natural camouflage thanks to their colors, and they can be wielded against an aggressor by making the animal look larger when the feathers are erect (Much like a cat can make its fur stand up to make it look bigger and more threatening.)

For many tribes, the significant role of raptors in spiritual beliefs has meant that these feathers indicate a level of honor for the person who possesses one. Eagle feathers may be given as a sign that a person has accomplished a great deed. At a modern powwow, if a feather falls to the floor, all action stops until the feather can be safely and appropriately lifted from the ground.

The Eagle feather law

If you cannot prove that you are a member of an American Indian tribe, and you are caught possessing an eagle feather, you can be fined up to $25,000 and also face a possible prison sentence.

There are several laws on the books prohibiting owning an eagle feather. These include the Endangered Species Act, the Migratory Bird Treaty Act, and the Lacey Act. However, there is also a law known as the Eagle feather law (Title 50 Part 22 of the United States Code of Federal Regulations) which provides exceptions to these laws that allow Native Americans to own eagle feathers for use in religious ceremonies.

A Native American must apply for a permit and prove his or her tribal affiliation before being allowed to purchase an eagle feather. And the feathers acquired must be used only in a religious ceremony, and cannot be sold as a collectible or for use on clothing or headwear as adornment.

The Eagle feather law has been repeatedly challenged over the years. The argument is that the law is unconstitutional and violates the First Amendment, which states, "Congress shall make no law respecting an establishment of religion. . . ."

Beads

Many types of beads have been developed and used by Native peoples:

- **Bones:** Animal bones were often hollowed out and worn as beads. The bones of birds and turtles especially made for nice tubular beads.

- **Teeth:** Mammal teeth were often strung together or sewn onto garments. The teeth of foxes, bears, coyotes, wolves, elks, and other animals native to a tribe's area were used as jewelry.

- **Claws:** As they did with mammal teeth, Natives often made great use of the claws of bears, big cats, wolves, and other predatory animals with large articulated claws.

- **Ceramic:** These were made from clay and heated and shaped into tubes, hollow balls, and barrel-shape beads. Because of their organic makeup, though, many ceramic beads didn't survive very long.

- **Copper:** Metal beads were made from copper, both that brought by Europeans and copper from local sources, such as the Great Lakes region.

- **Shells:** Both the aforementioned quahog, whelks, and other types of shells were used to make ornaments and beads for clothing and jewelry.

- **Stones:** Naturally ground rocks were often pretty and of a size that lent themselves to drilling and stringing. Turquoise, in particular, has long been associated with Native American jewelry of the Southwest tribes and its vivid color spectrum, ranging from bright blue to blue-green to yellow-green.

Footwear

The most well-known item of Native American footwear is the moccasin.

This versatile, easy-to-make, super-comfortable shoe is an example of how function mandates form. Native Americans needed a foot covering — a shoe — for walking through forests, across rocky areas, in sand, and on trails. Since they used the resources of nature available to them, the earliest moccasins resulted from a single piece of tanned hide — usually deer, bear, moose, or elk — that was folded up over the foot and sewn together.

There were several types of moccasins:

- The Northwest moccasin was two piece and had a soft sole.
- The Southwest moccasin two piece and had both hard and soft soles.
- The Southeast moccasin was two piece and had a hard sole.
- The Northeast moccasin was one piece and had a soft sole.

From their earliest forms as a plain, one-piece slipper-like shoe, the moccasin evolved, depending on the area in which the tribes lived and hunted. Modifications, again, came into being based on function. The form was adapted according to need. Some of these improvements included

- Doubling the thickness of the sole
- Adding flaps of leather or fur — cuffs of a sort — for warmth and to further protect the feet
- Connecting the moccasin to leggings
- Adding a tongue to further cover the top of the foot
- Adding beads for decoration

For a detailed look at the different types of moccasins by tribe and area, check out the Map of North America with Native American Varieties of Moccasins (www.nativetech.org/clothing/moccasin/mocmap.html). (We like the Mi'kmaq moccasin with the center seam and folded-down ankle flaps. In case you were wondering.)

The other common forms of Native American footwear were sandals and boots. Also, in the northern climes, the Inuits and Aleuts made snowshoes for trekking across snow-covered regions. Snowshoes (see Figures 14-3 and 14-4 for examples) were tennis racket–shaped footwear made from interlaced strips of leather.

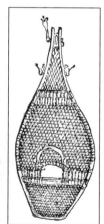

Figure 14-3: An Indian snowshoe.

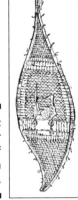

Figure 14-4:
Another
type of
Indian
snowshoe.

Sandals were often woven from plant fibers and were more common in the Southwest. Sandals from dry caves in west Texas can be 4,000 years old and still look like you could wear them today. Boots were leather and came up on the calf to just below the knee. Boots were made and worn in lieu of attaching leggings to moccasins.

Headdresses

The classic, traditional feathered headdress so familiar from paintings and movies is believed to have been created by the Sioux and then disseminated throughout the other Native tribes in the historical period.

The beautifully ornate feathered headdress was not just for adornment, or worn as a show of ostentatious tribal pride. Each feather in a warrior's headdress was *earned*, oftentimes for kills in battle, although feathers were also awarded for any act perceived by the tribe to be an act of bravery.

A young man often received his first feather upon entering adulthood. As you can imagine, it took a long time for a warrior to accumulate enough feathers to assemble them into a headdress. The finest headdresses used primarily eagle feathers, although feathers from other birds were also used for decoration and to fill it out.

Carrying out the deeds and acts of bravery required to "earn" a feathered headdress was difficult and took a long time. There are stories of warriors who earned only a few feathers throughout their lives. Each feather told a story, and a good comparison would be military medals earned and worn by soldiers for meritorious acts of bravery or for being injured in battle.

Traditional Dress Today

On September 21, 2004, Colorado Senator Ben Nighthorse, who is part Cheyenne, appeared at the opening of the Smithsonian's National Museum of the American Indian in full tribal dress.

And then he went to work. At the Senate. In full tribal dress.

Americans of Native heritage, whether they be full- or mixed-blood, today are embracing their past, and one of the ways they are doing this is by wearing Native American garments.

The clothing is almost always newly manufactured, although many Natives do own and wear on occasion an artifact from their ancestors, be it a leather pouch, or a beaded choker or bracelet.

Dressing for a powwow

A powwow is a gathering of Native Americans that includes marches, dancing, music, prayers and invocations, and Native foods. They are planned well in advance and are open to the public — both Natives and non-Natives. There is sometimes an admission charge and an organized program of events.

If you attend a powwow, don't go running into the dance circle uninvited. Also, you will see chairs set up in a circle just inside the perimeter of the circle. Do not sit in these chairs, thinking you've got a front-row seat at the event! These chairs are for the dancers and drummer.

Some of the traditional powwow events include

- ✔ **The Grand Entry:** The dancers enter the Dance circle while a very long drum song is played.

- ✔ **Dances and dance competitions:** Some dances are performed for attendees; other dances are done for prizes and awards.

- ✔ **Food vendors:** Native foods like Indian tacos, as well as typical "event" foods like hot dogs, hamburgers, and lemonade are sold.

- ✔ **Healing rituals:** Some powwows offer individual healing sessions with Native healers.

- ✔ **Interaction and picture posing:** Natives dress in full regalia for powwows and will often pose for pictures and answer questions about their outfits.

The regalia worn by Native Americans at a powwow is not, and should never be, called a costume. These outfits are handmade and are often decorated with revered family memorabilia, including sacred eagle feathers and beaded jewelry passed down from family elders and ancestors.

Powwows are opportunities for dancers and tribe members to gather with a sense of community and heritage, while also educating non-Natives about their culture, history, traditions, and garments.

Photographs should only be taken when you have the specific permission of the person being photographed, or when the event announcer says it is allowed. This varies from powwow to powwow.

Fashion looks to the past

Today, the influence of Native Americans on clothing is everywhere, and there are two facets to this presence:

- Traditional Native American garb boldly worn as a tribute to the traditions and past of Native peoples
- Native influences on ordinary Anglo clothing

Traditional regalia in the form of robes, dresses, jewelry, capes, shirts, breastplates, shawls, leggings, moccasins, and headdresses is available from retailers both in stores and online. Some of these garments are made by Native Americans, using as many traditional materials as they can acquire. Some are made by clothing manufacturers as replica items for people who don't require that the garments actually be made by an member of a tribe.

The other aspect of Native American influence on modern-day clothing is found in the presence of elements in garments that are unabashedly tribal — a fusion of American, European, and Native American styles, including

- Fringes on jackets
- Native patterns on dresses and skirts
- Pullover shirts with lace ties
- Suede fringed vests
- Beaded jewelry
- Patterned headbands
- Fringed and feathered handbags
- Ribbon shirts and tops
- Blanket coats

The Native American style has become commonplace in mainstream American clothing. Many Americans have worn a pair of moccasins or a turquoise ring or pendant. And many Americans own at least one thing — from a skirt to a pocketbook — with a little bit of leather fringe on it. Sure, there are those who have not purchased any clothing whatsoever bearing a Native American flair to it, but each year, almost all the major designers show fashions boasting at least a little Native style.

So, hoestõtse for success! (That's "dress for success" in Ojibwe and English!)

Chapter 15

Home, Native Home

*I*n the hierarchy of human needs, after our need for air, water, food, and sleep are satisfied, shelter and safety come next. This is universal for all human beings, and Native Americans developed innovative and creative ways to create a wide variety of shelters to provide this necessity. Each unique structure reflected not only their local climate, but also made excellent use of the array of natural resources available to them.

Trees were used for wood; plants for thatch; earth for mud. Native Americans looked around and asked themselves, "How can I use what I see to create a place to live?" (Maybe they didn't sit around actually asking each other that question. But you get the point.)

This chapter explores the many housing styles invented by different tribes, which are still in use today or have inspired other contemporary styles.

Wooden Homes

The original Native people were practical environmentalists. And many Native Americans today continue to "think green." Regarding the earliest Indigenous people, the key word is "practical."

For many tribes, the natural world played a large role in spiritual life. For this reason, it didn't make sense to exploit nature to the point of devastation — it would be like sacrilege. Trees were used for raw wood for building. The bark was used for roofing and siding. Grasses and branches were also used for protective covering and shelter. Saplings were used as cord. Many tribes had specific prayers for the construction of a new dwelling that acknowledged the role of both the community and the environment in bringing it forth. This section looks at a few of the most common Native American homes and dwellings, from simple lean-tos, to the legendary and undeniably iconic igloo, the only house built from snow.

Plankhouses

Plankhouses were constructed in a range of sizes, the larger ones for use as an extended family residence. The design of the plankhouse is long and rectangular, with a sloped, inverted "V" roof. Like a barn without a wide door at the end. This type of house was common in areas where the forests were extensive enough to accommodate harvesting.

Plankhouses were common among the northern California and Pacific Northwest Indian tribes.

They were built by the Tlingit, the Yurok, and other tribes of the West and Northwest, but the construction varied according to the tribe. Tribes in the Northwest Coast built houses of red cedar, spruce planks with vertical boards and an inverted V-shaped roof. Plankhouses had one door, which was sometimes round; they had no windows, and there was a pit in the center of the floor where the heating and cooking fire was built. A hole in the roof allowed the smoke to escape.

The really large plankhouses often housed more than one family, and woven cedar mats were used to create individual "rooms" of a sort for sleeping and private activities.

Commonly, a ledge or bench was constructed inside the house at about waist height for sitting and storage. Some houses were marked by the presence of totem poles that identified the clans or moieties of the houses.

For a virtual tour of the inside of a Yurok plankhouse, visit www.virtual guidebooks.com/NorthCalif/RedwoodPark/PatricksPoint/ YurokHouseInteriorL.html.

Longhouses

The Mohawks, Oneidas, Onondagas, Cayugas, Senecas, and Tuscaroras refer to themselves collectively as the *Haudenosaunee*, which means "People Building a Long House." This confederacy was perceived to be an enormous, invisible longhouse stretching from coast to coast and housing all the families of the six tribes. That's a beautiful image, isn't it?

Not to be flip, but longhouses (see Figure 15-1) were *long*. The typical longhouse was between 180 and 220 feet long, but evidence of a 400-foot longhouse has been found in upstate New York.

Longhouses needed to be long, as they were designed to house several families, each of which needed its own sleeping and storage bunks and spaces, as well as its own central fire. There was a hole in the roof above each fire, and this would tell visitors how many families lived in a particular longhouse. Some longhouses were big enough to house a hundred (or more) people.

Longhouses were built by placing poles in the ground at specific intervals based on the planned finished length. Long logs would then be attached to the poles lengthwise for strength. The roof was made of sheets of bark that were attached to the tops of the support posts after they had been bent toward the opposite side of the frame. Bark was also used for the walls.

Figure 15-1:
A longhouse.

Hogans

The hogan is a Navajo dwelling that is one of their most sacred of built places. Hogans can be described as male and female, based on their construction. They have been used as both a home and a place for rituals.

- ✔ Male: This one uses a forked stick placed facing south, onto which a straight pole is propped facing north. East and west poles are then placed. It is pyramidal in shape and is used only for rituals. Its walls are a combination of branches, strips of bark, and earth. A smoke hole is left at the top, and the poles are put in place in the specific order of east, south, west, north.

✓ **Female:** The female hogan was originally dome-shaped, but after the 1900s and the prevalence of the railroad running through Indian lands, the availability of surplus, straight railroad ties resulted in new, octagonal-shaped structures. These newer hogans have eight sides and are much larger than the male hogan. Logs are interlocked as in a log cabin, and the roof is domed. These larger hogans were ideal for family living, but are also a place where sacred rituals are performed.

First Man and First Woman, with help from Coyote and Beaver, built the first hogan, and these places are considered a spiritual necessity for Navajos today. Many modern Navajo will construct a hogan on their property for ceremonial uses — even while living in a much more contemporary home.

Chickees

Have you ever been to a park or beach area where there was a roofed, open-sided pavilion under which there were picnic tables, and sometimes barbecue grills? People often congregate beneath this structure to escape a brief shower at the beach, or when the sun just gets too darn hot.

We can thank the Seminole Indians of Florida for this type of sheltering structure, which is called a chickee. The chickees were originally developed by the Seminole as structures that could be quickly assembled and disassembled while people were on the run in the 1800s from American soldiers.

Chickees have no walls, but that's okay, since the climate where they were invented was always warm. The original chickees had a thatched roof that was supported by logs. Today's modern versions use either steel or wood support beams and a wood or shingled roof.

Some chickees had a raised floor, allowing sleeping and comfort off the ground, but the sides were still wide open.

Chickee means "house" in the Seminole language.

Tipis

In contemporary American culture (at least for the past century or so), the tipi has become so associated with Indians that many Native Americans today feel its image has devolved into a stereotype.

It's not so much that the tipi (see Figure 15-2) has become an offensive slur, but more that it's now almost trite from overuse (as well as from misuse, oftentimes conflating all Native Americans tribes into one huge tipi-inhabiting clan — that just ain't so), and, thus, is commonly not given the respect the dwelling deserves. As is common with many aspects of Indian culture, there is a spiritual component to the erection of a tipi and to its occupancy.

Tipis have been used by Plains tribes for thousands of years, according to archaeologists, who have identified rings of rocks believed to have been used to hold down the tipi covers. Today, many people in Plains tribes continue to use tipis, but not as permanent housing. At Crow Fair, an event held by the Crow Nation in Montana, many people bring tipis to camp in during the days of the fair. This event has been described as the "tipi capital of the world!"

"Tipi" is the Sioux spelling of the word. Also commonly used in mainstream cultural writings are "tepee" and "teepee."

The exterior of the tipi is made from hides. Flaps controlled by poles or ropes allow a fire to be built inside the dwelling. These openings also serve as a ventilation source. During cold winters, an interior lining is often used for additional warmth. The tipi's cone shape is remarkably stable in high winds, as long as the support poles are securely anchored.

Tipis are also portable, which allowed tribes to set up villages as they followed herds of buffalo, move to uncultivated lands, or established camps (see Figure 15-3) near streams for the fishing seasons.

The poles of the tipi served a dual purpose: They could be used for a travois. (See Chapter 16 for more on the travois.) And in an example of true utility, the poles from a single tipi could provide the travelers with six or more travois for transporting.

Figure 15-2:
A tipi.

Figure 15-3:
An Indian
village.

Other Indian Dwellings

There were dozens of different types of Native American dwellings, and their conception and construction were dependent on:

- **Resources available:** Lots of trees? Few trees? Lots of moist earth? Lots of reeds? Easy availability of animals whose skins could be used for construction? More rocks than anything else?
- **Climate:** Dry and hot? Rainy? Windy? Snow and cold?
- **Geographic area:** Was the area close to a river and villages were relatively permanent? Was the area noted for migrating herds that had to be followed? Were interlopers and enemies likely to force tribes off their land, thus requiring portability?

The Europeans were amazed by the variety of dwellings Indians had created in adaptation to their surroundings.

Wigwams and wickiups

A wigwam (see Figure 15-4) is a form of dwelling that is commonly dome-shaped with a sapling frame that is then covered with hides or bark, which was then commonly covered with grass or thatch.

Wigwams were commonly used in the U.S. Northeast. In other areas, especially the southwestern United States, the same type of structure is called a wickiup.

Figure 15-4:
A wigwam.

Igloos

The igloo is a cold-climate domed shelter built with blocks of snow, and it is one of humankind's truly innovative structures. Igloos were used by people in the Western Arctic, including Greenland. The film *The Journals of Knud Rasmussen* (see Chapter 24) made by Zacharias Kunuk has a great scene of people building an igloo. Most indigenous shelters are designed with only what's available in nature, but the igloo really wins the prize for doing the most with what could reasonable be described as the least.

Igloos are the ultimate in environmentally friendly housing in that they are constructed only from a renewable and recyclable resource — snow!

Igloos are made from snow blocks that are cut from snow using special knives. The blocks are placed in a spiral pattern so that each is slightly leaning on the next. An igloo might have a tunnel entrance that was slightly sunken in the ground to trap the cold outside air at a lower position relative to the living quarters inside.

Igloos are very sturdy structures, and their construction takes advantage of the physical properties of snow. After an igloo was constructed, but before a smoke hole was carved out, a lit oil lamp would be placed inside the dome of snow blocks. The heat from the lamp would eventually melt the snow blocks slightly, which would refreeze with exposure to the cold outside air, providing a layer of ice over the inside that was both insulating and strengthening to the structure. Over time, as people lived inside, the snow blocks would eventually become more ice than snow. There are stories that people could even stand on top of an igloo without fear of it caving in.

Snow is a magnificent insulator. The interior temperature of a well-built igloo could range from around freezing (32 degrees Fahrenheit/0 degrees Celsius) to the 40s (Fahrenheit) and warmer.

An air hole is always made in the top of the igloo, since a human's exhalations could cause a build-up of carbon dioxide if it is not vented, which could be lethal.

The Inuits know not to build a fire inside an igloo. Smoke inhalation and melting snow could combine to make it a very dangerous situation. Candles or small oil lamps are okay, though.

Interestingly, scientists that have studied the temperatures inside igloos and analyzed how body heat, combined with the snow's insulating properties, affect internal air temps, have determined that, believe it or not, the best way to be the warmest inside an igloo is to be naked.

The radiating heat from a nude human body serves to warm the interior air to its maximum. Human body heat is captured inside clothing, instead of emanating up, so being clothed actually results in a person being *colder*. (Heat rises, after all.) But, we can hear you wondering, won't the snow floor be a tad chilly on a person's . . . y'know? Sure, but one can always sit on a coat or a sweater, while still allowing the mini-furnace that is our body to heat the air. Maybe that's why some Inuits and other Arctic region Indians were known to sometimes line the interiors of their igloos with skins and hides?

Earth lodges

Earth lodges are also called sod houses, and they are constructed almost solely from sod either above or below ground. Many tribes used some form of earth lodge, but the ones used by Plains tribes such as the Mandan and Hidatsa are known to have been in use in the 19th century. George Catlin painted many pictures that show people and their lodges. If you want to stand inside an earth Evidence of an earth lodge was found by archaeologists during excavations on Macon Plateau and this structure is believed to date to nearly a thousand years ago. The Macon earth lodge has been reconstructed, down to the bird-shaped altar made from earth inside the building.

Regarding the earth lodge, there's a bit of crossover with other Native American homes, since many other types of dwellings use sod as a building material for walls and even ceilings.

The Earliest Apartment Buildings

In the Southwest, around 900 years ago, ancient Pueblo peoples built apartment complexes using adobe, which is a brick made from straw and dried mud.

These structures were amazing, and many still stand and can be visited. Inside the cliff dwellings of the Anasazi at Mesa Verde, for example, "suites" of rooms connect in very efficient design layouts, and evidence of communal rooms where the floor's cooking and heating fire still survive.

At the Pueblo Bonito ("pretty village") site in New Mexico, some archaeologists estimate the number of rooms as between 600 and 800, and housing over a thousand people. By any standards, that is quite the multi-person dwelling.

The interior rooms were connected by hallways, and access to the outside was via a main courtyard where kivas — below ground ceremonial areas — were located. For a virtual tour of the Pueblo Bonito ruins, check out the University of Colorado's QuickTime "visit" at `www.colorado.edu/Conferences/chaco/tour/pbtour/fs2.htm`.

Native American Housing Today

In June 2005, 56 percent of the United States's 4.5 million Native Americans owned their own home. But this number jumps to greater than three-quarters when specifically looking at homeownership on Native American reservations. Nationally, the overall U.S. homeownership rate is around 70 percent. (Source: U.S. Census Bureau.)

There are around 300 federally recognized reservations in the United States. About half of the U.S. Native American population live on reservations; the others live in houses, apartments, and mobile homes in both urban and rural areas. Interestingly, though, the percentage of apartment dwellers among Native Americans is a fraction of American apartment occupancy rates. The U.S. Census Bureau tells us that 27 percent of Americans nationwide live in apartments. That rate is only 5 percent for Native Americans on reservations. Here's how the housing breaks down:

- **Single-family homes:** 56 percent all Native Americans; 75 percent plus on reservations (U.S. average: 70 percent)

- **Mobile homes:** 12 percent all Native Americans; 14 percent on reservations (U.S. average: 7 percent)

- **Apartments:** 28 percent all Native Americans; 5 percent on reservations (U.S. average: 27 percent)

What is life like on a reservation where half of the U.S.'s Native Americans live? The answer varies based on the reservation.

Some reservations are enormous, equal or larger than some states. (The total number of acres of reservation land in the United States is 55.7 million.) On many reservations, poverty is high, as are unemployment, alcoholism, and crime.

The vast majority of reservations are not involved in gaming, and many tribes refuse to exploit mineral rights for coal and oil deposits beneath their lands. Most tribes that refuse to allow exploitation do so for cultural reasons.

The Mohawk Steelworkers

Mohawk David Rice, in a 2002 interview with *Indian Country News*, said the only way to walk around on girders 110 stories off the ground without a safety harness or a net is to put one foot in front of the other, look straight ahead, and never, under any circumstances, *look down*. Yikes. Sounds like good advice, eh?

During the interview, Rice tells about the time he actually did freeze while walking across a girder with a bucket of bolts on his shoulder. What did he do? He stood there until the paralysis passed and then, "I just walked to safety."

This incident is an interesting metaphor for Indian self-sufficiency. He had to save himself, because he knew no one would come out to help him. That's apparently one of the rules of high-rise work: better to lose one man than two.

Rice was working on a building in lower Manhattan on September 11, 2001, as were many Mohawk ironworkers, and after he realized what had happened, he averted his gaze from the smoke rising into the air from the World Trade Center.

Mohawk steelworkers began in the late 1880s working on the Quebec Bridge across the St. Lawrence River. When the first design of the bridge collapsed in 1904, 33 of the 75 workers that were killed were Mohawks. Since then, Mohawks have become known as some of the finest steelworkers in the world.

A resume to be proud of

The following are just a few of the projects in and around New York — and also across the country — that Mohawk steelworkers helped get off the ground:

- ✔ The Quebec Bridge
- ✔ The Empire State Building
- ✔ The Chrysler Building
- ✔ The Triboro Bridge
- ✔ The George Washington Bridge
- ✔ The Pulaski Skyway
- ✔ Rockefeller Center
- ✔ The Verrazano Bridge
- ✔ The West Side Highway
- ✔ Madison Square Garden
- ✔ The Golden Gate Bridge
- ✔ The World Trade Center

Chapter 16

Tools and Transportation

Animals provided food, clothing, tools, weapons, pouches, and oils, and people worked to ensure that the animals were accorded the respect that they deserved for providing all of this. In addition to using most parts of an animal out of respect for that creature, efficiency and frugality dictated people's behavior.

Indians made use of everything from the animal's fur, skin, teeth, and nails, to its bladder (for carrying), urine (for tanning), and, in the case of sharks on the eastern coast, its liver (for oil). The Calusa, for example, along Florida's southwest coast, went after great white sharks from which they would obtain more than 75 gallons of liver oil, which was used as a dietary supplement for its nutrients.

This chapter explores the ins and outs of all the uses the Indians made of animals.

Hunting and Trapping

Animals were both hunted and trapped. Also, the seas and lakes were harvested for fish, which was mainly used for food.

Bow and arrow

The ubiquitous bow and arrow has long been associated with Indians, although the weapon had a long history in Europe and Asia before it appeared in the area now known as Iowa around A.D. 500.

American Indians used the bow in battle (see Chapter 11) but its more common use was in hunting.

Bows were made from a flexible wood that was cut thin and then bent into a curved shape and held taut at both ends by a string made of sinew or a fiber. The arrows (see Figures 16-1, 16-2 and 16-3) were made of wood and feathers. (One valued type of wood, called Bois d'Arc, was traded from the Southeast throughout the country.)

A keen-eyed Indian archer could often down an animal with one shot. It was also said that the finest archers could get off six bulls-eye shots in a single minute.

Figure 16-1:
A bow and
arrow.

Figure 16-2:
Hunting
arrow.

Traps

Traps were used to snare all manner of animals, birds, and fish, and allowed Native hunters to set many in a range of locations and return to them later.

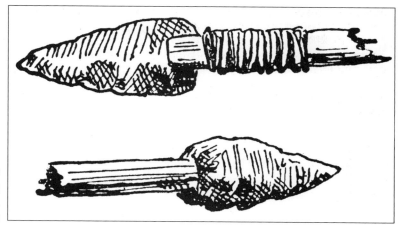

Figure 16-3:
Arrowhead.

Pit trap

Large animals were commonly caught with a *pit trap*. A pit would be dug and covered with camouflage and then animals would be steered or chased toward the pit. Once they fell through the reed or branches covering, they'd be killed and removed.

In some instances, the hunter would actually hide in the pit (obviously the pit would have to be wide enough and deep enough), and then bait would be placed on top of the pit's covering and secured so that it could not be removed. When a bird landed on the trap, or a small animal wandered onto it, attracted by the bait, the hunter would burst up out of the hole and kill his prey.

Deadfall trap

Another type of trap is the *deadfall trap*, so named because something heavy *falls* on the prey, and said prey is then *dead*!

Deadfall traps commonly attracted

- ✔ Ermine
- ✔ Mink
- ✔ Otter
- ✔ Wolves
- ✔ Weasels

This type of trap can be made with nothing but sticks, cordage (plants can be drawn and wound into cords if actual twine or string isn't available), and something heavy, like a large rock or a heavy piece of log. The heavy object is propped up so that when the bait is taken, the stick holding it up falls away and the object drops onto the animal. If the object is large and heavy enough, and the animal of a smallish size, the blow would usually kill it. If not, it would at least trap it beneath the object so the hunter could retrieve it and deal it the killing blow.

There are some terrific QuickTime movies of deadfall traps being constructed and tripped at the Wildwood Survival Web site on their page http://wildwoodsurvival.com/survival/traps/paiute/paiute01.html.

Fish weir trap

A *weir* is an enclosure made of netting or stakes that is set in a stream and used to catch fish. Metal, hinged, spring-loaded traps came later, in the early 1800s. Beaver traps were carried by members of the Lewis and Clark expedition.

Snare trap

An animal caught in a snare trap — rabbit, fox, small cats — would strangle to death from the rawhide loop they inadvertently stuck their head through.

Some snares would choke the trapped animal on the ground. Others used the bent wood that would release when tripped and suspend the animal off the ground, literally hanging them until they died. Since a snare trap is constructed of natural materials, it would essentially be invisible to the prey, blending in beautifully with its surroundings, and the animal would be trapped before it realized it had "stepped on a landmine," so to speak (and to shamelessly mix metaphors!).

Carrying the Load

Bowls and baskets were utilitarian and used for:

- **Harvesting:** Corn, berries, fruits, shells, stones, and other items of value to Indians were all carried in baskets.

- **Cooking:** Pottery bowls were placed in a fire pit or over a ground fire. Food could also be cooked in baskets by placing heated rocks into a tightly woven basket.

- **Fishing:** Clams and fish were collected and carried in open-weave baskets.

- **Storage:** Grains and other foodstuffs were stored in both pots and baskets.

- **Burial:** Sometimes decorated pots were placed in graves with the deceased. For some tribes, a hole would be put in the pot to symbolically kill it.

Baskets

Baskets (see Figure 16-4) were commonly made from plants and reeds that were abundant in the region, and the strands would be wrapped around support rods made from branches cut and trimmed to size.

Native tribes by the coasts wove some of their baskets loosely and widely so there were holes through which water could drain. Fish and clams would be caught and harvested and tossed in the basket, usually with lots of water, which would then drain out. These types of open-weave baskets were a clever and simple solution that:

- ✔ Drained excess water
- ✔ Reduced weight
- ✔ Allowed air to circulate through the harvested seafood

Smart.

Baskets were also often decorated with symbols and designs. Each tribe had their own styles of baskets and design patterns (see Figure 16-5). Because of their fragility, very few baskets have survived the passage of time, although pieces of woven mats and basket fragments have been found in rock shelters in the Lower Pecos region of Texas from up to 2,000 years ago. Plant fibers rot, thus their lack of durability and longevity.

The Burke Museum of Natural History & Culture in Seattle, Washington, has a terrific display of burden baskets and their Web site offers an amazing online exhibit of their holdings. Check it out at `www.washington.edu/burke museum/baskets/index.html`.

Figure 16-4:
Basket.

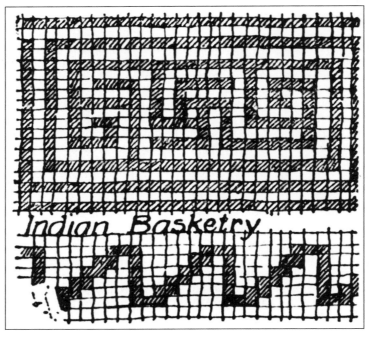

Indian Basketry

Figure 16-5:
Basket
pattern.

Bowls

Native American bowls were sometimes made of wood, but were mostly pottery. Bowls were also made from gourds that would be dried out and allowed to harden.

The story goes that Native Americans discovered the craft of pottery by accident. They purportedly covered their woven baskets with clay mud to protect them, and perhaps so they could be placed over a fire for cooking purposes. To their surprise, the mud hardened! It was probably one of those sudden light bulb moments: Some long-gone Native American man or woman was watching their fire and suddenly discovered that the mud was now a hard shell. A solid, hard-shelled container . . . how nifty! Or something akin to that probably leaped into their mind.

All Native American pottery was made by hand, since the potter's wheel was a European invention. Indigenous people (in Central America) had the wheel; for some reason, it was never adapted for use in throwing pottery.

All the Native American cultures — North, South and Southeast, Central, and Southwest — made their own bowls. As early as 2500 B.C., the Archaic Indians along the west coast of North America were making bowls (and baskets).

Other containers

Deerskin pouches and bags were also common among Native Americans. Many Europeans noticed that the Indians always had some sort of bag or pouch around their waist or slung over their shoulder.

These carry-alls were made from deerskin, animal bladders, and woven fabrics and were used to carry

- Tobacco
- Medicinal herbs and other medicines
- Food
- Good luck totems
- Ammunition
- Sewing supplies
- Flints for starting fires
- Cornmeal for mixing with water and making a quick meal
- Small tools

Also, Native Americans made sheaths and scabbards from deerskin and other materials and hides for carrying daggers and knives.

Puzzle pouches

The Iroquois, Mohawk, and other woodland Indians made a special type of leather pouch that was known as a "puzzle pouch." Why? Because it was a puzzle as to how to open it!

The pouch was made with interwoven strips of leather in such a way that if you didn't know how to open it, you'd have to figure it out or have someone show you.

The pouches were also apparently used in a game in which some object was placed in the pouch and then the pouch was passed around and players had to guess what the object was.

NativeTech.org has a page on their site where you can learn how to make an actual Native American puzzle pouch: `www.nativetech` `.org/clothing/pouch/puzzlepouch/` `puzzlepouchinstructions.html`.

Puzzle pouches seemed to have been made solely for fun. Not that there's anything wrong with that.

Travel Plans

How do you get around when you have no wheeled transports and you haven't yet been introduced to the horse? Or the stagecoach? Or the Chevy Tahoe?

You walk, or you use the waterways. And that's precisely how Native Americans traveled throughout the North American continent in the 16th and 17th centuries.

This section looks at some of the more common means of transportation by both Native Americans in the lower North American continent and the Inuit tribes up north.

Dugout canoe

If you "dig out" a log, said log is now "dug out," right? And that's exactly how dugout canoes were made. First, a fire would be set down the middle of the log to efficiently get rid of the central portion. Next, using hand tools, the log was chopped at and gouged out until it was deep and open enough to comfortably fit one or more people.

The natural buoyancy of the wood made this simple vessel one of the most useful and ubiquitous forms of transportation for Native Americans. Wooden paddles were likewise carved from tree branches and small logs and used for steering.

Bark canoe

Unlike the dugout canoe (see Figure 16-6), a bark canoe was built in steps and comprised of two separate parts: a wooden frame and a bark outer shell. The bark was almost always birch, and it would be removed in a large single sheet and then stretched out and shaped to fit the wooden frame.

The appeal of these types of canoes is that they were very light and, thus, very portable. They could also be easily manned by a single paddler, and large quantities of goods could be easily transported in its large hull. The downside was that they were more fragile than the solid, one-piece dugout canoes. But they were also quickly repairable. The thin bark hull was susceptible to damage from rocks and other natural impediments, but with some spruce gum and a small piece of spare spruce bark (carried along for exactly this eventuality), it could be easily patched.

Kayak and umiak

The Inuits in the Arctic regions invented the kayak and the umiak more than 4,000 years ago. The difference between the two is that the kayak is a covered boat and the umiak is an open boat.

The original kayak was made of wood and then covered with seal or walrus hide, including the top deck. There is a hole left in the center of the kayak for the paddler. The design of the boat meant that the pilot would remain relatively warm and dry while on the cold waters of the Pacific Northwest. The kayak was propelled by a two-headed paddle so the pilot did not have to switch hands.

Kayaks are still in use today and kayaking is a popular sport. But what was true in the past is true today: If a kayak overturns, the kayaker goes with it! The boat and pilot are, in essence, one unit. Thus, a little training (and a lifejacket) is probably a good idea before hitting the white-water rapids on your vacation.

The umiak, on the other hand, was open, like a canoe, but instead of a wooden or bark hull, it was likewise covered in walrus or seal hide. Umiaks held several people (also unlike the kayak, which was limited to one, sometimes two people) and could transport supplies and goods easily.

Umiaks were also used for fishing and whale-hunting expeditions.

Figure 16-6:
A canoe.

Bull boat

Now, this was a weird one.

Picture a floating bowl. Got it?

That's a bull boat.

Bull boats were made from birch wood that was shaped into a round shape and then covered with buffalo skin which had not been "de-haired." We can only imagine the difficulty to navigate these vessels, yet they were common among several tribes, especially the Mandan and Hidatsa.

Snowshoes

All snowshoes don't look like tennis rackets strapped to a person's feet.

Okay, I'll admit it, though: That *is* the image most of us are familiar with, and movies and television have perpetuated this version of the snowshoe.

The truth, however, is that each tribe designed snowshoes to accommodate the snowfall in their region, and there were many styles created. Many were modeled on animals' feet and paws; some were designed for specific types of snow: deep and wet; fluffy; in forests; on plains, and so forth.

Apparently, no one knows when the snowshoe was invented, but it's not a surprise it was. The earliest snowshoes were being used in central Asia between 4,000 and 6,000 years ago, and it is believed that the Indians who migrated across the Bering Strait (see Chapter 2) brought them with them.

Here's a rundown of the types of snowshoes a few different "cold weather" tribes used:

- ✔ **Huron:** Paddle-shaped
- ✔ **Ojibwa:** Pointed tip
- ✔ **Athabaskans:** Upturned toe
- ✔ **Attikamek:** Square toe, tight finely woven midsection

The snowshoe was one of those inventions that illustrates and truly validates the adage about necessity being the mother of invention. In order to hunt buffalo and other animals and survive, Native peoples needed to be able to walk across deep snow without sinking into it. Clever application of wood-working skills, along with sophisticated weaving, plus a soupcon of attentive observation of how animals walked across snow led to one of the most useful innovations of all time. (Until the snow blower came along, of course.)

Today's snowshoes are hi-tech and boast modern designs. They come in handy if you happen to live in an area that gets heavy snow. If you live year-round in Phoenix, though, then your tennis racket is probably the closest thing to a snowshoe you'll ever lay your hands on. (And we hope you don't mind that we just perpetuated a snowshoe stereotype!)

Plank canoe

The Chumash people were from an area that is now southern California. They were the inventors and sailors of the plank canoe, a vessel known as a *tomol* in their native language.

These boats were between 10 and 30 feet in length and were commonly made from redwood and pine. The tomol may have been one of the only Native water vessels that was assembled in part using glue.

This is how a typical *tomol* was built:

- ✔ The length of the boat was decided on and a one-piece flat floor was made.

- ✔ The depth of the boat was decided on and thin wood planks were stacked up on each side of the boat, edge to edge until the desired height was reached and these planks were then glued into place using a cement made from pine tar and asphalt called asphaltum, also known as *yop*.

- ✔ Once the glue dried (and this is the clever part), small holes were drilled in the planks adjacent to each other and then twine made from plant fibers was threaded through the holes and tied tightly to add strength to the bond of the cement.

- ✔ Once all the planks were tied together securely, the Chumash then painted the seams with more asphaltum to make the sides of the boat as watertight as possible. They also plugged the holes with the sticky substance. This didn't always work to keep water out of the boat, though, and one crew member was always assigned to continuously bail out the inevitable water seepage while they were underway.

Battles on snowshoes

During the French and Indian War, two battles were fought that are now known as the First Battle on Snowshoes (January 21, 1757) and the Second Battle on Snowshoes (March 13, 1758).

The battles occurred in upstate New York and pitted the French and their Indian allies against the British.

The battles bear this name because, yes, the British were wearing snowshoes for both conflicts.

The wounded land

One of the more notable painters of the American West was Edgar Samuel Paxson (1852–1929), most known for what many consider his masterpiece work, *Custer's Last Stand.*

In 1877, Paxson traveled the Lolo Trail—a 200-mile-long trail that stretches from Lolo, Montana, to Weippe Prairie, Idaho, and which was traveled by the Lewis and Clark Expedition — for the first time, and in his journal he noted that the ground had deep, long gouges in it.

These wounds in the land were from the dragging poles of the many Indian travois that had traversed the trail.

Today, there are *tomol* boats in museums that were built from original Chumash plans. However, no completely intact *tomol* boat has ever been found by archaeologists and historians.

Travois

A travois was made of two long sticks that were crisscrossed so that the front end could be draped across the animal's shoulder and not fall off.

Dogs and horses were the animals most commonly used for pulling a travois, but they were designed so that a person could drag one (although if it was piled with heavy load, the odds are the human dray horse probably wouldn't be able to drag it very far without resting).

The rear of the travois was dragged across the ground. There was a skin or some type of woven mesh covering stretched between the two rear ends of the sticks for carrying goods or people.

"Travois" comes from the Canadian French word *travail*, which means a frame for restraining a horse.

The travois was used widely in the fur trade in Canada. The benefit of its flat-bottomed design was that it could be dragged with very little resistance over even the rockiest or roughest terrain.

Initially, these wooden sleds were pulled by dogs (and, as mentioned, [unlucky] people). After the horse was introduced into Native American culture in the 16th century, it replaced dogs when the sleds were built larger and became heavier to pull.

Sled

A sled has two parallel runners across which slats of wood or leather are placed. It is pulled across snow or ice by people or dogs. (And it was often Native women who pulled the sleds.)

The Sioux used buffalo ribs for the cross-slats; most of time they were made from stripped and cut-to-length wood.

Toboggan

The toboggan, which is technically a sled, too, does not have runners or skis. It, instead, has a flat bottom with a curved front and it is pulled by a rope.

The word *toboggan* comes from the Algonquian word *odabaggan*.

Since flat, wide boards were unknown to the Eastern Indians, toboggans were built from strips of bark, or thin pieces of wood strapped together.

"Get the sled"

Sleds weren't only used by Native Americans; settlers made good use of them as well.

The acclaimed HBO western, *Deadwood*, which takes place in Deadwood, South Dakota, during the gold rush of the 1870s, was about miners who flocked onto Indian territory to make their fortune.

Because the Deadwood camp was illegal and not part of the United States, there were no laws, and a death a day from violence (or accident) was common Saloon owner Al Swearengen, the camp's de facto leader, owned a large wooden sled with runners. The thoroughfare of the town was either sandy dirt or mud, depending on the weather, and the sled's runners made it easy to pull it through town regardless of the condition of the ground.

Whenever a body needed to be transported to Doc Cochran's (or to Wu's pigsty), Al's employees would hear him shout down from his office, "Get the sled."

Part IV

All in the (Native American) Family

In this part . . .

Today, families are nuclear, blended, or dysfunctional. (Just kidding. Sort of.)

Native American tribes are structured a little differently — clans and bands are the organizational units — and in this part we'll learn how tribe members combine and interact with each other, and who does what in the American Indian family both in the past, and in these modern times.

You'll also learn about Native languages, both spoken and written, and study Indians' religious practices and faiths.

Chapter 17

Tribes, Clans, and Bands

*F*amilies have always come in all shapes and sizes, and this has been true since the earliest days of human civilization, up through today's advanced, technologically based societies.

At any given time in world history, human civilization has existed within a range of evolution and development, instead of all the people on earth being at a specific stage at the same time.

In the year 2000, for example, there were cultures and societies on planet earth that were, by any definition, primitive — lacking clean water, access to electricity, the ability to conceive and construct complex buildings and structures like bridges and other modern infrastructures, no access to medical care, and basic needs like food and shelter commonly going unfulfilled.

And at the very same time in that year 2000, there were cultures and societies on earth that were living, in a sense, in the future: They had unrestricted 24-hour electricity, water and sewage needs taken for granted, food of all kinds and varieties everywhere, advanced medical care a phone call away, wireless communications, Internet access.

The one constant regardless of a culture's stage of development, though, has always been the family and, on a larger scale, community. This fact always was, and still is, the guiding principle for American Indians.

Indians have many familial and societal constructs, with family always being the core of their society. In this chapter we look at these various forms of Native American community, particularly tribes, clans, and bands.

Coming to Terms in Indian Society

When talking about Indian society, it is important to remember that tribes are both political and cultural units. A tribe can be split into different groups, all of which are recognized as independent nations by the federal government. Within a tribe, there may be smaller groupings according to an individual's lineage or religious affiliation. Some tribes have religious societies and some have clans that are usually based on family relationships.

The tribes that are recognized as sovereign entities by the U.S. government are labeled as tribes or bands. In the case of Alaska, historical circumstances have meant that what might have been construed as a tribe in the lower 48 are instead incorporated as "Native Villages." These villages have the same authority as tribes, but what would have been a tribe farther south may be spread throughout several villages.

Clans exist among some tribes and a person belongs to a specific clan based on their family relationship. For some tribes, clans that existed in the past are no longer recognized because that information was lost during removal. Other tribes that were able to remain in their traditional territory continue to maintain strong clans.

A complete list of the tribes recognized by the federal government is published at regular intervals in the Federal Register.

The leader of a tribe is frequently called its chief, but today, the leader may also be the chairman of the tribal council.

The role of the chief has changed greatly over the years. The members of the De Soto expedition described rulers in the Southeast who had influence over large regions and who were described as *Caciques,* a word for leader the Spanish learned from the Taino. Anthropologists refer to these rulers as paramount chiefs, and ethnohistorical research indicates that they may have had influence over many smaller communities, each of which had its own leader.

In the 18th and 19th centuries, Europeans and Americans came to understand that one tribe might have more than one chief and that each individual had a different level of authority within the tribe. Among the tribes in the Southeast, both war and peace chiefs could be present and each had their own set of responsibilities.

By the time that the 20th century rolled around, the U.S. was trying to force tribes into a less traditional form of government. The Custis Act forced tribes to adopt the tribal council as a governing body, and the chair of the tribal council became the nominal ruler of the tribe. Today, many tribes continue this form of government, while maintaining some form of chief. The process whereby a chief becomes leader has changed as well, and today, men and women are elected to the role.

In Alaska, the combination of the Alaska Native Claims Settlement Act and the Indian Reorganization Act has resulted in Native Villages that have a tribal chair and Native corporations that handle the funds and resources for the tribes. A Native village may have multiple levels of governance.

(See Chapter 10 for more information on specific chiefs.)

American Indian tribal chiefs are the ones who are often remembered, by name, when certain tribes are spoken of — even by white people! Most Americans have heard of such tribal leaders as Geronimo, Crazy Horse, Cochise, and Sitting Bull.

The following list highlights some of the more unforgettable tribal chiefs:

- American Horse (Sioux)
- Black Elk (Lakota)
- Big Bear (Cree)
- Bigfoot (Lakota)
- Joseph Brant (Mohawk)
- Cochise (Apache)
- Crazy Horse/Tashunkewitko (Lakota)
- Dull Knife (Cheyenne)
- Geronimo/Goyathlay (Apache)
- Little Wolf (Lakota)
- Hole-in-the-Day (Ojibway)
- John Ross (Cherokee)
- Joseph (Nez Perce)
- Little Crow (Kaposia Sioux)
- Little Turtle (Miami)
- Little Wolf (Cheyenne)
- Low-Dog (Lakota)
- Ohiyesa/Dr. Charles Alexander Eastman (Santee Sioux)
- Pontiac (Ottawa)
- Red Cloud (Lakota)
- Red Jacket (Seneca)
- Santana (Kiowa)
- Sequoya (Cherokee)
- Sitting Bull (Hunkpapa Sioux)
- Spotted Tail (Brule Sioux)
- Standing Bear (Lakota)
- Tecumseh (Shawnee)
- Wilma Mankiller (Cherokee)
- Wolf Robe (Cheyenne)
- Wovoka (Paiute)

Today, the tribal chief is often the public face of modern tribal nations, but even though it is commonly an elected position, power is often consolidated in a Tribal Council with a leader elected or appointed and known as the Chair of the Council.

Men Ruled the Roost? Hardly

There was never, nor is there now, a "universal" model for Native American family structure. Some tribes have always been *matriarchal*; some have always been *patriarchal*; and there have always been tribes that were, in a sense, a commingling of both types of structures: the men "ruled" in certain situations; the women, in others.

We list the basic definitions of these two types of societal, tribal, and family structure in the following list:

- ✔ **Matriarchal:** This term describes a society in which power and property are controlled and held by women and are passed down through matrilineal descent. The mother's lineage is what determines power, control, heritage, and inheritance.

- ✔ **Patriarchal:** This refers to a society in which men are in charge. They have the power and authority, they own the property, they make the decisions.

There are also other variants of Native American familial organization besides the mother and father-based makeups, including:

- ✔ **Bilateral:** When both the mother and father's ancestry is of equal importance.
- ✔ **Patrilocal:** When the woman moves in with the man's family.
- ✔ **Matrilocal:** When the man moves in with the woman's family.

The Role of Women

A patriarchy is defined as a social system in which men are regarded as the authority within the family and the larger entity of the society, and in which power and possessions are passed on from father to son. At the time of the first European incursions into the new world, Europe had been, and continued to be, for the most part, comprised of unabashedly patriarchal societies.

And this is not surprising when we consider the political, judicial, and financial structure of these societies: They were monarchies. The king ruled everything. Thus, families mimicked this paradigm by considering the father of the family to be the king of his castle, in the, y'know, "a man's home is his castle" sense.

Thus, these patriarchal Europeans were both perplexed and surprised by the dominant role Native American women played within their families and tribes.

- ✔ Where was the passivity they had long demanded from the women in their own societies?

> ✔ Where was the deference to the male as the authority figure?
>
> ✔ Why were women allowed to make decisions, tell their husbands what to do, and assert such authority?

Although it is risky to assign a completely egalitarian profile to Native American families and tribes (since it's not really accurate in every case), there is no denying that the social makeup of Indian communities was much more democratic and classless than those in Europe.

How can this be? The Europeans asked. Didn't God make Adam first? Eve came from Adam's rib, their Christian dogma taught them. This meant that females were inferior and should be submissive, right?

A world of differences

All those rhetorical questions sum up the difference between the European gender mindset and that of the Native American.

European patriarchal males *allowed* women privileges and determined what rights and authority they had in their own families, and in society as a whole. Native Americans, on the other hand, respected the balance of nature and recognized that women and men each have equal roles to play.

Native American women wielded great power, and nowhere was this more evident than in the Iroquois tribes in the northeastern United States. Women of the Iroquois nation owned land, made important tribal decisions, and were recognized for their ultimate strength: the ability to give birth to new tribe members, thereby guaranteeing the continuation of the tribe. Today, important decisions for the Haudenosaunee are not made without consultation with and approval from the Clan mothers.

The Native American perspective of women is summed up beautifully — and with absolute truth — in this quote from Oglala Lakota Sioux warrior and compatriot of Crazy Horse, He Dog: "It is well to be good to women in the strength of our manhood because we must sit under their hands at both ends of our lives."

Workin' for a living

Native American women had many duties.

They worked so hard, and at so many tasks, that it was repeatedly noted that Europeans thought that women were slaves! When they witnessed them working their tails off, so to speak, they couldn't comprehend that women were honored and held in high regard by the tribes.

Some of their tasks included

- ✔ Assessing the domestic supplies needs and then making, by hand, whatever carrying devices, cooking pots, and work tools the family needed.
- ✔ Being responsible for the home and its construction. In some Pueblo and Plains tribes, the women were the actual homeowners and could divorce their husbands simply by putting his things outside the house.
- ✔ Being the primary "chef" for the family.
- ✔ Making sure that there were adequate supplies of water at all times.
- ✔ Raising, disciplining, and schooling the children.
- ✔ Taking care of the vegetable crops.
- ✔ Tanning and working with all the hides brought back by the men

Homemakers

The Native American woman was honored and protected because of her ability to bring new life into the community.

Women were the "life bringers" and the nurturers. They cared for the children, kept the home running smoothly, and were experts at skills ranging from cooking and weaving to crafts and farming.

Columbus noted (in fact, he was one of the first) how hard Native American women worked. He specifically stated that he felt that the women of the tribes he came into contact with worked much harder then the men did.

This is something of a misinterpretation of the social and cultural mores, practices, and customs of tribes, but it does emphasize that the role of the Native American woman was critical to the functioning of a tribe.

Craftspeople

The list of things that Indian women made sounds like an inventory of an aisle at Home Depot. And it also emphasizes just how hard women worked and how long their workday was.

They made

- ✔ **Cooking equipment:** Pots were made from pottery, bowls, too, and were used for cooking food in, storage, and as serving bowls. The Southwestern Indians used pottery. The Northwest Indians used tree bark to make containers for carrying and storage. Wood and woven baskets were also common.

> ✔ **Tools:** Native villages needed a wide variety of tools for working the fields, mixing clay and food, digging, scraping, polishing, and for use inside the room. For the most part, it was the women who took care of these needs.
>
> ✔ **Medicines:** Women were responsible for the gathering and sorting of the specific herbs and plants that could be used for healing and medicinal purposes.
>
> ✔ **Clothing:** American Indian women were responsible for making all the clothing for their family.

Farmers

American Indian women tilled the fields, gathered water for the crops, and took care of harvesting the grown vegetables.

It should be acknowledged that many Indian tribes kept slaves — both African and captured Indians from other tribes — and that they also took care of some of the agricultural work and domestic duties for families and the tribes as a whole.

Children

The familial and societal dynamic vis-à-vis children in Native American culture was, in a sense, a contradiction of terms.

Children were, at the same time, indulged and expected to behave in a certain way and achieve key growth and maturity milestones.

Child's play

Did Native American children have toys and play games and enjoy the free-spirited joy of childhood?

Every tribe, of course, had different attitudes toward children's play, as well as different expectations of children as they grew into adulthood, but, yes, Indian children did play games, and play with toys during childhood.

Girls played with dolls made from corn stalks, cattails, and other natural materials. Boys commonly played with miniature bows and arrows, and other hunting-themed toys, exposing them early on to their future responsibilities — feeding their families and learning how to utilize the bounties of their natural world.

The voyage to adulthood for Native Americans began almost the moment an Indian child was born.

Elders and parents taught by example, emulating both the habits of animals and Indian men.

Rituals and trials

Every culture has its own "coming of age" rights of passage.

- ✔ Jewish children have *bar* and *bah mitzvah* ceremonies.
- ✔ Some tribal African children track and hunt an animal.
- ✔ Catholic children experience the sacrament of confirmation.
- ✔ Australian aboriginal children go on "walkabout," during which they follow the tracks of their ancestors.

First menses

A young Native American woman's first menstrual period was a momentous event in her life, and it changed both the perception of her within the tribe, and also her role. She was no longer a child. She was now a woman, capable of bearing children.

The Navajo believe that Grandmother Moon determines a woman's cycles. Thus, a woman's menstrual period is often referred to as Moon Time. The Navajo puberty ceremony is called the *Kinaalda*.

Some tribes would mount ceremonies for the puberty rites, sometimes standing around a sacred fire, sometimes painting the young girl's face. Depending on the tribe, there were sometimes strict proscriptions against certain types of clothing, with special emphasis on which colors could and could not be worn. Some tribes also forbade the young girl from drinking water from a well, instead demanding she use a straw.

So, why all the rules? The answer to that question is completely dependent on the belief systems of the individual tribes.

Oftentimes when the rites of passage were completed, there would be feasting, accompanied by dancing and singing to honor the presence of a new adult woman — a new lifebringer — in the tribe.

Vision quest

Some tribes had the concept of a vision quest in which individuals would put themselves under stress in order to understand themselves more fully. For some of the Sioux tribes, a person might undergo a sweat lodge ceremony and then retire to a high or isolated place in hopes of receiving a vision that would help them throughout their lives.

The Sun Dance

Many Plains tribes practice the Sun Dance, which is a ritual involving dancing, chanting, praying, self-mutilation, and fasting. Its purpose is to give thanks and to pray for blessings upon one's family and tribe.

The Sun Dance was made illegal when the U.S. government outlawed it in 1904 because of the flesh-piercing aspect of the ritual and likely as a means of breaking tribal religion to assist with assimilation. President Jimmy Carter legalized it during his time in office and it is now practiced openly.

Chapter 18

Native Languages

*T*here never was, nor is there now, a standard, "universal" language spoken by all Native Americans.

In fact, such a language doesn't even exist. Members of tribes, if speaking in their own tribal language, will likely not be understood by members of other tribes, nor will what they hear spoken by others be understood by them.

An Impossible Question?

How many spoken Indian languages were in existence when the Europeans first arrived on the North American landmass?

It's a very good question, yet it is a question that has been a daunting challenge to answer for scholars, historians, and Native Americans for centuries.

Some sources state unequivocally that it is a question that is impossible to answer: Many encyclopedias state bluntly that it is simply not possible to know the number of languages that were spoken in the New World before the Europeans arrived. It's also impossible to know with certainty the number of people who spoke however many languages were being spoken.

Not possible.

So how do we "speak" intelligently about Indian languages? By concentrating on geographical areas and discussing the tribes of the area and the many individual languages they spoke.

Historians generally agree that there were nine basic Native American spoken language families:

- **Algic (Algonquin):** Parts of the midwestern United States, the Northeast, and most of Canada

- **Iroquoian:** The areas that are now upstate New York, plus a small pocket down in the heart of the U.S. South

- **Muskogean:** Mainly the deep South, including Alabama, Georgia, and parts of Florida

- **Siouan:** Central and northern U.S., including the Dakotas, Nebraska, Kansas, down to Oklahoma and Arkansas

- **Athabaskan:** The Southwest, mainly New Mexico, Arizona, and parts of northern Texas; also, Alaska, California, Oregon, Washington, and parts of the northern Pacific Coast

- **Uto-Aztecan:** The West, including Utah, Nevada, parts of California and Colorado; plus the Comanche area of Texas

- **Salishan:** The Northwest, including parts of Washington, Idaho, and the western third or so of Montana

- **Aleut:** The Aleutian peninsula

  Inuit: Interior Alaska

- **Mayan:** Parts of Mexico

- **All others:** Pockets scattered throughout the continental U.S.

The Slow Extinction of Native Languages

If a Native language is only spoken by adults, and is not routinely and consistently taught to the younger generations of a population, the language is considered "moribund"; that is, on its way out. (And I'm not speaking only of Native American languages here, but of all languages around the world in general.)

This means that it's almost a certainty that the Native language is unlikely to survive for many more generations, because as the elder generation that speaks it dies off, there is no one from succeeding generations knowledgeable enough in speaking and writing the language to continue its use.

It is estimated by linguist Michael Krauss, head of the Alaska Native Language Center, that there are only 175 Native American languages — from an original pool of languages numbering into the many, many hundreds — being spoken today and that close to 90 percent of them are moribund.

Could you repeat that, please?

Some Native languages have the characteristic of "polysynthesism" which basically means there's no difference between a word and a sentence.

Languages that use this concept take several ideas and create a single word expressing the concept of the original compilation of thoughts.

An example of this, according to Native American linguistic expert Edward Sapir, is this oft-quoted word from the Southern Paiute language:

Wiitokuchumpunkurüganiyugwivantümü

This translates to "They who are going to sit and cut up with a knife a black female (or male) buffalo."

A 16-word construct is manifested in a single, 34-character word.

Another example is this Wichita word:

Kiyaakiriwaac'arasarikita'ahiiriks

which means "He carried the big pile of meat up into the top of the tree."

(Source: David S. Rood, "North American Languages." *International Encyclopedia of Linguistics* 3 (1991):110–115.)

Today, the word "Wannabe" is a Pan-Indian pejorative term for non-Indians who express their longing to be Native American by doing things like practicing tribal rites or renaming themselves things like Wolf Moon Woman. It can be translated as "wacky non-Indians who thinks they are expressing much-needed sympathy or solidarity with Indian people, but who are really just making fools of themselves."

The "English only" movement

How did so many Native American languages die off?

There are several reasons, but one of the most significant reasons was the fact that Indian languages were deliberately "exterminated" during the boarding school period in America (beginning in the 1880s and continuing for decades) when Native American kids were punished if they spoke their Native language or did anything that could be considered tribal.

Today, efforts to pass laws making English the official language of the U.S. inadvertently continue this assault on Native languages. It is ironic that the U.S. would try to suppress Native language, given that some of these have been invaluable in our military efforts. Would the War in the Pacific have been won if the Navajo language had been extinguished prior to the recruitment of the code talkers? Would troops in WWI have been saved if Choctaw children had not learned how to speak to one another and if those children had not grown up and decided to fight on behalf of a country of which they were not yet citizens?

Can the damage be repaired?

First of all, why is it important to preserve the few remaining Native American languages?

Cultural diversity is one reason. Many historians, scholars, and ethnic people feel that a knowledge of many languages is beneficial for society in general. It opens people up to new ideas and ways of saying things, and eliminates the natural aversion many people have for anything different from what they're used to.

Restoring dead languages and furthering the use of moribund languages are no easy tasks. In fact, they are extremely difficult, especially when there are few Native speakers of a language still living.

In 1990, the U.S. House and Senate addressed this problem by passing the Native American Languages Act of 1990. And in 2006, the Esther Martinez Native American Languages Act of 2006 was made Public Law, adding to the resources available to schools and Native groups to ensure the "survival and vitality" of Native American languages.

Will the day come when the average American will have the opportunity in his or her day-to-day life to hear Native American languages spoken conversationally in the mainstream of American society?

Considering the fact that the American Indian population in on the upswing and is projected to grow steadily over the next several decades, the answer to that question is "possibly."

Sign Language

When people who do not speak a common language meet and need to work something out, they often resort to sign language. Columbus communicated with the Taino through sign language, but it is unknown how his gestures might have communicated the idea "I am here to subjugate you, enslave some of you, and bring devastation and disease upon your community." But then again, maybe he wanted to hide all that and simply tried to ask for food and water.

In 1540, explorer Francisco Vázquez de Coronado wrote of the Comanche in his journal, "That they were very intelligent is evident from the fact that although they conversed by means of signs, they made themselves understood so well that there was no need of an interpreter."

There was not a common signing system used by all Indians. There were some regional systems that developed. Some of the Great Plains tribes used a common system. But some of the gestures in the Northeast might have a different meaning in the Great Plains, the Southwest, or the Southeast.

Besides being the name of an utterly wonderful movie, smoke signals were used by some tribes who lived in clear areas to communicate with other tribes a distance away. This type of communication would never work in a forested area, but on the open plains or desert could have been effective. There was never a universal code of signals.

Little Written Down?

Until the 1800s, no tribe had an individual written language. In 1821, the Cherokee Nation adopted a syllabary invented by Sequoyah, and this script is still in use today. Prior to this, however, tribes maintained information and stories through oral accounts and through pictures.

Tribal history and stories were kept by men and women and were passed along through the generations in verbal recitation. Today, storytelling maintains its importance to Indian people, as is seen by the popularity of performances by people like Tim Tingle (Choctaw) and Gayle Ross (Cherokee).

Some of the traditional stories were written down by tribal members after they had acquired the skills to read and write. This practice has been controversial, however, because for some stories, the timing and nature of their recitation is important. Many stories that talk about the origins of people and the natural world are meant to be told as a practice of reverence for the world and are thus only told at certain times of the year or at certain times of day. Writing these down could mean that they might be read or told at inappropriate times, by and to inappropriate people. It's kind of as if somebody started randomly saying Mass while riding the bus to work in the morning.

Many tribes used drawings to express complicated ideas. These drawings are all tribal-specific, and anthropologists sometimes puzzle long and hard over the meaning of some of the earliest pictures. Paintings on rock shelters and cliff walls have been interpreted as representing hunting scenes, religious activity, or aspects of the natural world (see Figure 18-1). In West Texas, the Lower Pecos region has 4,000-year-old paintings and pictographs that may represent religious activity, but the exact meaning is completely unknown, as the descendants of the original artists are unknown.

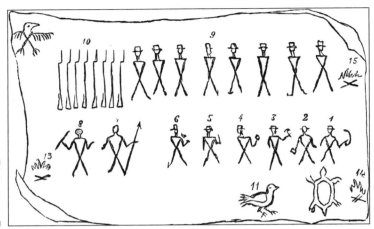

Figure 18-1:
Some Indian
pictograms.

In the 19th century, tribes on the Plains began to record images on ledger books and these have been studied and collected by art historians and anthropologists. The ledger drawings are sometimes in the style of hide drawings and sometimes take the form of Winter Counts, or calendars.

Simple symbols that appear on traditional clothing or jewelry are actually representations of complex, ancient ideas. The spirals that appear on southeastern beaded sashes may represent the serpent and consequently bring to mind stories about its role in protecting the people. For the Choctaw, the circle-and-cross motif represents the stickball game, but at least one anthropologist has noted the similarity of this design to an ancient Mississippian design of skulls and crossed bones, thus relating a modern design to a motif that goes back 3,000 years.

Today, artists from Jaune Quick to See Smith reinterpret traditional imagery to make social commentary.

Language As (the White Man's) Weapon

Racist language against American Indians was, unfortunately, quite common in the 18th and 19th centuries.

One ignoble example (perhaps) was by none other than that American icon, Mark Twain.

In an 1870 issue of the magazine *The Galaxy*, Twain published an essay called "The Noble Red Man" which was, in essence and on the surface, a scathing excoriation of how Indians had been portrayed in James Fenimore Cooper's novel *The Last of the Mohicans*.

Twain approaches the topic by first listing all the attributes Cooper assigns to Indians, and then providing an alternate assessment of the "noble red man," one which is, at the same time, both dreadfully racist and quite derogatory.

Was Twain being satirical? One could make the case, perhaps, that his "compare and contrast" structure in the piece was used for ironic effect. But his final line that everything he wrote describing Indians was "from personal observation," combined with the merciless and, let's face it, vicious assessment of a "typical" Indians leads to the inevitable conclusion that he wasn't kidding around.

No matter how we twist and turn the words, and no matter how we attempt to recast our perception of the essay, there's no denying that Twain sounds like he means every word of it.

Language As (the Native American) Weapon

Sadly, modern writers have internalized the opposing concepts of Noble and Savage and this is teeth-grittingly frustrating to a modern Indian person who has to contend with either being thought "Noble and Stoic" or "Stupid and Dirty."

Despite the tensions between the enforced English language and the traditional ways of conveying stories, many Indian people have embraced writing as a tool, and as a weapon. The Miwok poet Wendy Roses has noted that having a universal language has had unintended consequences, in that for once, tribal members can now all communicate with each other and can unite to fight together against common threats.

Additionally, Indian people have seized the opportunity to begin to portray ourselves as we really are. Forget whatever you've learned from either Cooper or Twain, or Louis Lamour, for that matter. If you want to read *real* Indian writing, try Louise Erdrich, Leanne Howe, or Susan Power. *The Shell Shakers*, by Howe, contains Indian people who are wise, Indian people who are greedy, Indian people who are silly, and Indian people who are finance moguls. Reading real Indian literature is one of the best ways to understand real Indian people.

Chapter 19

The Faith of Their Fathers ... And How Native Americans Worship Today

*H*armony and balance: That's probably the single best description of the totality of Native American spirituality and its wide range of structured religious practices. In fact, if it were a *Jeopardy* question, the answer would be, "These two words best define Native American spirituality." And of course, we'd ring in with, "What is harmony and balance, Alex?" This chapter explores the many elements that make up the harmony and balance of Native American spirituality.

In the Beginning ... Native Peoples' Creation Myths

Creation myths, or *creation stories*, are deeply important to the members of the cultures that believe them.

These myths are sacred legends that explain the beginnings of the universe and of all life everywhere. They provide a grounding, and adherents believe that they answer the inevitable questions all thinking people have: Who am I? Why am I here? Where am I going? Plus, the notion of an all-knowing, eternal arbiter of a person's actions provides a moral framework within which people can live their lives. As different as Native American religions and creation mythologies are from Judeo-Christian dogma, they share some similar "definitive abstractions," so to speak, and offer the same comfort to believers.

How important are these myths? Important enough that people of certain religions who hold true their own creation myths often want them accepted and taught as fact, rather than as fable or fiction.

The Elements and the Deities

One of the biggest differences between traditional Native American religious beliefs and Judeo-Christian dogma is the absence of the concept of original sin — the notion that man was created perfect, sinned and offended God, and was cast out of Paradise, only being allowed to return if repentance is made.

In many tribal religions, natural elements are seen as representations of sacred powers/forces. Some of the common elements running through many Native American creation myths, include

- **Animals and Birds:** Different tribal religions imbue different animals with specific roles or powers. Animals such as coyotes, rabbits, hummingbirds, buzzards, and snakes appear in various tribal stories.

- **Insects:** Many tribal myths include insects. Spiders are important to many tribes, but technically, these are arachnids.

- **Water:** For many tribes, water is considered the source of all life and all material things in the universe. A Cherokee creation myth, for example, states that in the beginning, all there was, was water. The Hurons, too. A Creek creation myth claims that all of existence was completely underwater at first. What's fascinating about the ubiquitousness of water in Indian creation myths is that their essential meaning is that all life came from the sea. We know that that is, in fact, true, and that 3.8 billion years ago, life started in the seas, and that the seas sustain life today. Pretty clever, those early mythmakers, eh?

- **Trickster figures:** These animals play larger than life roles in many Native mythologies. They cannot be thought of as deities or gods in the general sense, but are more like hero figures.

- **Deities:** According to the detailed and well-researched Godchecker.com Web site, these are the top ten most important Native American gods:

  - **Raven:** Common to the Pacific Northwest tribes, the Raven is known to be a trickster, and legends state that he created the land of Earth by flying above the seas with a stone in his mouth and dropping it when he tired. The stone expanded and became all the dry land we know today. The Raven is also known to be ceaselessly hungry and forever seeking food, and it is said he is also responsible for placing the Sun, Moon, and stars in the sky. Busy guy.

- **Coyote:** Another trickster, stories about Coyote are common among Southwestern tribes, and are also known in California, the Plains (the Menominee), and among the Plateau Indians, including the Nez Perce. Coyote is credited with many creation achievements, including the creation and placing of the Milky Way Galaxy, the making of the star Arcturus (he was juggling his eyeballs and threw one a tad too high), and he is also responsible for humans dying once and forever (unlike plants that bloom again in the spring).

- **Kwatee:** Another of the trickster figures, this guy is known in the Pacific Northwest as a changer of worlds and is credited with creating human beings from his personal body dirt and sweat. (Now there's an uplifting thought, eh?) And Kwatee is also a slayer of monsters. He is best known for killing the monster that was living in the depths of Lake Quinalt in Washington state. It seems that said monster swallowed Kwatee's mother, and then his brother, which ticked Kwatee off to no end. So he threw hot rocks into the lake, which caused the water to boil and kill the beast. When the monster's corpse floated to the surface, Kwatee eviscerated it and freed his brother from the entrails. All in a day's work! Kwatee retired some time ago and is now a mountain.

- **Rabbit:** A trickster figure whose fame has crossed cultural lines, Rabbit is thought to have had his exploits adapted to become the Brer Rabbit stories, but may also have influenced the movie *Donnie Darko* (with its creepy giant rabbit that may or may not be a hallucination).

- **Sedna:** Sedna is honored as the original source of much of the food and clothing of the Inuit people. She started out as a good daughter, taking care of her elderly father, but was seduced by a no-good spirit in the form of a rich, good-looking guy with a fancy kayak. When her father tried to bring her back, the spirit raised a terrible storm, and in order to save himself, her father tossed her overboard, cutting off her hands when she clung to the side of the boat. Sedna dropped to the bottom, but her hands and fingers became fish and seals which continue to sustain the Inuit people. Sedna herself sunk to the bottom, where she keeps watch over the gates of life and death.

When a planet was discovered outside the orbit of Pluto in 2003, they named it Sedna in honor of the daughter sacrificed to the sea by her heartless father.

- **Windigo:** This Algonquin mythological creature, also spelled Windigo, would better be defined as a demon rather than a god. Why? Because it's a ravenous cannibal creature that eats any living creature it comes across. Plus, its heart is made of ice, and it's a skeletal giant and is commonly described as being hideously deformed. There are lots of legends about the Windigo, and none of them are good. Let's say you're stranded in a blizzard and you eat your fellow travelers? Bang: you're a Windigo. Dream about a Windigo? Bang: you're a Windigo. The first accounts of the Windigo legend appear in the writings of 17th-century explorers, but they referred to the monster as demonic, or a werewolf.

- **Wakan Tanka:** In Dakota and Lakota Sioux mythology, Wakan Tanka (or just Wakan, or Wakanda or Wakonda) is the name or term for the sacredness running through all of existence.

✔ **A First Man and First Woman:** Native American mythology has its own Adam and Eve story, and each tribe and culture seems to have its own interpretation and account of how First Man and First Woman appeared on Earth. The well-known Navajo First Man/First Woman creation myth states that they were created when a holy wind blew life into two ears of corn, and that the resulting First Man and First Woman were sent to Earth to prepare the world for the creation of all human beings.

✔ **Wind:** The sacred or generative wind is part of many Native American creation myths.

✔ **An underworld:** The dark and watery underworld is a common belief in Native American belief systems.

Tools of the Spiritual Trade

Throughout history, there has been a concerted, conscious effort by man to access the spiritual nature of ourselves. To see deeper, to know more. To *understand.*

The list of "tools" — both tangible and intangible — used in the quest for enlightenment is enormous, ranging from an array of mind-altering substances, to meditation, sensory deprivation, and sexuality.

Today, people commonly turn to books, the Internet, and other sources for assistance in both understanding their own psychology, and for assistance in achieving higher states of consciousness on the path to enlightenment. Early Native Americans depended solely on three things:

✔ *Physical "tools,"* as described in the following sections

✔ People we'd identify today as "*clergy*"

✔ *Themselves,* as they fasted and used various physical disciplines to attain focused, inner mental states

The Native American Church

The Native American Church has around 250,000 members and is legally allowed to use peyote in its religious ceremonies.

The relevant passage of the American Indian Religious Freedom Act of 1994 is:

> The use, possession, or transportation of peyote by an Indian for bona fide traditional ceremonial purposes in connection with the practice of a traditional Indian religion is lawful, and shall not be prohibited by the United States or any State. No Indian shall be penalized or discriminated against on the basis of such use, possession or transportation, including, but not limited to, denial of otherwise applicable benefits under public assistance programs.

This was an extremely important ruling that impacted the interpretation of the First Amendment — favoring a hands-off policy toward a specific religion — as well as mandating a new interpretation of U.S. drug policy. For the first time in U.S. history, an hallucinogenic was deemed legal to use simply by being a member of a particular denomination.

Peyote

Peyote is a form of spineless cactus that causes hallucinogenic effects when consumed. It has long been touted as a tool for achieving higher consciousness, for communicating with the supernatural, and for medicinal use. Its active psychedelic component is mescaline.

Members of the Native American Church use the hallucinogenic plant peyote in their religious ceremonies — and it's legal to do so, as long as you're a member of a federally recognized tribe.

Musical instruments

Plato said, "More than anything else, rhythm and melody find their way to the inmost soul and take the strongest hold upon it." Different tribes have used different musical instruments as part of religious activity.

Hide drums

Drums have long been important to Native peoples and are made for individual and communal use. Today, the drums that are an important part of powwow dances are constructed to be large enough for many people to sit around and play at the same time.

Many are constructed out of either a hollowed-out log, or a handmade wooden frame, and tight deerskin is stretched across the top. Water drums have water poured inside the drum body, with the liquid giving it a different sound. Water drums are usually made from clay, since water would rot the wood of a traditional drum.

Don't call a Native American drum a tom-tom. Sure, it has come to mean American Indian drum and is commonly used interchangeably, but tom-tom is not a Native American word. It's an old British word for a child's toy.

Flutes

Some tribes have used flutes in prayer and healing services and for personal meditation. They can be made from woods like cedar, walnut, and cherry, or from bones of important animals, like eagles.

Check out the International Native American Flute Association for more info on Native American flutes. Their Web site is www.worldflutes.org.

The Native American flute has a haunting sound, and that has a lot to do with its tuning — they're commonly tuned to a minor scale. They also have two chambers, one for air, and one for playing.

Today, Native American flutes are used for a wide array of types of music, and are no longer considered to be solely a solo instrument. New Age, World Music, and jazz, especially, are common genres where the sounds of the Native American flute can be heard.

Rattles

Rattles have been made from a wide variety of materials:

- Gourds
- Wood
- Hoofs
- Rawhide
- Turtle shells
- Shells
- Horns
- Animal teeth

The handles are wood or bones, and the rattles are filled with beads, stones, or seeds and shaken rhythmically during prayer and healing services.

The human voice

Chanting is an integral part of Native American music and song. Sometimes, actual songs with lyrics are sung; other times, syllables which are merely vocalizations of sounds are used, sung in tempo with the drums and rattles and commonly repeated.

The types of vocalizing can be

- ✔ **Call and response:** A chanter sings a phrase which the group responds to with a sung phrase. This is a common motif in stomp dance songs, among Southeastern tribes.
- ✔ **Solo:** A single chanter/singer is featured, either a cappella or accompanied by musicians.
- ✔ **Choral:** The entire group/tribe/gathering sings songs in unison. (And in most case, everyone knows the words, so no karaoke machine and TV screen are necessary.)

Foods

Many Native American tribes have harvest festivals where gratitude for the season's harvest is expressed and the bounty is eaten. The process of harvesting sometimes involved making sacrifices in thanks to the earth.

Stone and wood fetishes

Fetishes are animals or figurines depicting forces of nature carved from wood or stone that are sacred and believed to possess living powers that can be tapped through prayer and ritual.

Stone and wood carvings of each animal are prayed over for guidance and enlightenment, and sacrifices are made in supplication and respect.

The Totem Pole

The totem pole is an iconic symbol of Native American history and culture, but they are unique to the tribes of the Pacific Northwest.

One small area of the world — a strip of land from around Seattle to Juneau, Alaska — was the birthplace of the totem pole, and its creation was due to a combination of factors that included the idea of immortalizing historical events with carved images, and the abundant availability of suitable trees.

There were several types of totem poles, including lineage poles, house poles (both inside and outside the home), mortuary and grave poles, and ridicule poles.

The giant trees used

Totem poles were not carved out of living trees. Trees were cut down, pruned, and trimmed to create long logs which were then laid flat and carved. This allowed the carver to access all parts of the pole, including the rear. Although some totem poles were carved all the way around, some being carved today have hollow backs to reduce weight and are used mainly indoors.

The most common tree used for totem poles was a mature red cedar tree. Other trees used include spruce and fir trees.

What totem poles mean

Totem poles tell a story and they symbolically express pride in family and tribe.

Some important figures that appear on totem poles include

- Bear
- Beaver
- Crow
- Eagle
- Frog
- Goat
- Human
- Raven
- Thunderbird
- Whale

Each figure was deliberately placed according to its role in the story or history being conveyed. Sometimes, figures were deliberately carved upside down as a joke, or were placed within the figure of another animal.

House posts

A totem pole was sometimes placed outside the home as a means of identifying the family. Guess you could say they were one of the first address markers.

Totem poles were also sometimes placed inside the house for good luck, especially if the pole displayed an eagle.

The idiom "Low man on the totem pole" is something of a misappropriation of totem pole iconography. The University of Washington in Seattle tells us that there was never a "ranking" process regarding which figures were placed on totem poles or where. Once totem poles became known, an assumption was made that the figure on the bottom had to be the lowest ranking, but that's not generally the case. In some instances, perhaps the individual carver did deliberately place one figure below another, but the universality of "low man on the totem pole" being interpreted as referring to someone of little or no significance isn't accurate.

Grave markers

Totem poles were often carved for use as grave markers. Another death-related totem pole was known as the mortuary pole. The remains of the deceased were placed inside a carved pole commemorating their life, and the pole was then respected as though it were a grave or burial place.

Symbols of a family's heritage

Individual families often carved their own poles or commissioned poles to symbolically illustrate the history of their family. Their patron animal was included, as were other symbols representing family members and events from the family's past.

Ridicule poles

Sometimes, totem poles were carved and erected to mock or shame someone, or to tell the world that someone owed the chief money and hadn't paid. Enemies were often depicted upside down.

Think about the effort it took to create a totem pole before the days of power tools. All that cutting and dragging and carving. By hand. To commit all that effort to craft a pole designed to deride someone else sure does say a lot about Indian pride.

Christian Indians? Not a Contradiction!

Upon arriving in the Americas, Europeans found people who *seemed* to be worshipping rocks, and mountains, and the sky, and the lakes, and the ground, and the trees, and, dear heaven! even animals.

In all religious doctrines, there is a difference between "creation" and the "Creator." To the Europeans, Indians seemed to be worshipping creation, while Christians worshipped the Creator. This meant, of course, that the Native people were hopelessly misguided and it was the Europeans' mission to show them the light. (And yes, I'm being sarcastic, in case that didn't come across.)

This meant doing anything and everything possible to force them to abandon their traditional ways and beliefs and, instead, coerce them into accepting the Christian dogma of a triune God, with Jesus as the second person of this trinity.

Europeans also had a problem with the belief that everything is everything. That all of existence, all of nature is connected. That the Creator's spirit moves through all and, thus, all that is alive should be respected. Europeans heard this and said, "Nuh-uh." Humans are the top of the pyramid, according to the Bible, and nature is at our beck-and-call to use as we see fit. This ideology was grossly offensive to Native Americans then, and many still feel that way today.

Civilizing "savages" through Christ

There are none so fervent as those who believe they are carrying out orders from God.

The Europeans' belief that it was their sacred mission to convert the "heathen savages" to Christianity in the name of Jesus was an enormous part of their easy willingness to consider the Indians as "less than" European whites. This psychologically empowered them to either destroy or convert them, and justified in their minds any and all actions necessary to do one of two things: remove them, or transform them into good, upstanding Christians.

Native American Christians today

Christianity as practiced by Native Americans has evolved in a very interesting manner over the past century or so. Many tribes with members having strong Christian faith have also integrated aspects of traditional religion into the practice of this faith.

Tribes that have done this by and large see no conflict in an openhearted "mingling," a stark departure from the days when they were forced to abandon and actually denounce their ethnic beliefs and practices in order to become "good Christians."

Today, Catholic and Protestant churches where Native Americans attend Mass are decorated with Indian symbols and artwork. Christ is sometimes depicted in Native cultural garb.

Part V
In a Modern World Not of Their Making

The 5th Wave

By Rich Tennant

©RICHTENNANT

"Help me out here. Are these guys Pilgrims or Puritans? I can never tell them apart."

In this part . . .

There's no denying that the American Indian has it tough these days, due in large part to government policies of encroachment and elimination. But times are changing and things are clearly improving for Native Americans in America. Government programs help with education, housing, and health care. And more and more Indians are launching and successfully running their own businesses, achieving advanced degrees, and attaining high positions in the corporate world.

This part looks at how Indians and tribes are identified and defined these days, and also how Indians got into the casino business and what other areas of economic development are proving to be beneficial to tribal improvement.

You'll also find out about the very important practice of repatriation, and gain insight into the future of the American Indian in America.

Chapter 20

The Slow Dwindling
of Native Americans

*I*n the early 1600s, Dutch explorers arrived at Delaware Bay. Lots of Europeans followed, and it is estimated that by the end of the 17th century, after the arrival of said Europeans, a staggering 90 per cent of the Native American coastal population was dead. Disease was the primary culprit, followed by violence.

Depending on the demographic model used, and depending on who you listen to, the Indigenous population in the Americans before Columbus arrived in 1492 was . . . *impossible to know with certainty!*

Yes, you read that right. We don't know for sure. This is simply a reality that anthropologists, historians, and scientists have lived with for ages. (Although "argued about" might be a better way of putting it.)

This doesn't mean, however, that the aforementioned anthropologists, historians, and scientists have not come up with numbers. That they have done. And those numbers range from 8 million to as high as 145 million. Yes, there is that big a spread in the estimates, and no one knows for certain the exact number.

The number 40 million seems to appeal to experts as possibly being as close to correct as we can get. Although depending on the estimates they support, some find it impossibly high and others, yes, impossibly low. Can't we all just get along?

Today, there are 2.4 million full-blooded Native Americans in America. (That number approximately doubles when you count people who are *part* Native American.) Native American numbers are on the rise, though, and it is projected that by 2050, the Native population in American will be around 4.4 million, rising from 0.9 percent of the U.S. population, to 1.1 per cent.

Too Much to Defend Against

The drastic decline in the Native American population from the 16th century on was due to several reasons.

It's undeniable that the combination of assaults against the Indigenous populations — the exponential increase in deaths when the attacks piled on — hastened and expanded the fatality toll.

The Native Americans had five strikes against them. The array of physical, medical, military, economic, and cultural assaults included the following:

- **Disease from contagions:** This includes deaths from diseases carried by Europeans to which Native Americans were not immune, many of which were introduced into Indian society by the livestock and other animals brought to the New World by Europeans once the serious colonization efforts kicked in.

- **Disease from deliberate infections:** Smallpox-infected blankets. True story.

- **Warfare and battle losses:** Recurring violent conflict between Native Americans and Europeans caused an enormous number of deaths. Similar violent clashes between warring tribes also resulted in mass Indian deaths.

- **Starvation and exposure:** Forced removal of Native Americans from their lands to make room for white settlers often resulted in horror shows like the 1838 Trail of Tears, during which Cherokees were marched from Georgia to Oklahoma.

  (See Chapter 6 for more on the Cherokees and the Trail of Tears.) Many Natives died from starvation, illness, and exposure during the march.)

- **Extermination and slaughter:** Deliberate annihilation of Indians began when Columbus and his men returned to Hispaniola and slaughtered thousands of Taino Natives in three years. Official policies and a cultural mindset that reduced Native Americans to less than human made it easy to consider genocidal atrocities as no big deal.

Defenseless Against Dastardly Diseases

Transmittable diseases cannot be transmitted if there is no one to transmit them to.

Today, big cities are "target-rich" playgrounds for all manner of bacteria. The nature of modern society makes it easy for nasty critters to move from host (the office doorknob), to host (the guy who delivers the mail), to host (the boss's secretary), to host (the handle of the shopping cart), to host (you!)

This is why biological terrorism is perhaps the most frightening form of attack, because it's essentially a silent, invisible invasion. A terrorist nonchalantly drops a test tube filled with the smallpox virus on a crowded New York city sidewalk, or in an airport terminal, or on the stadium's cement sets at a baseball game. The vial, of course, shatters — and then the terrorist keeps on walking.

A week or so later, there's a devastating epidemic — because no has been vaccinated against smallpox for decades. We licked it in 1979. That's when it was considered "eradicated." But strands of the virus still exist in U.S. and Russian laboratories and there are new fears that these samples could end up in the hands of terrorists and smallpox could be used as a biological weapon. Some believe Russia manufactured tons of it during the Cold War when they ramped up their biological weapons programs.

Dense populations, like those in cities, means that disease transmission is easy. There are a lot of people meeting up with each other and this means that it's easy for bacteria and viruses to meet up with them as well. Because people are exposed to many different bugs, hardy populations are able to develop immune responses to the diseases. This is not to say that all diseases could be overcome. Remember that little event called the Black Plague? During the 16th and 17th centuries, European cities lived in fear of outbreaks of smallpox and of something called the sweating sickness. People typically reacted by fleeing the city or by shutting themselves away from others.

While Europeans had lived with the same set of bugs for centuries, when they brought these over to the Americas, the bacteria and viruses took advantage of the large amount of fresh vectors, so to speak.

Medical mayhem

Is it any wonder there was such a drastic decline in the Indian population once the Europeans set foot on the continent? The diseases the Native peoples' immune systems suddenly had to contend with included this vile smorgasbord of illnesses (and notice how many are bacteria-borne):

- **Bubonic plague:** An often fatal epidemic bacterial disease that affects the lymphatic system and then the entire body.
- **Chicken pox:** A contagious viral disease.
- **Cholera:** An often fatal intestinal disease commonly caused by drinking water contaminated with the cholera bacteria.

✔ **Diphtheria:** Often deadly infectious bacterial disease that damages the heart and nervous system.

✔ **Dysentery:** A lower intestinal bacterial disease that causes severe diarrhea and the passage of blood and mucus.

✔ **Influenza:** A contagious viral disease that can be deadly for people with weakened immune systems or other systemic problems.

✔ **Malaria:** An infectious disease caused by a parasite transmitted by the bite of mosquitoes infected with the bug.

✔ **Measles:** A very contagious acute viral disease causing spots that cover the entire body, a high fever, and a sore throat.

✔ **Mumps:** An acute contagious viral disease that causes fever and a swelling of the salivary glands, and can also damage the pancreas, testes, and ovaries.

✔ **Pleurisy:** A serious lung inflammation that is often the result of a systemic viral or bacterial disease like tuberculosis.

✔ **Scarlet fever:** A contagious bacterial disease caused by an infection and causing fever and throat problems.

✔ **Smallpox:** The killer. A highly contagious viral disease causing back pain, high fever and the development of small pustules on the skin. Smallpox has a fatality rate of approximately 30 percent.

✔ **Typhoid fever:** A bacterial infection of the digestive tract, sometimes fatal, that is caused by eating or drinking salmonella-contaminated food or water.

✔ **Typhus:** A bacterial infection spread by ticks and fleas on rats that causes high fever and delirium and can be fatal.

✔ **Whooping cough:** An infectious bacterial disease that causes violent coughing and a very recognizable shrill inhalation sound.

✔ **Yellow fever:** An often fatal viral infection spread by mosquitoes and causing liver damage, hemorrhaging, high fever, and vomiting of blood.

A review of these horrific ailments makes it clear that the odds were stacked against the Indigenous populations when these diseases entered their environment.

But Indians dying from European diseases did not mean they were always intentionally infected. As mentioned, a lot of the death toll was due to just plain "biological bad luck" — immune systems that had never been exposed to European diseases and, thus, were unable to fight them off.

The first epidemics

In the Autumn 1988 issue of the journal *Social Science History*. Dr. Francisco Guerra states that the first American epidemic to devastate an Indigenous population was the 1493 influenza epidemic, almost certainly brought from Spain to Hispaniola during Columbus's second trip to the island.

When Columbus returned, he brought with him livestock that were the probable source of the virus.

The mainland was next.

The 93

From the 16th century (c. 1520) through the early 20th century (1918), no less than 93 confirmed epidemics and pandemics — all of which can be attributed to European contagions — decimated the American Indian population.

These 93 epidemics were a potpourri of disease, and some of them were sexually transmitted. Native American populations in the American Southwest plummeted by a staggering 90 percent or more.

The Europeans were of the belief that the deaths of the Natives was because God was on their side. The Indians, on the other hand, believed that God had abandoned them and looked to the "evidence" that their healers were helpless in the face of disease outbreaks that were catastrophic. Suicide, alcoholism, and Christianity were the solutions many Indians turned to. Unfortunately, what could have helped them — antibiotics, for one — had not yet been invented.

An epidemic is an outbreak of a disease that spreads rapidly through a group of people. A pandemic is when epidemics of disease spread widely, often raging through several states, or regions, or even countries at the same time.

The Columbian Exchange

The Columbian Exchange is the term used for the rapid and widespread exchange of, well, just about *everything* after Columbus landed in the Americas in 1492.

The "Columbian" Exchange was named after Christopher Columbus, not the South American country of Colombia.

There were three basic "categories" of things exchanged during the Columbia Exchange:

- ✔ Animals
- ✔ Plants
- ✔ Diseases

This massive exchange also included human beings, both in the form of colonists and slaves, and is considered one of the most significant cultural interminglings in the history of civilization.

Smallpox during the American Revolution

The British had better immunity to smallpox than did the Continental Army, but in the end, it didn't help them win the war.

In 1775, there was a smallpox outbreak in the North among the soldiers of the Continental Army and, thanks to George Washington's brilliant decision to vaccinate all his soldiers, it was quelled quickly enough so as not to decimate the troops. (It did spread to the southern armies, though, where it wreaked havoc.) Washington himself was immune to smallpox: He had contracted it when he was 19 during a visit to Barbados with his ailing brother.

Yes, the story of Europeans deliberately infecting Native Americans with "toxic" blankets and other items is true.

By the spring of 1764, smallpox was epidemic among the Indians of the area. It seems indisputable that the linens had "the desired effect."

Wasn't the Black Death worse?

If we compare the death toll of Native Americans killed by European diseases to Europeans killed by the Black Death from 1347 through 1350, it seems like the Indians were hurt more than the European population.

Approximately one-third to (from some estimates) one-half of Europe's population was killed by the Black Death, which was actually bubonic plague. Yet it's estimated that three times that percentage — 90 percent to 95 percent — of the Native American population on the North American continent was wiped out during the 400 years of the 93 epidemics.

It really boils down to a sort of "apples and oranges" comparison: The Black Death killed a smaller percentage of its victim population, but the disease did its dirty work in a very short period of only four or five years. The European diseases that killed the Indians, on the other hand, plagued the population for almost four centuries, but the death toll was a much higher percentage of the Indigenous population.

Fighting

It was almost always about land and control: keeping it, or stealing it.

Indians fought with Indians over land; Europeans fought with Indians over land; heck, even Europeans and Indian allies fought with other Indians over land. And the body count climbed each time forces came to blows.

Experts differ on the prevalance of violent battle in the pre-Columbian era, but after guns were introduced to the Indian populations, warfare became more frequent and far more deadly.

In 1675, approximately 6,000 Indians died or were enslaved in King Phillip's War in colonial New England. The war lasted two years and it is estimated that one in ten from both sides died in the conflict. (See Chapter 11 for more details on this often-overlooked war.)

Starvation

Forcing Indians onto reservations and away from their hunting grounds and proven growing lands resulted in a great many deaths by starvation.

Also, the deliberate extermination by Europeans of the life-giving buffalo caused Indian tribes to starve and disintegrate. By 1895, the buffalo was essentially extinct. The Plains Indians suffered most from loss of the buffalo. And, again, if we follow the money, we'll see why the animal was exploited to the point of "almost" extinction:

- Their hides were worth a lot of money.
- They were in the way.

How did the tribes of the Plains Indians replace the meat they got from the buffalo?

They didn't.

Extermination

As late as the late 19th century, there was pervasive racism against Native Americans, and all too much accepted talk about eliminating them completely as a race.

University of Hawaii professor David Stannard uses the term "holocaust" to describe what the Europeans did to Native American people in the quarter of a century following Columbus's arrival at Hispaniola in 1492.

Statistics bear him out. And those statistics are grim:

- In 1492, the population of the Caribbean islands was around 8 million Natives.
- By 1496, the population was down to between 4 and 5 million.
- By 1508, the population was less than 100,000.
- By 1518, the population was less than 20,000.
- By 1535, the population was virtually extinct.

And how did all these people die?

Horrifically, is how, and the intensity of the effort to not simply eliminate the Natives, but to do it as sadistically and cruelly as possible, is an undeniable dark stain on European colonization of the New World.

Professor Stannard's use of the term "holocaust" was deliberate, since it is now interpreted to mean a deliberate extermination, and that is precisely what the Spanish conquistadors intended: extermination of the Natives in any and all ways possible.

There is controversy over Stannard's use of the term "holocaust" because it implies abundant intentionality. The term, right or wrong, is now associated in large part with the idea of intentional genocide. (And the term "ethnic cleansing"

What about Aztec human sacrifices?

Is it true that the pre-Columbian Aztecs in Meso-america performed ritual human sacrifices? Yes.

Did the numbers of people sacrificed affect population numbers of the Indigenous people in the post-Columbian years? Probably not, since the number of human sacrifices were small compared to the population. Some experts estimate an Aztec population of around 19 million, which dropped to 2 million or less by 1581 — but not because of the their practice of sacrificing approximately 20,000 people each year to the gods. (No group would continue a cultural tradition like sacrifice if it impaired their own ability to survive.)

The Aztec population decline is believed to have been caused by smallpox.

is often commonly used today to describe the deliberate extermination of people based solely on their race or ethnicity.) Some critics assert that genocide was not the primary purpose of western colonization, and they've got a point. Trade was. Follow the money, and all that, right?

Nonetheless, the disease fork of the three-pronged Columbian Exchange mentioned earlier did serve to exterminate the Native peoples quite effectively, although it's reasonable to say that killing off Indigenous people with European diseases was not the master plan of the colonists.

Today's Challenges

The American Indian population is on the upswing.

Today, Native Americans do not have the brigade of assaults they had to contend with in the past. Yet, that said, it cannot be denied that the injuries impressed upon the Indigenous populations from the 15th century on took a toll, and their effects are lingering even today.

To put it plainly, everything in America is worse for the Indian than for other racial groups. Comedian Chris Rock, during one his comedy specials, made the point that even blacks don't have it as bad these days are American Indians. As he said (and I'm almost certainly paraphrasing), "When was the last time you saw two Indian families eating at a Red Lobster?"

Of course, one major problem facing Native Americans is just that — the sense of being invisible. Not every Native person looks like they're a descendant of Sitting Bull. Some look like they might be more related to Thomas Jefferson, while others could be the niece of Dr. Martin Luther King, Jr. Chris Rock may very well have seen two Indian families together, but not recognized them as such!

Despite the dark night of the colonization, Native people have come forward into the present day, changed in some ways, but strong in every way that matters.

In Chapter 22, we compare realities. There you'll find statistics that do not paint a pretty picture for the American Indian.

In all categories — health, income, education, employment, and so forth — the Indian lags behind white America.

Chapter 21

What's a Tribe, Who's an Indian, and What's the BIA Got to Do With It

*N*ative peoples were managing their own affairs quite well when the first Europeans arrived. Yet, to the colonists, Native people were a problem that had to be dealt with.

So what did the U.S. government do? As is typical for centralized bureaucracies throughout recent history, they created an agency to handle things.

A Bureau of Indian Affairs came into existence on March 11, 1824, but was then known as the Office of Indian Affairs. This chapter examines this agency as well as its earlier versions, and takes a look at how these agencies have impacted and still impact Indian tribes today.

The Evolution of Indian Agencies

As far back as 1775, the colonists established agencies to deal with the Indians. They had to. Treaties needed to be negotiated, plus they wanted to somehow get the Indians on their side during the War for Independence, or at the very least, secure their neutrality.

Indians were the original occupants of the land, and yet European expansion took a decidedly less accepting view of their presence.

The 1775 Continental Congress addresses the Indian issue

In 1775, the Second Continental Congress allocated 40,000 pounds to dealing with the Indians, appointed the first commissioner of Indian Affairs, and created three departments of Indian Affairs, northern, central, and southern.

Also, the Congress considered a proposal from Benjamin Franklin titled "A Sketch of Articles of Confederation." Included in Franklin's Articles was Article X, which stated:

> No Colony shall engage in an offensive War with any Nation of Indians without the Consent of the Congress, or great Council above mentioned, who are first to consider the Justice and Necessity of such War.

And in Article XI, Franklin proposed that "A perpetual Alliance offensive and defensive, is to be enter'd into as soon as may he with the Six Nations; their Limits to be ascertain'd and secur'd to them; their Land not to be encroach'd on . . ."

Neither of Franklin's Indian-related articles made it into the final Articles of Confederation.

John C. Calhoun's bold move

In March 1824, President James Monroe's Secretary of War John C. Calhoun, a staunch proponent of slavery (he once delivered a speech to the U.S. Senate titled "Slavery a Positive Good") and nullification (the principle that states could declare null and void any federal law they didn't agree with) created the Office of Indian Affairs after getting fed up with Congress.

The Office was part of the War Department and Calhoun named his pal Thomas L. McKenney as its first head.

The Office of Indian Affairs (which, for a time McKenney called the Indian Office) was a huge endeavor, with little authority and a small staff.

According to its Letter of Appointment, the responsibilities of this Office included the following duties:

- To take charge of the appropriations for annuities and current expenses
- To examine and approve all vouchers for expenditures
- To administer the fund for the civilization of the Indians

> ✔ To decide on claims arising between Indians and whites under the intercourse laws
>
> ✔ To handle the ordinary Indian correspondence of the War Department

This rasher of duties was daunting, and it wasn't long before McKenney became frustrated with both the workload and the fact that essentially he had no authority whatsoever.

In 1826, McKenney put forth a bill in Congress that would create a Commissioner of Indian Affairs who would actually be given supreme authority and not need to run every decision by the War Department. The bill failed, but with Lewis and Clark's support, it was reintroduced and passed both houses in 1832 and was signed into law that same year.

What the BIA does

Here's how the agency defines their mandate today:

> The Bureau of Indian Affairs (BIA) responsibility is the administration and management of 55.7 million acres of land held in trust by the United States for American Indians, Indian tribes, and Alaska Natives. There are 564 [2004 statistics] federal recognized tribal governments in the United States [226 are Native villages in Alaska]. Developing forestlands, leasing assets on these lands, directing agricultural programs, protecting water and land rights, developing and maintaining infrastructure and economic development are all part of the agency's responsibility. In addition, the Bureau of Indian Affairs provides education services to approximately 48,000 Indian students.

The BIA is part of the U.S. Department of the Interior and is overseen by the Assistant Secretary for Indian Affairs, who reports to the Deputy Secretary of the Interior.

According to an Equal Opportunity publication from the U.S. Army, the following are the Bureau of Indian Affairs responsibilities:

✔ Overseeing over 300 reservations

✔ Leasing of mineral rights

✔ Developing of forest lands

✔ Developing and directing agricultural programs

✔ Protecting water and land rights

75 percent of the BIA's 13,000 employees are Native American.

Cobell v. Kempthorne: Bad news for the BIA?

Cobell v. Kempthorne is one of the largest class action lawsuits ever filed in the United States.

It basically alleges that the U.S. government, specifically the Department of the Interior, has mismanaged Indian trust assets for decades. The defendants in the case are the Department of the Interior and the Department of the Treasury.

The case was filed in 1996 and, in 2001, the plaintiffs successfully convinced the judge adjudicating the case to shut down the BIA Web site on the grounds that the BIA could not be trusted to adequately protect its data. The site has been unavailable to web surfers ever since.

The plaintiff Elouise Cobell alleges that "the case has revealed mismanagement, ineptness, dishonesty, and delay of federal officials." And when one looks over the list of stipulations the U.S. government has agreed to, it seems like the charges are accurate. The IndianTrust.com Web site says that the case's intent is "to force the federal government to account for billions of dollars belonging to approximately 500,000 American Indians and their heirs, and held in trust since the late 19th century."

So what else are the plaintiffs asking for? They also want a complete reform of the Indian trust system.

The case has been split into those two parts and, so far, neither result has been achieved.

One of the problems with the whole Indian trust system is fractionation: There are parcels of land owned by hundreds of Indians, and overseen by the Department of the Interior, resulting in many owners receiving rent of around five cents a year. Yet, it costs the U.S. government tens of thousands of dollars to manage the property each year.

A "complete reform" of the system, considering the existing rules (for example, all assets held in trust must be probated, even if the account is worth less than a penny, and the probate costs could be tens of thousands of dollars), seems almost impossible.

What It Takes to Be a Tribe

In the United States, a tribe is not a tribe unless the BIA says so.

Sure, there are countless Indian tribes in America that are, in fact, tribal nations, but in order to receive benefits from the Bureau of Indian Affairs, a tribe must be officially decreed a tribe, and not every tribe that applies is deemed a tribe, even if their history goes back to the times of the First People.

The criteria for being federally recognized as an Indian tribe consists of seven requirements. These specifications are found in Federal Regulation 25 CFR Part 83.

They are

1. The petitioner has been identified as an American Indian entity on a substantially continuous basis since 1900.

2. A predominant portion of the petitioning group comprises a distinct community and has existed as a community from historical times to the present.

3. The petitioner has maintained political influence or authority over its members as an autonomous entity from historical times until the present.

4. A copy of the group's present governing documents including its membership criteria.

5. The petitioner's membership consists of individuals who descend from a historical Indian tribe or from historical Indian tribes which combined and functioned as a single autonomous political entity.

6. The membership of the petitioning group is composed primarily of persons who are not members of an acknowledged North American Indian tribe.

7. Neither the petitioner nor its members are the subject of congressional legislation that has expressly terminated or forbidden the federal relationship.

What it takes to be officially designated an Indian

The BIA not only decides what's a tribe, it also decides who's an Indian.

According to the Bureau of Indian Affairs, in order to be officially defined as an American Indian a person must meet *all* of the following criteria:

- ✔ Their blood quantum must be at least ¼ American Indian.
- ✔ They must be listed as a member of a tribe that is federally recognized.
- ✔ They must be able to definitively trace their Indian ancestry back at least three generations.
- ✔ They must be formally approved by BIA officials.

These criteria are problematic. For decades now, American Indians have been encouraged (and, let's face it, often hectored) to "mainstream" — to become an integral, integrated part of American society. Since the days of the first immigrants to arrive in the U.S., this has entailed getting an apartment or buying a home in a city or town, and working a job nearby. It's the American way, and today's immigration issues aside, it is the traditional approach to becoming an "American."

Blood quantum quandaries

Blood quantum is the percentage of Indian blood in a person.

Many people do not like being told that to be legally proclaimed an Indian, they must meet a blood percentage requirement. The Bureau of Indian Affairs demands a Certificate of Degree of Indian or Alaska Native Blood (known as a CDIB) to establish eligibility for BIA programs, including funding and services.

According to the U.S. Census Bureau, anyone who says they are Native American is counted as a Native American.

This is what the BIA has to say about the CDIB. (And note how they make a point of telling you what it *doesn't* mean, too.)

> A Certificate of Degree of Indian or Alaska Native Blood (CDIB) certifies that an individual possesses a specific degree of Indian blood of a federally recognized Indian tribe(s). A deciding Bureau official issues the CDIB. We issue CDIBs so that individuals may establish their eligibility for those programs and services based upon their status as American Indians and/or Alaska Natives. A CDIB does not establish membership in a federally recognized Indian tribe, and does not prevent an Indian tribe from making a separate and independent determination of blood degree for tribal purposes.

A determination of a Native American's "blood quantum" doesn't involve visiting a clinic or doctor's office and having blood drawn. The determination as to percentage of Indian ethnicity is made solely through an analysis of a person's parents and grandparents.

So, you can't get a CDIB unless you're a member of a federally recognized tribe, but a CDIB doesn't establish membership in a federally recognized tribe. And how is the blood quantum determined? Again, from the BIA:

> Your degree of Indian blood is computed from lineal ancestors of Indian blood who were enrolled with a federally recognized Indian tribe or whose names appear on the designated base rolls of a federally recognized Indian tribe.

Blood was used to determine lineage well before the United States began using it to determine American Indianness. In England, blood was used to establish inheritance eligibility. In Virginia, in 1705, the state went so far as to define "mulatto" as "the child of an Indian and child, grandchild or great-grandchild of a Negro."

Today, the BIA requires a ¼-blood quantum to be eligible for services. Many tribes, however, often require less for membership.

And many tribes are offended at even being asked about it.

The anti-BQ brigade

The blood quantum laws were established to determine the "amount of white" in a person, which many Indians and other ethnic minorities consider racist. The complaint, and it's a valid one, is that white people do not need to have the degree of their "whiteness" confirmed to apply for and be eligible for federal programs like student loans, energy assistance, small business loans, rehabilitation services, and so forth.

The Nipmucs: The State? Yup. The Feds? Nope.

One tribe that did not succeed in being granted federal recognition is the Nipmuc tribe of Massachusetts.

Beginning in 1980, the Nipmuc Nation began the process of applying for federal recognition by sending a letter of intent to the BIA. After correcting "deficiencies" the BIA found in their paperwork, the Nipmuc application was finally put on active status in 1995. (No, that's not a typo — it took 15 years to move up to "active" status, although part of the delay was because of time and financial constraints. The Nipmuc Nation is a small tribe, and legal costs to pursue the process of gaining federal recognition can be daunting.)

The Nipmucs, which had been granted tribal recognition by the state of Massachusetts in 1976, had plans to open a casino once federal recognition was granted.

However, they were denied federal recognition by the BIA in June 2004. A BIA press release stated, "Indian Affairs Aurene M. Martin today issued a Final Determination in which she declined to acknowledge a group known as "The Nipmuc Nation" from Sutton, Mass. The Nipmuc Nation group does not meet four of the seven mandatory requirements for Federal acknowledgment."

The requirements the Nipmucs failed to meet were 1, 2, 3, and 5. (See "What It Takes to Be a Tribe" earlier in this chapter.) On September 23, 2004, the Nipmucs filed an appeal with the BIA. The appeal was denied on June 15, 2005.

Some anti–blood quantum activists have gone so far as to compare the BIA's fixation on blood ratios with the Nazi obsession with blood purity and their goal of creating an Aryan race. The point is also made that no other ethnic group is ever systematically queried as to the percentage of their Italian, or Irish, or Hispanic, or Jewish lineage.

There is a movement afoot these days to abolish the blood quantum requirements of the BIA. An online petition titled "Blood Quantum Does Not Determine Identity" currently has more than 5,500 signatures. The opening passage of the petition states "Native America does not believe that the BIA or any other government organization has the right to determine who is or is not Native American by degree of blood. There is no other group in America that is ever asked who they are by how much blood," which sums up the rancor many Natives feel toward this government requirement. (You can view and sign the petition at www.petitiononline.com/0001/petition.html.)

Other Native American people believe that without requirements for blood quantum or tribal rights to restrict membership, tribes would be inundated with people who have no Indian ancestry or culture at all wishing to receive tribal benefits. Being an enrolled member of a tribe is akin to receiving citizenship in one's own nation.

When the BIA says no

There are 564 federally recognized governments in the U.S., but there are many more tribes that want to be added to that list.

When the BIA says no, the tribal nation can appeal the decision. The BIA provides a detailed summary of what specific qualifying criteria the tribe failed to meet. The tribe can provide whatever documentation they wish to counter the BIA's reasons for refusing recognition.

This is a lengthy process and, if a negative decision is rendered on the appeal, the tribe can no longer challenge the BIA, but can file a lawsuit in U.S. District Court contesting the decision. For many small tribes, the legal costs of pursuing such a lawsuit are prohibitive.

Chapter 22

Native Americans: Today and Tomorrow

*W*hat is life in America like these days for Native Americans? And is it possible for an entire ethnic group to suffer from post-traumatic stress?

Make no mistake about it: If there is any single ethnic group that underwent trauma warranting subsequent stress, it is the American Indian.

But time passes, and the American Indian is now a vibrant and productive member of the American melting pot, a rich color in the American ethnic quilt. Sure, there are problems, and many of them are due to what they went through in the past (covered at length elsewhere in this book) but now there are Native American PhDs, and physicians, and engineers, and teachers, and computer programmers, and business owners, and writers.

This chapter looks at the state of the American Indian today, and what is on the horizon for this earliest inhabitant of what is now the United States of America.

An Indian By Any Other Name . . .

Columbus didn't make it to "India," so why do we still call the Natives (and all their descendants) that he encountered when he did finally sight land "Indians"?

And how do Native Indigenous people feel about being called Indians? Has the term become politically incorrect? An insult? A slur? Is "Native American" the proper way to describe people who had been here for thousands of years when the Europeans first arrived? Have we witnessed an evolution of an ethnic/racial identifier, as we did when culture and society went from Negro, to Afro-American, to Black, to African American?

But what about the inaccuracy of the term? Isn't a woman born in Boston to Italian-American parents a "native American" in the strictest sense of the term? And can't the same be said about any single person born on American soil?

This is a real issue, and there is real resistance to granting only descendants of pre-contact Indigenous people the title Native American, yet many Native Americans prefer it — but not all.

So what should these 4.1 million people be called then?

The fact is that the phrase *American Indian* is a legal descriptor. Consider:

- The Bureau of Indian Affairs
- The National Museum of the American Indian
- The National Congress of American Indians
- The American Indian Heritage Foundation
- The *American Indian Art Magazine*
- The American Indian Movement (AIM)
- The American Indian Science & Engineering Society (AISES)

. . . and so forth.

Yet, the repatriation law (see "Repatriation: Resting in Peace" later in this chapter) is titled the Native American Graves Protection and Repatriation Act, and many other bills and laws use the term "Native American."

As is the case with many ethnic groups, Means has decided to reclaim the inaccurate and often abused term *Indian* and declare it as his and his peoples' own, and to do so with a fierce sense of ethnic pride and entitlement.

Today, many Indians prefer to be identified by their tribe. And this makes all the sense in the world when you think about it.

White people from the U.S. and Europe say, "I'm an American." "I'm a German." "I'm Scottish." And since tribes are sovereign nations, identifying ones nationality by stating the name of their "nation" — Choctaw, Navajo, Sioux, Apache, and so forth — is appropriate and solves the problem of trying to find a way to establish ethnicity by using the term *Indian* — which, while it is the legal term, is still historically errant — or "Native American," which can rankle Americans who claim the same sobriquet based on being born in Dubuque or Scranton.

We have used both terms interchangeably in this book because that's what countless Indians and Native Americans do.

The truth is that the term "Indian" has morphed into a true identifier, and everyone knows what it means. Many Native Americans take no umbrage at being addressed as an Indian, its historical inaccuracy notwithstanding.

Repatriation: Resting in Peace

Repatriation is the returning of cultural artifacts and human remains and bones to Native American tribes.

The U.S. government states, "The Native American Graves Protection and Repatriation Act (NAGPRA) is a Federal law passed in 1990. NAGPRA provides a process for museums and Federal agencies to return certain Native American cultural items — human remains, funerary objects, sacred objects, and objects of cultural patrimony — to lineal descendants, culturally affiliated Indian tribes, and Native Hawaiian organizations."

For the museums that comprise the Smithsonian Institution, the National Museum of the American Indian Act (NMAI Act), passed in 1989 and amended in 1996, governs repatriation.

Repatriation is a complex process for both tribes and the institutions holding remains. From the outside, it can seem like museums and tribes would be at each other's throats over the right to possess and control Native American remains. In fact, while in the beginning, challenging situations arose, today it can be more common for tribes and museums to work together to determine cultural affiliation. In addition, by beginning to work together on repatriation, tribes sometimes decide to work more closely with archaeologists on other avenues of scientific inquiry. Many Native people have even chosen to become archaeologists in part because of having to work on this issue for our tribes.

These are the official definitions from the Smithsonian's National Museum of Natural History's Repatriation Office regarding artifacts and remains:

- ✔ **Culturally affiliated human remains:** The legislation defines these as human remains with whom a demonstrable relationship of shared group identity can be shown to an existing federally recognized American Indian tribe, Alaska Native Village, or Regional Corporation or Native Hawaiian organization, based on a preponderance of evidence.

- ✔ **Associated and Unassociated Funerary Objects:** Funerary objects are items that, as part of the death rites of a culture, are believed to have been intentionally placed with an individual at the time of death or later. An object is considered to be "associated" if the human remains with which it was originally interred are present at the National Museum of Natural History.

- **Sacred Objects:** These are specific ceremonial objects that are needed by traditional Native American religious leaders for the practice of traditional Native American religions by their present-day adherents.

- **Objects of Cultural Patrimony:** An object having ongoing historical, traditional, or cultural importance central to the Native American group or culture itself, rather than property owned by an individual Native American, and which, therefore, cannot be alienated, appropriated, or conveyed by any individual regardless of whether or not the individual is a member of the Indian tribe or Native Hawaiian organization and such object shall have been considered inalienable by such Native American group at the time the object was separated from such group.

- **Remains of Individuals whose Identity is Known:** The return of the remains of named individuals to lineal descendants was an established priority for the National Museum of Natural History, even prior to the passage of the NMAI Act. This policy continues to be in effect. Very few of the individuals whose remains are in the collections of the National Museum of Natural History are known by name.

- **Objects Acquired Illegally:** In accordance with long-standing Smithsonian policy, the National Museum of Natural History may repatriate any materials acquired by or transferred to the National Museum of Natural History illegally or under circumstances that render invalid the Museum's claim to them. (Source: Smithsonian Institution Repatriation Office.)

As per the National Museum of the American Indian Act, the National Museum of Natural History has issued detailed reports on cultural artifacts and human remains held in its collection for dozens of cultures and ten culture areas.

What does it matter where the remains are?

It may be difficult for non-Natives to understand just how important repatriation is. Imagine if you had always thought that your grandparents and your grandparents' grandparents were resting quietly in their graves and suddenly learned that this was not the case. For American Indians, the removal of human remains and funerary objects is just one more in a long line of insults, To make matters worse, it is sometimes the case that remains were destroyed or lost by the scientific institutions who were supposedly caring for them. When American Indian remains were taken to museums, they were often thought of only as "specimens" for scientific study, and not as beloved human ancestors. Repatriation is the process through which the human nature of the remains is returned to them.

In addition, repatriation has meant that Native people have become more involved in the practice of anthropology and archaeology. Because tribes were forced to work with museums and archaeologists in order to bring remains home, tribal members began to acquire specialized knowledge in museum studies and archaeology. Today, there are many Native American archaeologists, all of whom hold the highest standards of scientific integrity while still maintaining cultural values.

These reports are painstakingly compiled upon tribal inquiries and then disposition is decided upon in consultation with tribal leaders. The Repatriation Office defers to the tribes regarding the cultural identification and significance of individual items.

Native American Stats

Native Americans are the fourth-largest minority group in the United States after Hispanics, Blacks, and Asians, yet their overall state of affairs as a group is in many cases Third World grim. A third of all Native Americans live on reservations, where the quality of life can range from excellent to abominable.

Income

Money changes everything, money makes the world go round, money is the root of all evil, money burns a hole in your pocket, money is time, money doesn't grow on trees . . . choose whichever cliché you like. The reality is that the dominant force in everyone's life is how much one earns and how much one spends.

The statistics for Native Americans when it comes to earning in the U.S. do not paint a pretty picture:

- The median U.S. income in the United States in 2005 was $46,326. For Native Americans? $33,627.

- The poverty rate in the United States is around 13 percent. For Native Americans? Around 25 percent.

- The poverty rate jumps to almost a third for Sioux, Navajo, and Apache tribe members.

- In 2005, just under 16 percent of the U.S. population had no health insurance. For Native Americans? Around 30 percent have no coverage.

- In 2000, around 34 percent of the American workforce were employed in professional or management occupations. For Native Americans? Around 26 percent. (Source: U.S. Census Bureau.)

- The percentage of homeowners in the U.S. is around 66 percent nationwide. For Native Americans? Around 56 percent.

- Native Americans are incarcerated at a rate 38 percent higher than the national per capita rate. (Source: U.S. Department of Justice.)

- Native American families, on average, are larger than the average American family: 3.06 people versus 2.59. Yet the number of single-parent Native American households — and we're speaking of both motherless and fatherless households — exceeds the average number of single-parent American households.

✔ For almost three decades (since the 1980 census), the Pine Ridge reservation in South Dakota has been declared one of the ten poorest counties in America. The reason? No jobs.

✔ A quarter of Sioux, Navajo, and Pueblo households are run by a woman without a husband present.

The situation is improving slowly for Native Americans, and education is, as has long been touted, the silver bullet when it comes to pulling minorities out of poverty and improving their living conditions.

Education

Educational levels of Native Americans are below the national average, yet they have grown significantly over the past few decades.

In the year 2000, 70.9 percent of Native Americans had graduated from high school. At the time, the national average was 84.6 percent. In terms of higher education, only 11 percent of the Native American population had earned a bachelor's degree, compared to more than double that — 24 percent — for the rest of the U.S. population. (Source: U.S. Census Bureau.)

Yet these numbers are much higher than the same statistics as recently as 1990.

Occupations

How bad is unemployment for Native Americans?

This is not a simple question to answer, because Native American unemployment figures are often difficult to ascertain accurately. Someone is considered "unemployed" if they are available for work, able to work, and actively sought a job in the past four weeks.

Graduation day

Tribes in which a high percentage of its members are high school graduates:

✔ Creek

✔ Choctaw

✔ Iroquois

There are many Indian reservations and villages where there are no jobs. People there commonly don't look for work because they know it's often futile. Also, there are Natives who choose to focus on seasonal subsistence strategies like hunting and fishing and are what the federal government considers "voluntarily idle"; that is, not in the workforce through choice.

Also, when tribal governments control, through sovereignty, all aspects of a tribe's existence, including infrastructure, employment, and law enforcement, and yet resources are not in place to expand and improve, stagnation is inevitable, along with its unavoidable result, poverty.

In the past few decades, the numbers of Native American and Alaska Native businesses have climbed.

For example, a 1997 U.S. Census Bureau industry breakdown report found that 14 percent of the construction businesses in the U.S. were owned by Native Americans or Alaska Natives. Likewise, 17 percent of service businesses and 8 percent of retail businesses.

In 2002, Native American–owned businesses — which number over 200,000 firms — did around $27 billion in sales. The state with the most Native American–owned businesses is California, followed by Oklahoma, Texas, New York, and Florida. The number of Native American–owned businesses with 100 or more employees was 178, and these businesses did a total of close to $6 billion in sales.

Alcoholism and the Native American

Five of the top ten causes of death among Native Americans are related to abuse of alcohol. This is about four times the rate in America as a whole.

According to U.S. Department of Health and Human Services, alcohol abuse among 13-year-old Native American children is ten times the national average — 1 percent vs. 0.1 percent. *Yes, 13-year olds.*

And sadly, the suicide rate among Native Americans is 1.5 times the national rate, and alcohol plays a role in a great many of these tragic deaths.

So how did Native Americans get into so much trouble with booze? And why does alcohol have such a statistically significantly higher rate of damage and destruction among Native Americans?

The legendary Blackfoot chief Crowfoot summed up alcohol's nefarious impact on his people:

> The whiskey brought among us by the traders is fast killing us off. We are powerless before this evil. We are unable to resist the temptation to drink when brought in contact with the white man's water. Our horses, buffalo robes, and other articles of trade go for whiskey.

Alcohol became a factor in the Indians' lives from their earliest encounters with the Europeans. It quickly became a form of currency, and traders exploited its effects in many ways, most notably in trade deals that they were able to skew in their favor.

Is it true that Indians lack a gene to process alcohol? Or perhaps the better question is, is there actually a verifiable genetic component to alcohol abuse? Can alcoholics justifiably claim that being an alcoholic is due to their genes?

The answer to these questions seems to be yes. In a 1994 study funded by the National Institutes of Health at the Indiana Alcohol Research Center at the Indiana University School of Medicine, Dr. Ting-Kai Li discovered that Native Americans do not possess what he describes as "protective genes."

But the trend in the Native American community is toward controlling alcohol and minimizing the deleterious effects of alcoholism, and this has been ongoing for years. In 1999, Yvette Joseph-Fox, the Executive Director of the National Indian Health Board, revealed in a statement before Congress that Native Americans as an ethnic group abstain from alcohol in greater numbers and percentages than any other ethnic group in America.

Mineral Wealth and Offshore Banking: Native American Economic Bright Spots

There's more to Indian moneymaking than casinos. (See Chapter 21 for more.) The Blackfeet have their own bank.

The exploitation of natural resources on tribal lands has been a good source of income for some tribes, but this comes with its own set of challenging issues.

The banking Blackfeet

In 1999, the Blackfeet Tribe of Montana chartered their own offshore depository called Glacier International Depository. As a sovereign nation, the Blackfeet are exempt from federal and state banking regulations and were, thus, free to launch their own "offshore bank."

The GID has only foreign depositors, and they make it clear that no funds are kept in the United States and no depositor funds are kept on Blackfeet tribal land. The GID serves foreign depositors who desire anonymity and security.

The GID has been a winner for the Blackfeet, although after the terrorist attack of September 11, 2001, they have been faced with increased scrutiny thanks to the Patriot Act. All international financial transactions are now scrutinized, and many foreign investors have shied away from GID because of the hassles.

Yet, by any standard, the endeavor is a success. In May 2006, GID announced that they had signed an exclusive agreement with FranTech Switzerland Licensing of Zurich, Switzerland, to market GID's foreign depository services licenses (called "Global Cash Management") through FranTech's network of 600 agents in 220 countries to governments around the world.

The Blackfeet's success has certainly spurred interest in other tribes in expanding into the international banking business.

Money from mineral rights

According to the Division of Energy and Mineral Resources Management of the Bureau of Indian Affairs, in fiscal year 2000 mineral resources royalties from American Indian leases in the continental United States totaled almost $245 million:

- **Gas:** 45 percent
- **Coal:** 27 percent
- **Oil:** 22 percent
- **Other:** 6 percent

Under the BIA's Mineral Assessment Program, tribes can request a wide array of assistance from the BIA, including:

- Provide economic evaluations of energy and mineral resources to Indian mineral owners as requested.
- Provide studies on the current and expected energy and mineral market conditions.
- Provide expert technical advice in geology, mining engineering, renewable energy resource assessments, design and engineering, petroleum engineering, and geophysics to Indian mineral owners.

An excellent guide to tribal energy resource development can be found at the Department of Energy's site, Guide to Tribal Energy Development: Fossil Fuel Resources at `www.eere.energy.gov/tribalenergy/guide/fossil_ fuel_resources.cfm`. The site offers downloadable PDFs organized by tribe detailing the development programs each tribe has embarked upon. Reports are available for tribal lands located in Colorado, Montana, New Mexico, North Dakota, Oklahoma, South Dakota, Utah, and Wyoming. Truly a noteworthy compilation of detailed information.

These services are providing opportunities for tribes to reap benefits from valuable resources on and beneath the lands they own. In addition to traditional mining operations, tribes are looking to the wind and the sea, and the forest and the rivers for ways to profitably utilize lucrative natural resources and provide a steady income for their people.

For example, tribes today are involved in:

✔ Oil, gas, and coal mining operations throughout Indian lands

✔ The development of wind farms and tidal plants for generating electricity by the Passamaquoddy, the Omaha Sioux tribes, and the Ewiiaapaayp

✔ The building of hydroelectric plants utilizing rivers as an energy source by the Colorado River Indian Tribe

✔ Development of biodiesel plants by the Nez Perce

✔ Use of biomass — logging and mill residue — as a power source by the St. Croix tribe

Prior to April 2005, the Division of Energy and Mineral Resources Management reported to the Depart of Trust Services of the BIA. Today, the Division reports to a newly formed agency, the Office of Indian Energy Resources and Economic Development.

The development of mineral resources on tribal lands can be problematic, though, when the infrastructure involved puts the environment at risk. Particularly difficult are the cases where sacred sites are impacted by development. Mining operations may threaten important mountains. The use of water in coal mining may impact sacred springs. Lumbering operations may lead to changes in the sacred landscape or in animal habitat. While natural resources seem like an obvious source of revenue for tribes, they are not without a high cost to the tribes.

The Top Ten Tribes Today

Table 22-1 details the top ten tribes in the United States and their numbers, in descending order:

Table 22-1	Top Ten Tribes
Tribe	*Population*
Cherokee	302,569
Navajo	276,775
Sioux	113,713
Chippewa	110,857
Choctaw	88,692
Pueblo	59,621
Apache	57,199
Lumbee	52,614
Iroquois	47,746
Creek	40,487

These tribes make up 0.41 percent of the U.S. population.

Here is a "snapshot" of each of the top ten today. (See Chapters 6 and 7 for more information on the Five Civilized Tribes and other major tribes.)

Cherokee

The Cherokee Nation is the largest tribal group in the United States. They comprise three separate federally recognized bands:

- **The Cherokee Nation,** 250,000+ members (www.cherokee.org)
- **The United Keetoowah Band of Cherokee Indians,** 10,000+ members (www.unitedkeetoowahband.org/)
- **The Eastern Band of Cherokee Indians,** 13,400 members (www.nc-cherokee.com/)

Navajo

The Navajo are the second-largest tribal group in America today in terms of population, but they possess the largest tribal reservation, with land covering 27,000 square miles in the states of Arizona, New Mexico, and Utah.

In 2003, Navajo tribal revenue was $137 million, with most of it coming from mining royalties, but the tribe's poverty rate is 43 percent, and unemployment among Navajos is a staggering 42 percent.

Sioux

The Sioux are the third-largest tribal group in America and there are many federally recognized Sioux tribes. The Pine Ridge Reservation, home to the Oglala Sioux Tribe, in South Dakota — a 2-million-acre expanse the size of Connecticut — is the second-largest reservation in the country.

The Sioux Wars in the second half of the 19th century resulted in the Wounded Knee Massacre, during which 153 Sioux were killed by the U.S. military. In 1973, Sioux members of the American Indian Movement occupied Wounded Knee for seventy days, resulting in 300 arrests. Six years later, the Sioux were awarded $105 million from the U.S. government for lands that had been taken from them.

Chippewa/Anishinabe

"Chippewa" is the term most used in the United States for this tribe, but tribal members prefer to be known by their original name: Anishinabe; in Canada, they're known as Ojibway.

The Chippewa are the fourth-largest tribal group today, and Anishinabe tribes have lands mainly in Minnesota, Wisconsin, and Michigan (as well as in Canada). There are around 150 individual Chippewa bands or tribes.

Choctaw

The Choctaw people, the fifth-largest tribal group in the United States, are one of the Five Civilized Tribes (see Chapter 6 for more details on the Five Civilized Tribes) and today are organized into three bands: the Mississippi Band of Choctaw, the Jena Band of Choctaw in Louisiana, and the Choctaw Nation of Oklahoma.

During World War I, Choctaw tribe members served the U.S. as code talkers, paving the way for the Navajo code talkers of World War II.

Pueblo

The Pueblo Indians, are not, strictly speaking, an individual tribe. There are many different tribes that are organized as Pueblos. Two of the more well-known are the Hopi and the Zuni.

Most Pueblos are in Arizona and New Mexico, but there is one Pueblo in far west Texas.

Apache

The Apache are organized into six separate groups, the Western Apache, the Chiricahua, the Mescalero, the Jicarilla, the Lipan, and the Plains Apache (formerly the Kiowa Apache). Cochise and Geronimo were both Apache. (See Chapter 10 for more information on Native American chiefs.)

Today, Apache tribes have territory in Oklahoma, Texas, Arizona, and New Mexico.

Lumbee

The status of the Lumbee Tribe is that they are the eighth-largest Native American tribe in the United States, yet they are not federally recognized and are, thus, not eligible for BIA services and all other benefits of federal recognition.

Iroquois

The Iroquois Confederacy — also known as the Haudenosaunee (which means "People of the Longhouse" or "People Building a Longhouse") — was originally comprised of five tribes — the Mohawk, Oneida, Onondonga, Cayuga, and Seneca. The Tuscaroras joined later.

Today, the six separate tribes are still extant and live in the U.S. mainly in New York, Wisconsin, and Oklahoma. There are also Iroquois in Ontario and Quebec.

Creek

These days, many Creek Indians prefer to be identified by their original name of "Muskogee." The Creek were known as one of the Five Civilized Tribes. Today, the federally recognized Creek tribes have territory in Alabama and Oklahoma.

In partnership with the Oklahoma State University system, the Muskogee (Creek) Nation operates the College of the Muscogee Nation in Okmulgee, Oklahoma.

How Native Americans Ended Up in the Casino Business

The Mashantucket Pequot tribe operates the Foxwoods Casino in Mashantucket, Connecticut. Foxwoods is the largest casino in the world and, since its launch in 1993, has paid more than $2.4 billion to the state of Connecticut (through March 2007) as the state's share of the take. Foxwoods offers concerts, restaurants, shopping, golf, salons and spas, hotels, and, of course, a staggering array of gambling opportunities. And a Native American tribe owns it all. The Mashantucket Pequots have used their money to advance many causes dear to all Native people. They gave one of the largest donations to help establish the National Museum of the American Indian and they built an incredible museum of their own up in Connecticut.

Foxwoods' sole in-state competitor, the Mohegan Sun Casino, is the second-largest casino in the world and, since its launch in 1997, has paid $1.7 billion to the state of Connecticut (also through March 2007). Like Foxwoods, Mohegan Sun offers many of the same amenities and also like Foxwoods, an Indian tribe runs the show. (The Mohegans are not to be confused with the Mahicans or the Mohicans.)

For many tribes, launching a gaming enterprise was the path to self-sufficiency and, in many cases, great wealth. The Seminoles were poor before starting the Indian gambling phenomenon; now the tribe leaders fly around in private jets.

There are currently around 360 Indian gaming establishments in the United States. Of the more than 560 federally recognized tribes, just over 200 of them have their own casinos. And of the casinos that do exist, the majority of them are nowhere near as profitable as the casinos in Connecticut, or on the West Coast. Most tribes who have gaming enterprises make a modest amount of money, but of course, every little bit helps.

One recent study estimated that just over 10 percent of the Indian gaming establishments in the United States generate close to ¾ of all the revenue from Indian gambling.

But there is no denying that gambling has been an economic boon for Native Americans, as well as the states in which they're located.

The Seminoles were first

The Seminoles were the first Native American tribe to offer high-stakes gambling when they opened a bingo parlor in Hollywood, Florida, in 1979. The jackpot was $4,000, and the crowds quickly flocked to the place.

Today, the Seminole tribe of Florida has seven casinos in the Sunshine State, owns the line of Hard Rock Cafes (which they purchased in 2006 for close to a billion dollars), and the tribe provides a dividend to each of its 3,300 members in an amount rumored to be in excess of $40,000 per year. (And this is *per person*. So if it's a family of five . . . well, do the math.)

There is also a significant population of Seminoles in Oklahoma and they, too, are in the casino business with six gaming establishments throughout the state, including the Mystic Winds Casino in Seminole, and the Rivermist Casino in Konawa. As is typical for most casinos, slots and blackjack are the big draws, although the Rivermist also offers off-track betting.

The 1988 Indian Gaming Regulatory Act

In 1988, there were several tribes running gaming joints and the federal government, as federal governments are often wont to do, decided new laws were needed to regulate said Indian gambling enterprises. The Feds admit as much in two of the first Findings of the Act:

The Congress finds that

- ✔ Numerous Indian tribes have become engaged in or have licensed gaming activities on Indian lands as a means of generating tribal governmental revenue.

- ✔ Existing Federal law does not provide clear standards or regulations for the conduct of gaming on Indian lands.

Three types of gambling were defined in the Act:

- ✔ **Class I:** This covers traditional Indian games with minimal prizes or non-monetary prizes awarded. The tribes had total jurisdiction over this type of gambling.

- ✔ **Class II:** This covers bingo, and games like bingo, including punch cards, pull tabs, and other like games. This category also included what are called "non-banked" card games. Non-banked card games are when players play only against each other and there is no "bank" or "house" to beat. Again, the tribes were in charge of these types of games and the IGRA didn't establish any legal guidelines.

✔ **Class III:** This category is the big one, the one that can be summed up in those two magic words that so many tribes love these days: casino gambling. Class III gaming includes:

- Slot machines
- Blackjack
- Craps
- Roulette
- Baccarat
- Texas Hold 'Em poker
- Faro
- Video poker
- Video lottery
- Keno

In other words, Class III games are games where you can win a bundle, or lose your shirt. These are the games under federal jurisdiction, and the IGRA was written so that new regulations can be implemented whenever the Commissioner of the National Indian Gaming Commission sees fit.

Sharing the wealth?

There's a widespread misconception among many Americans that all Native Americans are getting rich from the casino business, and that tribes that have hugely successful gambling operations distribute their profits to all the Indians in America.

This couldn't be further from the truth, although the tribes that *do* have gaming businesses and share the proceeds end up paying out sometimes enormous monthly checks for official tribal members. For example, the Pechanga Indians of California own a casino in Temecula, California, that provides each tribe member with a check for around $15,000 a month. Fifteen grand a month equals a $180K a year income for simply being part of a tribe. Not bad.

Tribes that make money through gaming enterprises — like the Mashantucket Pequot tribe in Connecticut — are sovereign nations. As the Native American Rights Fund explains, if a state earns big bucks from their lottery, they have zero responsibility to share it with another state. It's the same thing with tribes and gaming earnings.

Part VI
The Part of Tens

In this part . . .

This part contains fascinating lists of books, movies, museums, and cultural centers that anyone interested in Native American history should be aware of.

The movie picks range from mainstream hits (*Dances with Wolves*) to eclectic films shot solely with Native actors and in Native languages. The books range from general histories to encyclopedias. The museums include all-inclusive institutions like the Smithsonian's National Museum of the American Indian, to event-specific places like the Wounded Knee Museum in South Dakota.

A splendid time is guaranteed for all!

Chapter 23

Ten Native American Museums and Cultural Centers

• •

*T*hese museums and cultural centers are located all over the United States and each provides their own unique look at the history and culture of Native Americans.

Some, like the Smithsonian's National Museum of the American Indian, cover the complete history of all Native American tribes; others, like the Cherokee Heritage Center and the Iroquois Indian Museum, cover the history of specific tribes.

If you plan to visit any of the museums and have questions, call or e-mail the venue, or visit their Web site before you hit the road.

The National Museum of the American Indian (Smithsonian Institution; Washington, D.C., New York, Maryland)

The National Museum of the American Indian can justifiably be considered the gold standard of American Indian museums, and it is associated with the gold standard of educational and research institutes, the Smithsonian Institution. A must-see when you're in D.C., or NYC, or even Maryland!

For more information on open hours and admission prices, you can contact the National Museum of the American Indian at 202-633-1000 or go online to www.americanindian.si.edu.

The Indian Museum of North America (South Dakota)

This museum is part of the Crazy Horse Memorial project in the Black Hills of South Dakota.

For more information on open hours and admission prices, you can contact the Indian Museum of North America at 605-673-4681 or go online to www. crazyhorse.org.

The Museum of Indian Culture (Pennsylvania)

This museum covers a wide range of Indian culture and boasts programs that include the Spring Corn Festival, the Roasting Ears of Corn Festival, and A Time of Thanksgiving Festival.

For more information on open hours and admission prices, you can contact the Museum of Indian Culture at 610-797-2121 or go online to www. museumofindianculture.org.

The Plains Indian Museum (Wyoming)

This museum is part of the Buffalo Bill Historical Center in Cody, Wyoming and has one of the largest and finest collections of Plains Indian art and artifacts in the country.

For more information on open hours and admission prices, you can contact the Plains Indian Museum at 307-587-4771 or go online to www.bbhc.org/pim/index.cfm.

The Indian Pueblo Cultural Center (New Mexico)

This center is dedicated to the preservation and perpetuation of Pueblo Indian Culture, History, and Art.

For more information on open hours and admission prices, you can contact the Indian Pueblo Cultural Center at 800-766-4405 or go online to http://www.indianpueblo.org/ipcc/.

The Anasazi Heritage Center (Colorado)

The Anasazi Heritage Center is a museum that presents exhibits and programs about the Ancestral Puebloan (or Anasazi) culture in the Four Corners region.

For more information on open hours and admission prices, you can contact the Anasazi Heritage Center at 970-882-5600 or go online to www.co.blm.gov/ahc/index.htm.

The Museum of the Cherokee Indian (North Carolina)

This museum offers exhibits and programs that tell the story of the Cherokee people and their ancestors using computer-generated images, animation, and audio and visual presentations.

For more information on open hours and admission prices, you can contact the Museum of the Cherokee Indian at 828-497-3481 or go online to www.cherokeemuseum.org.

The Iroquois Indian Museum (New York)

The Iroquois Indian Museum is an educational institution committed to fostering an awareness of Iroquois culture using Iroquois art and the work of contemporary Iroquois artists as a means of experiencing and understanding that culture.

For more information on open hours and admission prices, you can contact the Iroquois Indian Museum at 518-296-8949 or go online to www.iroquoismuseum.org.

The Mid-America All-Indian Center (Kansas)

The Mid-America All-Indian Center houses a museum, a kiva for special events, and a gift shop. They present exhibits on the Plains indians and other tribes throughout the U.S. and Canada.

For more information on open hours and admission prices, you can contact the Mid-America All-Indian Center at 316-262-5221 or go online to www.theindiancenter.org.

The Wounded Knee Museum (South Dakota)

The Wounded Knee Museum describes itself as a "narrative museum" that tells the story of the 1890 massacre of Lakota Indians during the last major military operation against American Indians.

For more information on open hours and admission prices, you can contact the Wounded Knee Museum at 605-279-2573 or go online to www.woundedknee museum.org.

Also Worth Noting . . .

A list of museums cannot leave out the groundbreaking Mashantucket Pequot Museum in Mashantucket, CT. (http://www.pequotmuseum.org).

Also worth a visit are the:

- The Alutiiq Museum (Kodiak, Alaska; www.alutiiqmuseum.org/
- The Eiteljorg Museum of American Indians and Western Art (Indianapolis, Indiana; www.eiteljorg.org/)
- The Makah Culture and Research Center (Neah Bay, Washington; www.makah.com/)

Chapter 24

Ten (Plus) Worthy Movies and Documentaries about Native Americans and Their History

· ·

*T*hese movies, miniseries, and documentaries are listed in chronological order and are all fascinating cinematic looks at Indian history.

Some great directors and actors have turned their attention to the stories of Native Americans; likewise some brilliant documentarians (most notably Ken Burns, of course) have produced works that expanded on our knowledge of the American Indian in a passionate and artistic search for the truth.

Little Big Man (1970)

Dustin Hoffman plays the 121-year-old title character in this irreverent, somewhat revisionist anti-Western that tells the story of Custer's Last Stand and other Indian history from the non-white point of view.

> **Director:** Arthur Penn
>
> **Writers:** Thomas Berger (novel), Calder Willingham (screenplay)
>
> **Cast:** Dustin Hoffman, Faye Dunaway, Chief Dan George, Martin Balsam
>
> **DVD:** Paramount Home Video, 2003, 139 minutes, PG-13
>
> **Note:** Another movie about Indians from the seventies worth checking out is *A Man Called Horse*.

Powwow Highway (1989)

Two Northern Cherokee men, Buddy and Philbert, who live on a reservation in Montana have to leave their tribe — and their important tribal council meetings — to bail out Buddy's sister, who has been arrested on drug charges in Santa Fe, New Mexico.

Basically, a buddy road trip set in the Native American zeitgeist, this film is a look at life in Native America today, and the two unforgettable characters powerfully illustrate just how taken for granted among Indians is the sense of community and respect for the past.

There is a plot of sorts — Buddy's sister was arrested solely as a trick to get him out of Montana just before a referendum on an important land deal that he would have voted against — but it's more entertaining and insightful as a look at a modern culture still coming to terms with modern America.

Powwow Highway was one of the first films that included Native input into the characters and, like *Smoke Signals*, it drew heavily on Native humor. While not everything about the film is precisely accurate, there's a lot that they get right.

> **Director:** Jonathan Wacks
>
> **Writers:** Janet Heaney and Jean Stawarz (screenplay); David Seals (novel)
>
> **Cast:** A. Martinez, Gary Farmer, Joannelle Nadine Romero, Amanda Wyss, Margot Kane, Wes Studi
>
> **DVD:** Anchor Bay, 2004, 91 minutes, R

Dances with Wolves (1990)

To this day there are Martin Scorsese fans who are still upset that *Dances with Wolves* beat *Goodfellas* for the Best Picture Oscar in 1990. It's wise to avoid weighing in on that argument, except to say that the Academy probably should have declared a tie that year.

While this film did much to redress the previous stereotype of Native peoples as bloodthirsty savages, it did so only for the Lakota at the expense of the Pawnee. This film is not widely praised by Native people because it adheres too closely to the romantic stereotype of the "Noble Savage." To its credit, it was among the first mainstream films that accurately depicted Native American humor and chose to have actors speaking in a Native language.

The movie tells the story of John Dunbar, a Union general who meets and bonds with a Sioux tribe. After fighting side-by-side with the tribe against a savage Pawnee tribe, he is accepted into the tribe and named Dances with Wolves (because he did, indeed, dance with his pet wolf, Two Socks.)

He falls in love with a white woman — Stands With a Fist — who had been adopted by the tribe after her family was killed by Pawnee.

Director: Kevin Costner

Writer: Michael Blake (novel and screenplay)

Cast: Kevin Costner, Mary McDonnell, Graham Greene

DVD: MGM, 2003, 236 minutes, PG-13

The Last of the Mohicans (1992)

A love story during the French and Indian War.

This film is an Oscar-winning adaptation of the James Fenimore Cooper novel that tells the story of a white man raised as a Mohawk who falls in love with the daughter of a British general.

Director: Michael Mann

Writers: James Fenimore Cooper (novel); John L. Balderston (adaptation); Paul Perez (adaptation), Daniel Moore (adaptation); Philip Dunne (1936 screenplay); Michael Mann (screenplay); Christopher Crowe (screenplay)

Cast: Daniel Day-Lewis, Madeleine Stowe, Russell Means

DVD: Twentieth Century Fox, 2001, 117 minutes, R

Christmas in the Clouds (2001)

Now, *this* is a rare bird in the aviary of movies about the American Indian.

Why? Because it's about an upscale ski resort run by affluent Native Americans. That plot alone is worthy of being singled out. Well-off Native Americans? Yup. It's about time that the successful Indians in America were given their due.

The romantic comedy plot is simple: The manager is trying to impress an incoming restaurant reviewer and wacky confusion ensues that could easily be cleared up with a couple of lines of dialogue, but that would have made for a super-short movie and we wouldn't have been treated to warm and funny scenes that work to resolve everything in a heartwarming way.

Graham Greene steals many scenes as the vegetarian chef who insists on telling diners the histories of the animals they're eating. Tim Vahle plays the romantic male lead role and is of the Choctaw tribe in real life.

Director: Kate Montgomery

Writer: Kate Montgomery

Cast: Timothy Vahle, Sam Vlahos, Mariana Tosca, M. Emmet Walsh, Graham Greene, Rita Collidge, Lois Red Elk

DVD: Hannover House, 2006, 96 minutes, PG

Atanarjuat (2001)

Atanarjuat means "The Fast Runner" and is the first movie shot completely with Inuit actors, a 90 percent Inuit crew, and in the Inuit language, Inuktitut.

It takes place in the frozen north and is the story of an Inuit community that not only has to survive in a hostile environment, but also has to contend with the personal squabbles, rivalries, jealousies, and infidelities that are part and parcel of any close-knit — emotionally and physically — community.

The movie boasts several memorable scenes and is unlike anything most moviegoers have ever seen.

Director: Zacharis Kunuk

Writer: Paul Apak Angilirq

Cast: Natar Ungalaaq, Sylvia Ivalu, Peter-Henry Arnatsiaq, Lucy Tulugarjuk, Madeline Ivalu, Pauloosie Qulitalik

DVD: Columbia Tristar Home, 2003, 172 minutes, R

The Native Americans (Documentary, 1994)

A terrific six-part documentary on the history of Native Americans. The six parts in this TBS production are:

- Vol. 1: The Nations of the Northeast
- Vol. 2: The Tribal People of the Northwest
- Vol. 3: The Tribes of the Southeast

Northern Exposure: The *absolutely* greatest TV depiction of Native Americans *ever*

Northern Exposure debuted on CBS in 1990 and was immediately noticed by viewers, of course, but also by people who pay attention to the portrayal of Native Americans in the media. Why? Because many of the characters on the show were Indigenous people — Native Americans, Inuits, and so on — and for the most part they were played by Indigenous people and portrayed realistically.

The most memorable Native character (as well as being the most ubiquitous throughout the run of the show) was Marilyn Whirlwind, transplanted New Yorker Dr. Joel Flesichman's calm, inscrutable receptionist. Talk about oil and water! Marilyn was played by Cayuse-Nez Perce actress Elaine Miles. In a 1993 interview with *Radiance* magazine, she expressed her feeling that she was representing all Native Americans: "I've found out that I'm not just myself or my family or my tribe, but I'm representing all Native Americans."

Other Native characters included Ed Chigliak, a half-Native Alaskan who was a budding filmmaker and a shaman-in-training (played by Apache Darren Burrows); Menominee Lester Haynes Apesanahkwat); and One Who Waits (played by Dakota Floyd "Red Crow" Westerman).

✔ Vol. 4: The Natives of the Southwest

✔ Vol. 5: The People of the Great Plains, pt. 1

✔ Vol. 6: The People of the Great Plains, pt. 2

Directors: John Borden, George Burdeau, Phil Lucas

Cast: Joy Harvo (narrator), John Mohawk

DVD: None, but used Turner Home Entertainment VHS tapes of all six parts are commonly available online at Amazon, eBay, and elsewhere, individually, and in a set.

500 Nations (Documentary, 1995)

Kevin Costner does a serviceable job as host and reins in what could have easily descended into self-righteousness. His tone throughout his intros for the docu's several parts is respectful and informative. (A lot of people think it was his way of making up for *Dances With Wolves.* Ouch.)

500 Nations itself is very watchable, yet it is limited in the scope of its coverage of Native American history. It focuses on specific events and personalities for its individual episodes, but it is certainly instructive and well-researched in the topics it covers.

In terms of style, it is very Ken Burns–esque, with its zoom ins on photos and pans across paintings, and it manages to be both educational and entertaining at the same time and is recommended.

Director: Jack Leustig

Writers: Roberta Grossman, Jack Leustig, Lee Miller, W. T. Morgan, John Pohl

Cast: Kevin Costner (Host), Gregory Harrison (Narrator)

DVD: Warner Home Video, 2004, 376 minutes, Not Rated

Lewis & Clark: The Journey of the Corps of Discovery (Documentary, 1997)

Another Ken Burns classic — a fine documentary on the Corps of Discovery well worth the 240 minutes of your time.

Director: Ken Burns

Writers: Ken Burns (book); Dayton Duncan (book)

Cast: Adam Arkin (voice), Hal Holbrook (voice), Murphy Guyer (voice), Sam Waterston (voice), Matthew Broderick (voice)

DVD: PBS Paramount, 2005, 240 minutes, Not Rated

Smoke Signals (1998)

This movie is based on short stories from Coeur d'Alene author Sherman Alexie's collection *The Lone Ranger and Tonto Fistfight In Heaven,* and tells the story of two young Coeur d'Alene men — Victor and Thomas — who take a bus trip to claim the ashes of Victor's father.

Smoke Signals won the Sundance Audience Award in 1998 and portrays Indians today living in a world not of their making, yet (and often humorously) remembering the world of theirs that was unmade by whites.

Director: Chris Eyre

Writer: Sherman Alexie (book, screenplay)

Cast: Adam Beach, Evan Adams, Irene Bedard

DVD: Buena Vista Home Entertainment, 1999, 89 minutes, PG-13

Skins (2002)

This film by Native American director Chris Eyre (director of 1998's *Smoke Signals*) won the 2003 IFP Independent Spirit Awards, and is considered a raw and realistic portrayal of life on a modern Indian reservation, a place where alcoholism is nine times the national average and where Mount Rushmore is considered a blasphemous desecration of sacred mountains.

Two Sioux brothers — one a cop, one an alcoholic Vietnam vet — live angry, stilted lives and, as is often the case, one turns to crime to vent his rage.

As the mask of drama boasts both a laughing and crying face, *Smoke Signals* and *Skins* are Chris Eyre's laughing and crying looks at his own culture, people, past, and problems.

These two films paint a stark portrait of what happened when vast numbers of an entire race of people were systematically marginalized and, in many cases, destroyed in the name of, and for the purpose of, white expansionism.

> **Director:** Chris Eyre
>
> **Writers:** Adrian C. Louis (novel), Jennifer D. Lyne (screenplay)
>
> **Cast:** Eric Schweig, Graham Greene, Gary Farmer, Noah Watts
>
> **DVD:** First Look Pictures, 2003, 87 minutes, R

Images of Indians: How Hollywood Stereotyped the Native American (Documentary, 2003)

This documentary is only 25 minutes long and we haven't seen it.

But we wish we could. It doesn't seem to be available on DVD and was apparently aired on TV in 2003, but it does have an Internet Movie Database listing and the cast alone — everyone from Wes Studi and Russell Means, to Iron Eyes Cody and Elaine Miles — makes it worth seeking out.

Images of Indians shows a slew of clips from movies over the years that illustrate the portrayal of Indians and, by highlighting particular moments, the stereotyping and racist rendering of Indigenous people becomes obvious.

We include it here on the chance it shows up on TV one day, or a DVD is released, so you'll at least be aware of it. This is the kind of program that often magically appears one day on the shelves of local public libraries, even if it's not available for sale.

So now you know what to keep an eye out for when you visit your local library!

Directors: Chris O'Brien, Jason Witmer

Writers: Brock DeShane, Jeff Hildebrandt, Chris O'Brien, Jason Witmer

Cast: Nicholas Schatzki, Casey Camp-Horinek, Ward Churchill, Chris Eyre, Dr. Jacquelyn Kilpatrick, Russell Means, Elaine Miles, Dr. Peter C. Rollins, Wes Studi

DVD: None

The Journals of Knud Rasmussen (2006)

This is the story of a 1922 encounter between Inuit Natives and European explorers and is co-directed by Zacharias Kumuk, the director of the acclaimed *Atanarjuat*.

It is told mainly from the Inuit's perspective and includes some interesting moments, and heartbreaking depiction of how Christianity came to the Inuit.

It is a rich story about the conflict between ancient cultures, different religions, men and women, and the living and the dead, and it notable for its reliance on Inuit actors and the use of Inuktitut dialogue.

Director: Norman Cohn, Zacharias Kunuk

Writers: Eugene Ipkarnak, Madeline Ivalu, Herve Paniaq, Pauloosie Qulitalik, Lucy Tulugarjuk, Abraham Ulayuruluk, Louis Uttak (all for Inuktitut dialogue)

Cast: Pakak Innuksuk, Leah Angutimarik, Neeve Irngaut, Natar Ungalaaq, Samueli Ammaq

Index

• D •

• *M* •

• N •